ON A MOVE

ON A

Philadelphia's Notorious Bombing and

a Native Son's Lifelong Battle for Justice

MOVE

MIKE AFRICA JR.
WITH D. WATKINS

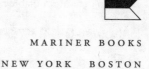

MARINER BOOKS
NEW YORK   BOSTON

The Mariner flag design is a registered trademark of HarperCollins Publishers LLC.

HarperCollins books may be purchased for educational, business, or sales promotional use. For information, please email the Special Markets Department at SPsales@harpercollins.com.

FIRST EDITION

Designed by Chloe Foster

Library of Congress Cataloging-in-Publication Data

Names: Africa, Mike, Jr., 1978– author.
Title: On a MOVE : Philadelphia's notorious bombing and a native son's lifelong battle for justice / Mike Africa Jr.
Other titles: Philadelphia's notorious bombing and a native son's lifelong battle for justice
Description: First edition. | New York : Mariner Books, [2024]
Identifiers: LCCN 2024008851 (print) | LCCN 2024008852 (ebook) | ISBN 9780063318878 (hardcover) | ISBN 9780063318892 (ebook)
Subjects: LCSH: MOVE (Organization)—History. | Africa, Mike, Jr., 1978– | Africa, John, 1931–1985—Family. | Black nationalism—Pennsylvania—Philadelphia. | African Americans—Pennsylvania—Philadelphia. | Africa family. | Philadelphia (Pa.)—Race relations. | MOVE (Organization)—Bombardment, 1985. | Police-community relations—Pennsylvania—Philadelphia. | Philadelphia (Pa.)—Biography.
Classification: LCC F158.9.B53 A37 1995 (print) | LCC F158.9.B53 (ebook) | DDC 974.8/11043092 [B]—dc23/eng/20240226
LC record available at https://lccn.loc.gov/2024008851
LC ebook record available at https://lccn.loc.gov/2024008852

ISBN 978-0-06-331887-8

24 25 26 27 28 LBC 5 4 3 2 1

CONTENTS

AUTHOR'S NOTE   vii

1. THE BOMBING   1
2. THE ORIGIN OF JOHN AFRICA   4
3. THE BIRTH OF MOVE   14
4. RIZZO GETS MOVE ON A RUN   32
5. THE FIRST STANDOFF   42
6. BORN IN PRISON   55
7. JOHN AFRICA ON THE RUN   63
8. VIRGINIA   77
9. JOHN AFRICA VS. THE FBI   91
10. THE PRISON RIOT   110
11. RUMBLINGS OF DEFIANCE   118
12. MUTINY I   123
13. MUTINY II   138
14. LIFE WITH MY PARENTS IN PRISON   150
15. SAMBOR AND GOODE ATTACK   156
16. A NEW DAY   167
17. HITTING ROCK BOTTOM   182
18. BACK ON A MOVE   195

19. STEPPING UP 216

20. STEPPING IN 224

21. THE EXIT STRATEGY 240

22. SECURING THE PACKAGE 259

23. THE MAN WITH THE FREEDOM PAPERS 272

EPILOGUE 279

ACKNOWLEDGMENTS 289

AUTHOR'S NOTE

On a Move is based, in part, on the extensive archives of Louise Africa, LaVerne Africa, and Moe Africa. That includes roughly sixty thousand pages of records, five hundred audiotapes, and one hundred videotapes—all collected and sustained since the MOVE organization's early ideation in the late 1960s. Additionally, I conducted hundreds of hours of conversations with MOVE members over many years. Some of it is oral history, passed down to me as a child raised in the organization. Some is based on taped conversations. And some of the experience is based on my own memories, including what happened to me personally, what I saw, and what I heard. Numerous newspaper articles and court records housed in the City of Philadelphia were also helpful in corroborating events.

I have changed some names and identifying characteristics to protect the privacy of the individuals involved, and I have reconstructed dialogue, including courtroom testimony, from the sources available to me. In all cases, I have upheld the integrity and truthfulness of this story.

ON A MOVE

Chapter 1

THE BOMBING

On Mother's Day in 1985, the Philadelphia Police Department (PPD) waged war on my family, the MOVE organization. It is the darkest day in modern Philadelphia history. The police dropped a bomb on my home—killing five of my MOVE brothers and sisters, six of my MOVE aunties and uncles, and destroying sixty-one houses. More than 250 of our neighbors were left homeless.

I still remember the black cloud of smoke from the fire above my West Philly block as it stretched across to New Jersey on one side and Delaware on the other.

"Evacuate! Evacuate!" echoed throughout the block.

More than five hundred uniformed officers wrapped in riot gear from head to toe stormed 6221 Osage Avenue around 6:25 a.m.—pounding on doors, spewing commands, and manhandling residents.

"Evacuate!"

Our neighbors, startled, with sleep still in their eyes, awoke to "Leave now!" and "You must evacuate immediately!"

Confused residents quickly rushed out of their homes holding all they could carry. Tow trucks were removing cars, and children scampered and scattered around the cops. Some homeowners and renters paused to demand answers.

"What is happening? Evacuate to where?" they asked. "Where exactly are we supposed to go?"

"Shut the fuck up! Evacuate!" cops spat back. "Evacuate!"

By 7:30 a.m., the PPD had blockaded the community, allowing newly crowned police commissioner Gregore Sambor—a giant, pale, block-headed, ex-military vet—to take center stage with his bullhorn. He screamed, "Attention! This is not a warning! Attention, MOVE! This is America!"

People nearby retreated in fear.

"You must abide by the laws of the American government!"

Me and my big sister Whit watched the scene unfold from my grandma LaVerne's house on Thirty-Ninth and Reno Streets, which is about four and a half miles away from the house on Osage Avenue that was under siege. But at this moment, just like every other moment, Osage Avenue was precisely where my heart and thoughts resided. It was where Tomaso, Delisha, Little Phil, Tree, Netta, Birdie, and all the other MOVE kids and I would run and hug and hide and fight and cry and make up and fight again and play and laugh until our stomachs ached, and learn and eat well and love hard. I wasn't living at Osage, but that was a part of me just as I was a part of it.

"What are those people doing?" I asked the room of frantic adults who'd gathered in LaVerne's living room. "Why are they towing cars? What's happening? I'm scared."

"Hush, Kita, hush!" LaVerne said, using a shortened version of the family nickname, Makita, that I share with my father.

LaVerne held a finger close to her mouth, as she drank in the news story. "I'm as confused as you are." She didn't say it, but I could tell she was just as scared as I was.

The sun typically gets an early start in May. Yet it was very dark out. The streetlamps clashed with the police lights on our TV screen, causing an identical glare on every local channel, where local reporters covering the story all wore the same look of disbelief on their faces.

We watched as the police sealed Osage Avenue on both ends with their trucks, paddy wagons, and tanks—as if our residential neighborhood was a foreign nation they were invading. Those tanks were full of cops hopping out and dashing in every direction across our television screen. We saw cops climbing onto the roofs with rifles on their backs; cops tucked off to the side with their pistols drawn; cops who didn't want to be caught on camera, waving off reporters; cops in huddles; angry cops; laughing cops; and, sadly, cops with their machine guns and pistols trained on Osage at every angle.

With teary eyes, LaVerne grabbed her things and rushed toward the front door.

"Where are you going?" I asked.

"Osage," she said. She didn't look back.

The siege on Osage Avenue wasn't the first confrontation between MOVE and the PPD. Seven years earlier, in 1978, they attempted to evict MOVE from the original headquarters, located in the Powelton Village section of West Philly. When MOVE refused to submit to PPD demands, police called in the fire department to flush them out. Firefighters shot four high-pressure fire hoses at MOVE's house; the kind of hoses that shoot water strong enough to snap bones, crumble bricks, and debilitate building structures. Those hoses aren't supposed to be sprayed anywhere near people, which was excellent for the PPD because they didn't see MOVE members as people worth caring about. MOVE had been under attack by Philly police for years. To understand why the attacks happened, you have to understand my great-uncle John Africa.

Chapter 2

THE ORIGIN OF JOHN AFRICA

Vincent Lopez Leaphart was the fourth of ten children. He was born on July 26, 1931. His family and close friends affectionately called him Benny—a play on the diminutive for "Vincent" that swapped out the *V* for *B*. The Leapharts lived in Mantua, a small neighborhood in West Philly. In the early 1900s, the neighborhood was full of white residents, but the Leapharts were part of a wave of African American families moving into the area. They were fleeing racial violence in the south that gave our family a German name and nearly white skin.

Benny's father, Frederick Eugene Leaphart, worked as a handyman, while his mother, Lennie Mae, had the more difficult job of raising their ten children.

Back in the 1930s, modern technology was a wood-burning stove to cook the food and heat the house. A washing machine was a scrub board and a wringer that you had to hand-crank to ring the excess water out before hanging the laundry on a clothesline to dry. And a refrigerator was a block of ice that an iceman delivered. Cooking for a family of twelve was no easy feat. Cooking for a family of twelve after chopping wood and lighting the fire while washing clothes on a scrub board was next-level difficult.

Lennie Mae was used to hard work, though. She spent most of her childhood helping her parents with all the household duties. Part of her dream for a better life when she left the south was to earn money outside of the home. So when she had her own family, she taught her older children to help the younger ones, and she got a job making beds and cleaning rooms in Atlantic City hotels. The hotels she worked in were more modern than her West Philly home. Exposure to air-conditioning that piped through the ventilation system in the building had a bad effect on her body chemistry. In September 1950 she fell ill with pneumonia, and at just forty-two years old she suddenly died.

The loss of Lennie Mae left a deep hole in the family. Benny was especially close to his mother. He spent a lot of time with her, especially when he was a young child struggling in school with a learning disability. Benny complained that he would immediately get a migraine when he saw mathematical equations. The school tried to help him with this, but he was determined not to learn what he felt was hurting him physically. So Benny was sent to a school for slow learners. That didn't help much. By fourteen or so, he was done with school for good, finishing at a third-grade reading level.

Because of his school issues, and being one of the older children in the Leaphart home, Benny spent a lot of time with his mother, helping her with chores and with the younger children. Her death left him very angry. In conversations with his family, he vented his frustrations about the hospital she died in. He believed that if his mother had been a white woman the hospital would have done more to save her. Considering the hostility toward Black people that was common and overt at the time, he might've been right.

That same year, in 1950, the United States went to war with Korea, sending nearly two million Americans to fight. A year later, when Benny was twenty years old, he was drafted to serve in an infantry unit in the army.

What happened in Korea changed Benny forever. He was already a skeptic of institutions because of what happened to his mother. After what Benny saw in the war, his skepticism only deepened. He felt that the American government's practice of legalized murder was still criminal behavior. Benny had grown to know and care for so many soldiers, including some of the South Korean soldiers, who were their allies. One time the Korean soldiers "captured" him and took him back to their camp because they thought he was one of them. It sounds crazy, but because of Benny's Native American ancestry, his race could be difficult to determine, especially when he was covered in military gear and battlefield grime.

Benny lived among the Koreans long enough to learn some of the language and to get to know the people. Watching the Koreans get shot down and blown to pieces was hard for him to take.

Aside from the people who were meaninglessly killed, the destruction of plant life and animal life was also overwhelmingly traumatizing for Benny. Rivers that were drinkable one day were contaminated by bombs and shrapnel the next day. Animals that were unable to escape a forest that the army set ablaze were charred to ash. The mountains, which Benny summited and where he felt closest to God, were bombed to smithereens. American soldiers launched bomb after bomb, shot bullet after bullet, and at no point did the death of any soldier from either side make any sense to Benny. For him, the real enemy was the US government, for invading Korea and tricking people into believing the invasion was a righteous thing to do. He quickly grew to believe that the true enemy was not who he was told to believe it was.

Benny served four years in the army and left with an honorable discharge. He stayed as long as he did only because his siblings needed money. After his mother died, his father was a broken man, unable to work and care for the family. Philadelphia's Family Court was going to split up the remaining four or five underage Leaphart children and move them to group homes. Benny, along with his brothers Fonnie and Marvin and their big sister Louise, wasn't having it. The brothers relied on their income from the military to help provide for the younger siblings. Louise got a job with Bell Telephone as a switchboard operator. They all held their jobs until the kids were old enough to be left alone by the courts.

When Benny returned from the war, he caught the eye of Dorothy Clark, who everybody called Dotty. She lived a few neighborhoods over from the Leaphart residence.

Dotty and Benny first met in the summer of 1953 and were married by March 1954. They had a strained love because they both wanted children but couldn't conceive. Throughout their marriage they had numerous miscarriages and false-positive pregnancies. As two people who deeply loved children, having none of their own drove a sadness between them and eventually, after nearly twenty years together, a permanent separation. Dotty was forever linked to our family, though. I remember her even in her later years bringing me and other children to her house for weekend visits. She was one of the most decent, polite, and warm human beings I ever met.

To financially support them after his military service, Benny worked as a drummer with a jazz band that toured nationally. He'd grown up about a mile away from where jazz great John Coltrane lived, and spent a lot of time in Fairmount Park directly across the street from Coltrane's house. Benny loved that park. It was where he got to convene with nature.

Already, Benny was showing a strong interest in animals, plants, landscapes, getting his hands in the dirt, and building things. He learned about craftsmanship from his father. And it came in handy. When his siblings couldn't afford furniture, Benny used salvaged lumber to build pieces so fine that people were shocked it didn't come from a furniture store.

As a drummer, though, Benny couldn't have been further away from the furniture making he loved. He was in New York City a lot, or on the road, playing with jazz musician Ornette Coleman.

He sent money home whenever his family needed it. In times of distress, they knew they could check the mailbox to find a letter and some cash that Benny had earned from playing. He always helped as much as he could.

While touring, Benny was also educating himself about global politics and activism. Having seen America with a clearer and broader lens, as a son and as a soldier, he believed that it was America's structural system and warped priorities around war, health, and the environment that led to millions of senseless deaths, including his mother's.

The government that was supposed to protect people, Benny observed, was the same government that turned a blind eye to racism, classism, and sexism. Benny came to believe that the United States government made people ill. He learned that the same government he risked his life for also took bribes from industrialists who created life-threatening products. For Benny, the culprit for all of life's suffering—be it animal life, plant life, or human life—was the government. He believed this to be true, from the most gigantic oil-spilling sea tanker to what seemed like a simple or an innocent product, like a plastic comb.

Benny's transformation from Average Joe Black American to Revolutionary was a slow progression. First it was his mom's death, then the Korean War. The civil rights movement made an impact, as well. Benny studied and drew inspiration from many leaders, especially Dr. Martin Luther King Jr.

Benny watched Dr. King and felt that his message of peace and love resonated with all the feelings he already had inside of himself. Still, he had a few significant criticisms.

Dr. King was a God-fearing, Christian man, but Benny felt that he was a masochist. The idea of not fighting your enemy back after they attacked you was a massive turnoff for Benny. Civil disobedience, as taught and preached by Henry David Thoreau, Mahatma Mohandas Gandhi, and then Dr. King, basically instructed people in search of liberation to fight their enemies with a cocktail of love, kindness, and hugs instead of punches. Benny's beliefs were rooted in love like Dr. King, but Benny was not a pacifist. He was not about to pray and wish you well if you were beating him with a nightstick or a baseball bat.

Dr. King once said, "We shall match your capacity to inflict suffering by our capacity to endure suffering. We will meet your physical force with soul force. Do to us what you will, and we will still love you, but be assured that we'll wear you down with our capacity to suffer."

That sounded like a joke to Benny. Remember, he served in the military and grew up in West Philly. As a kid, I heard the story from one of my aunts about a day when Benny was strolling through Powelton Village. A couple of white K9 cops on the beat were bored and decided to step to Benny.

"What are you doing out here?" hissed one of the officers. "I'll pull those dogs out the car and sic them on you, boy!"

Benny glanced at the patrol car and saw two caged dogs growling, foaming at the mouth, and moving enough to shake the car.

"Now I love dogs, but if you want to keep them dogs, you better keep them in that cage," Benny told the cops. "If your dog acts like a monster and attacks me, I'll treat him like the monster that he is."

That sums up Benny's mentality in a nutshell. He wasn't looking for trouble, but the man surely wasn't turning any down. He believed in the first rule of nature: self-preservation. To Benny, allowing your enemy to slap you, spit on you, or sic their dogs on you was absolutely a no-go. Further, Benny felt that Dr. King's pacifism incited more violence, which went against the reason for his protests in the first place. Allowing your enemies to slap you was not the path to earning respect. You couldn't be slapped into a space of equality. You had to fight for it.

Benny also felt people needed clarification about the difference between nonviolence and self-defense. Nonviolence does not eliminate one from practicing self-defense, Benny liked to say. All life defends itself. Lions protect themselves against enemies. Gorillas will pound on their chests and beat the hell out of somebody. Even plant life defends itself and has different mechanisms to continue procreation and self-preservation. Yet Benny believed that Dr. King's commitment to pacifism was unhelpfully misunderstood as being peaceful to the point of allowing brutality.

Another tidbit of disillusionment for Benny was Dr. King's marital infidelity. Rumors about Dr. King's affairs had been circulating throughout activist communities for years. It bothered Benny. A man should fight for his people, with the only reward being liberation—not sexual pleasures.

As Benny's journey as a revolutionary progressed, he started to question everything he was taught about the way people are "supposed" to live. He especially developed a deep resentment for Christianity. Christianity was the strongest tool used for maintaining slavery in America. Enslaved people's ancestral religions were beaten out of them and they were taught Christianity in its place. Benny considered that psychological warfare. He also felt that praising a God that you cannot see was senseless. This questioning of the Christian religion made it even harder for Benny to follow people like Dr. King, Ralph Abernathy, and other heralded Christian leaders of that time. It also made room for Benny to begin giving serious thought to his own approach to revolution.

Initially Benny wasn't planning to spearhead a movement. He just wanted to be a part of one. Fighting injustice takes hard work, and in order to make the most powerful impact for people's freedom, the leader needed to be strong-minded, strong-willed, and unimpeachable.

Benny researched Elijah Muhammad and the Nation of Islam. He loved the Nation, Minister Louis Farrakhan, and the powerful, dynamic sermons by Malcolm X. He further appreciated the Nation's mission to teach Black people a thorough knowledge of their history. However, Benny couldn't get past how Elijah Muhammad was able to live like a king while so many of his followers lived like peasants. Why did these so-called leaders get fancy meals, extravagant mansions, and special treatment while the followers were forced to survive living off sales of bean pies and the *Muhammad Speaks* newspaper?

Benny's thoughts and feelings would be fully vindicated later on, when Malcolm X began having the same issues with Elijah Muhammad and the Nation in general.

As Benny observed these other organizations, groups, and ideas, he noticed that none of them led with the understanding that all life is from one God. If people can be shackled and enslaved, so can animals. If animals can be bartered, so can water. All life is endangered by the same system. For Benny, there was not nearly enough emphasis on this fact.

Benny believed that all life is important and needs to be seen as equally important. Dr. King was fighting for civil rights and racial integration for people. Malcolm X and the Nation were fighting for the Black community. But who was fighting for the lions locked in cages at the zoo? Who was fighting for the tigers forced to jump through rings of fire in the circus? Who was fighting for the whales whose ocean waters were being polluted by the shipping industry? Who was fighting for the mountains blasted to bits by industrial miners? Benny saw that some groups fought for people but didn't fight for the environment. Some groups fought for the environment but didn't fight for people. Some groups fought for Blacks but not Asians. Benny was clear that all the fights had to be linked. If the air, water, and soil are polluted, then the people will be polluted as well. If the environment's polluted, in general, then everything will suffer. So everything had to be fought for together, totally—as one. It was what Christianity, Islam, and every other religion should've been, but clearly weren't.

Benny didn't blame America only. People all over the world had been systematically indoctrinated into a society based on exploitation and plunder, and they were conditioned to protect and perpetuate the very way of life that was keeping them down. He saw a sick cycle in place that imbued people with a love for things that were not natural and a resistance to what *was* natural. Benny called this phenomenon the reform world system, or the System for short.

According to Benny, any country that embraced big industry, technology, and science instead of living in a natural and organic way would face the same problems. Water is natural, the air is natural, naturally grown fruits and vegetables are natural. Technology and computers are not. Their creation and usage pollute the planet. Benny believed that the System was the cause of every problem that existed. Homelessness, extortion, corruption, murder, rape, prostitution, drug addiction, and war. Every problem. And Benny felt that there was only one solution to these problems: a true revolution.

With a tidal wave of insight and crystal-clear clarity, Benny felt he had his answer. He believed that the entire System needed to be destroyed, and that the only way to destroy it was to detach oneself from the trained addictions of the System and to embrace Mother Nature, who is the god of life. Benny referred to Mother Nature as Mama. He had a very personal connection to Mama and eventually encouraged others to connect themselves to her and to call her Mama, too. He believed that an acknowledgment of Mother Nature's power was the right mindset for destroying the System and healing the world.

Benny thought that to destroy the System, people needed to take the same type of approach that the System was taking to kill, enslave, and addict them. He would say things like:

"All of life is threatened because of the presence of this system."

"You need to be forceful to fight this system."

"We need to fight this system with everything we've got."

"We need to reject this system and everything about it."

"We need to eat the food that life gives us, not the poison that the System gives."

"We need to be strong like animals and not weak like how people have become."

"We need clean air, not polluted air. We need pure water, not poisoned water."

Benny wanted to get all this down on paper to spread his message further. His writing skills were subpar because of his stunted formal education, so he called on his many nieces, nephews, and siblings, and a few friends to help him compose his ideas and beliefs. This went on for years. Day after day, weekend after weekend, Benny dictated his thoughts about the System, his methods for combating it, and more. When he was finished, Benny had more than six hundred pages. He called it "The Analytical Book of Life." It detailed his mission, which he called his "work." From his writings: "My work is to show people how corrupt, rotten, and criminally enslaving the System is. My work is not done till all violations are put in the ground, processed, and cleaned up. I mean to do this, and ain't nobody gon' stop me."

After a couple of years of writing, constant thinking on his beliefs, and then years away on the road, Benny reemerged with a new name: John Africa.

Chapter 3

THE BIRTH OF MOVE

Benny's marriage to Dotty was nearing its end. He hadn't seen his family in a couple of years. His playing in the jazz band had kept him traveling around. He resurfaced with a phone call to his big sister Louise in 1972. "Hey, babe. How you doing, babe?"

"Benny?!" my great-aunt Louise said. Louise was a tiny woman. She stood four foot eleven and had a thin build of maybe a hundred pounds on a heavy day. She had a light-skinned complexion and the iconic afro that Black people wore in the 1960s and 1970s. Louise was a very principled person and she knew it. Her clarity of who she was made her feel comfortable being stubborn about things Benny strongly believed. She was not gullible or flighty. Like iron, her resolve had been forged by fire. If she stood by something, it was because it proved itself to be trustworthy. Everyone knew it took a miracle to change Louise's mind when it was about something she really believed in. She and her brother were close. He was happy to hear her voice after such a long time.

"Yeah, Louise! Yeah, babe! It's me!"

"Benny!" Louise said, all excited. "I spoke to Daddy today, and he told me you wrote a book. And he said it was good, too. In his words, he said you 'defied logic.'"

"Yeah, babe, I'm working hard to fight this system. And guess what else, my book is being taught three nights a week at community college. You gotta check it out."

Like Benny, Louise didn't like the way the System functioned. But she still believed it could be made into a better system for Black people with enough effort. She believed that as long as you worked hard and did what you were supposed to do, there was no way you could go wrong. And for the most part, that was the way her life was playing out. Louise came from the same ghetto Benny came from, the same house. But with hard work and dedication, she moved up the ladder. She earned herself the ideal American life. She got married to the love of her life, had a son who was a straight-A student, and bought a house on Osage Avenue that was as far from the bottom of West Philly as it could be. In fact, if she went across the street, she'd be in Cobbs Creek Park, which separates Philadelphia from the fancy suburbs. Louise was proud of her life, her family, and all her achievements.

She knew Benny was a hard worker, so she was proud to hear about him excelling. What shocked Louise was that her little brother, who could barely read or write, wrote a book.

"Okay, so what's it about?" she asked. "Dad said you covered many topics, but what's the book really about?"

Benny was tripping over his words, he was so eager to explain. "Oh yeah, I talked about the System and how it imposes on everyone, all life, all forms of life. The System uses school to make us obedient. They used processed food to make us weak. They use religion to subdue us."

"Religion? Wait, Benny," Louise said. "Wait, wait. Did you mess with my God in your book? Did you mess with my God?"

Louise was an old-school Baptist just like Dr. King and Coretta Scott. In fact, some of her early activism included corresponding with Coretta Scott King to support making MLK Day a national holiday. Louise told me that one of her greatest memories was taking her son Frank, when he was still in grade school, to hear

Dr. King speak in Philly in 1965. She adored church, attended services all her life, and decorated her house with lights and angels every Christmas. Now Benny was about to insult her God.

To Louise, her religion was just like her job: do the right things and it will serve you well. She was one of those old-fashioned people who never liked to try new things as long as the old things worked. She was always talking about how old cars were made better than the new ones. The old skates rolled better than the new ones. She would never start using something new unless the old one was discontinued. She was the same with religion. Her belief in the Bible was a staple in her family. There was community, love, and understanding. And if you followed up your prayers with a good heart, your prayers would be answered.

Benny paused, recognizing the waters he was stepping into. "Yeah, babe, he's gone. Your God is gone."

"Then I'm gone." Louise hung up the phone. She didn't plan to speak to Benny again unless he showed respect to her beloved Jesus.

But a few weeks later, the house across the street from Louise's, also on Osage Avenue, burst into flames. Louise was sitting at her kitchen table when she noticed smoke dancing around different sections of that house. Screaming fire engines immediately followed a strong burning smell. Louise ran to the window and saw a collection of trucks carrying fire hoses and battling a ferocious blaze.

She knew that three latchkey kids were normally inside. They were friends with Frank, and all around thirteen or fourteen years old. Their parents worked overnight, so to keep their kids off the street and away from trouble, they locked them in the house with a double-keyed deadbolt.

Other neighbors saw the fire and knew the kids were trapped inside, too. It was an unthinkable scenario. Louise saw hands from inside banging on the windows. She couldn't bear to watch. But God. Louise had God.

She ran into her kitchen, dropped down on both knees, and reached both hands to the sky. "Father God in the name of Jesus, please don't let them kids die in that house," Louise begged. "Lord, please bless the hands of the firefighters to get in there and rescue them babies. Lord, please let them find a way out, safe and sound. Keep the smoke and the flames at bay. Let the water do its job. Let the kids come out safely. Father please, don't let them kids die in that house. Don't let Frank's friends die. Don't let that mother and father come home to three less children. Lord, please!"

Louise's face was soaked in her own tears. She was scared and continued to pray—for the parents, for the children, and for Frank, who was looking on. Her final words to her God were, "If you let them kids die in that fire, you and I are through."

The three children all died in the fire. When she went outside, Louise saw them being carried out in body bags. Her devastation was total. How could such a thing happen? How could God let that happen? Something in Louise that she thought was solid as rock suddenly felt muddy.

Bewildered and probably a bit in shock, she grabbed Frank and walked past the fire trucks and all the commotion. She started walking and crying with Frank, landing six miles away at Benny's house.

Benny was carrying some wood into the house just then, to do some building. He spotted his sister in disarray, tossed the wood to the side, and ran toward her. "What's wrong, babe? What's wrong?"

Normally a mouthy person, Louise was silent.

Benny scooped her up and carried her over to the porch, where he sat her down and wrapped his arms around her small, trembling body. The two sat in silence until Louise parted her lips and told her brother what happened.

When she finished, she asked, "What did you say about that God?"

"I said he's gone," Benny answered.

"Yeah. He is," Louise replied. "Tell me more about what you believe."

Benny encouraged Louise to take some time to adjust before he heaped a bunch of new ideas on her. After a few months she was ready to listen. By that time, Benny's appearance had changed. He had strange, antenna-looking hair protruding from all over his head.

"Benny, what is that on your head?" Louise asked.

"These are locs," he explained. "It is obstinate to comb your hair when nature guides it to lock. Natural living is where we gotta get back to, babe.

"Just look how we live," Benny continued, meaning all of society. "This unnatural world ain't good for nobody, including the people that created it and keep it going. The System created this idea and uses religion to control people. But the only true god is nature. And the example of how we should be living is found in the example of wild animals that don't violate nature's course. Wild animals that have never been imposed on by the System follow the natural laws, not the System.

"You don't see whales praying to a fucking book. You don't see tigers going to no church. Only people. Only humans pray to this God that they say is merciful and great. But it's all designed to control people's minds, to keep people obedient and locked into a system. Religion ain't even natural."

Louise was trying to pay attention to Benny, trying to keep up. But she was stuck staring at his uncombed hair. Benny used to be a fly dresser with tailored suits and the neatest hair in the Leaphart family. The transformation to locs was too stark not to stare.

Benny noticed but didn't comment. He knew why she was staring, and it wasn't unusual. In 1972 locs were not popular. Bob Marley wasn't an international star yet. Most people in Philly had never seen them before.

Benny began to make regular trips over to his sister's house to continue explaining his book and his new beliefs about religion and natural law. Louise transformed from a person who wasn't willing to listen to her brother at all to being open to his ideas and practices. Finally, he thought she was ready to hear about the next phase of his movement-building.

Around then, Benny visited her with a man named Donald Glassey. Benny and Don lived on the same street and were neighbors. Don was average-looking in every way. About five nine and 150 pounds, with a touch of male-pattern baldness. He was an Honest Abe–looking type of white dude with a big heart and a strong interest in dispelling the myth that whites and Blacks couldn't work together. And he loved Black culture. Don had a Black girlfriend named Marie. They had a daughter together.

Don was the type of white dude that hung out with Rastafarians in Jamaica and bought marijuana by the pound. He once was detained for suspicion of drug smuggling. He was committed to shedding the white's man reputation of speaking with a forked tongue and backstabbing, and he was all-in with supporting justice for Black people.

Don loved Benny and his ideas, and he was one of the people who helped Benny get "The Analytical Book of Life" down on paper. That was also how it ended up in a classroom at Philadelphia's community college. Don was a sociology professor there and was happy to teach Benny's writings to anyone who showed up.

Don was also key with Louise. She was enthused to see a white man partner with a Black man in the name of change. The wounds from Dr. King's assassination four years prior were still raw. Little more than a decade earlier, Ruby Bridges was the first Black person to integrate an elementary school in the south. More and more, Black people and white people were starting to come together to champion equality and real justice. To Louise, whites and Blacks putting their heads together and creating ways to make a change seemed like the best idea ever thought up for Black people's liberation and equality.

Louise looked at Don and Benny. "Did he help you write your book?" she asked Benny enthusiastically.

But Benny thought she was being skeptical and was insulted. He pointed at Don and snarled, "No! He didn't write anything! He didn't conjure one word! He took dictation from me, and he put that down on the paper. He took the words I gave him, but he didn't write or develop any of this stuff. A Black man wrote this! I wrote this!"

Louise realized her blunder. "Benny, I wasn't trying to upset you. It's just—"

Benny cut in. "That's exactly why I changed my name to John Africa."

Louise moved to speak. "What?! I'd heard something about this. I've been wondering about it. Why did you change your name? And why to 'John Africa'?"

"Because Leaphart is a German name. And before long, once my message spreads into the world, people will try to say a German was responsible for this information. Fuck that shit. I know people will try to give a white man the credit for my work, just like they did Jesus Christ. All that suffering, torture, and eventual crucifixion, and the same system that murdered him took his message and his image and made it into some unrecognizable white motherfucker that they use to subdue and control every fucking body."

Don and Louise watched in silence with their mouths hanging open as Benny continued his rant.

"They did the same thing to Beethoven. They took the brilliance of this man and then gave credit to a white face. Before you know it, they're going to do the same thing with Dr. Martin Luther King Jr., if we let 'em. Every Black prophet, every Black messiah, every Black man that wields power and influence, the System wants to take him down. Because finally, they want to take down the Black man, period. Because finally, they want to destroy all life, period."

"All I did was write down what he told me to write down," Don confirmed. He held Benny's book up in the air. "These are all his ideas."

Louise spoke again, more cautiously. "Okay, so I get the Africa part of your name. Why the John part?"

"Because 'John' means 'graced by God,'" Benny replied, calmer now. "And the information that I'm delivering is most certainly godly. What could be more godly than the water? What could be more godly than the air? What could be more godly than the earth, children, the animals, life? And if these things are godly, then what could be more devilish than a motherfucker that supports a system designed to weaken and destroy these godly creations? My job as John Africa is to use what I can to direct the people to the natural way of life that is secure, healthy, and strong, and away from the unnatural, reformed world system that got everything fucked up. Long live John Africa!"

Louise wasn't sure what to say. She'd only ever known her brother as Benny. Nobody even called him Vincent, his actual first name. He was throwing a lot of new information at her. But I knew this woman personally. And I can imagine that she probably had a ton of thoughts that she was reserving for later, when Benny was less worked up. There was so much he was saying—including about religion—that would have given her pause.

In the end, it didn't matter. No one ever called Benny by the name John Africa, and he never told or encouraged anyone to.

John Africa was more like his pen name. Anytime he dictated his thoughts and had them written down, it was with the name John Africa. He wanted Africa to get the credit.

Louise was trying to make sense of this new information from her brother.

"So, Benny," she began, "if you know white people did these horrible things, and you're saying they did them, why would you have a white man with you? Why even allow white people near your ideas?"

"Because this is a strategic revolution. Don can get into places that my Black presence can't," Benny answered. "He can speak to people that won't even listen to a Black man. But if we are to make these changes in the world, it ain't only Black people that need to change. These white motherfuckers definitely need to change, too."

Benny believed that revolution was like fighting an adversary who is heavily armed. You can't expect to match the enemy's fire-power. So strategically, you must create situations that would make the enemy shoot themselves and one another instead of you. Benny believed Don could help with that.

Louise had known her brother as a sweet, kind, mild-mannered person, but now he had completely morphed into a fighter. Despite her concerns, though, her curiosity was piqued. "Okay, okay. What else is in the book?"

"Babe, the book is about the movement," Benny said, pounding his fist into his hand. "The movement of life. Because the true sign of freedom in life is movement. The enslavement of life is stagnation. The animals on the plains in Africa are free when they're free to move. The animals trapped in a zoo are not free; therefore, they stagnate. Running water in a stream is free, but still water becomes stagnant. There are children that roam free, but then there are children who are trapped in a fucking classroom—their energy is stifled.

"People are weaker now than they ever were before. Look at

these crazy motherfuckers out here doing all this crazy shit. God gave women every muscle they need to have a baby, and the System convinced women that the muscles God gave them are inferior to the speculum the doctors use to pry them open. People are more confused than ever before. Women have been having babies naturally in their homes since women and babies existed. Now, in the last fifty years every woman that gets pregnant automatically thinks she needs a hospital to give birth. It's the biggest scam in the world. Natural law is the only correct law to live by, and babe, let me tell ya, when women get into what I've written"—Benny pointed at the book in Don's hand—"they will have their babies at home just like they are supposed to.

"There's a System that's standing in the way of people living according to natural law, this fucked up System. There's also only one solution to this problem, destroy this whole fucking System so we can be free. We need to be free; the only way we can be free is to move. Destroy this fucking System so we can move.

"And that's what the fuck I'm going to do," Benny explained. "My book is nothing more than guidelines, the wisdom of life, the truth. And I know people will try to dispute it, but they'll all fail. Because you can't live without water, so why the fuck would you poison it? You can't live without air, so why the fuck would you pollute it? You can't live without soil, so why the fuck would you contaminate it with goddamn pollution, with pesticides?"

Benny explained how the System violated people and animals and nature every day. And because the System was made up of people, then those idiots were voluntarily violating themselves, and their families.

"The people that run the System don't have any respect for their own children. So how the fuck can they care about a poor Black man from the bottom of West Philly? How can they care about the poor Africans in the jungles?"

The love and care, and the fact that Benny showed the strong passion he displayed in Louise's living room on that day, was the beginning of MOVE as an organization. Louise didn't fully understand her brother anymore, but she knew his words felt right—and whatever he was building, she wanted to be a part of it. Her teenage son, Frank, listened in as Benny spoke. Before the conversation was over, Frank had already thrown away his comb and decided that he wanted to be a part of whatever his uncle Benny was doing, too.

Louise and Frank were not alone. Benny attracted a wide range of members and close supporters to MOVE, as he preached about the ills of the System from his home on Pearl Street in West Philly. Most of the original MOVE members were people who were from the Powelton Village area or were not far from where Benny grew up in the Mantua neighborhood, like Delbert, Janet, Janine, Merle, and Rhonda. Before long there were Red, Dirty Mark, Andy, Sam, Greg, Bob Moses. Jerome and Eddie were brothers, and Conrad was their cousin. Their grandmother lived on Pearl Street near Benny. They had heard this man had conceived a new way of life and could answer the serious problems they faced, and they approached him to see if that was true. Raymond, one of Benny's jazz band buddies, joined early on. Don was MOVE's first white member.

Moe, Big Jerry, and a guy named Will Smith (not *that* Will Smith) were three of Don's community college students. They got turned on to MOVE from Don's class readings and the discussions that followed. Phil was a gangster with a hairpin trigger temper that could easily result in him whipping somebody's ass, or worse. Phil had dark skin, thick locs of hair and one central incisor missing. Bert, Sue, Consuewella, DeeDee, Sandra, Cheryl, Lamont, Shongo, Steve Grossey, and Ray—every MOVE member had a different but important reason for joining MOVE. Big Jerry was a hulking, six-foot-five college football player about to turn pro, but he still felt dissatisfied with his life.

Conrad and Delbert couldn't find a better life in the military even though they risked their lives for the military. Delbert and Moe had physical health issues from separate car accidents that left them both physically impaired. The accident Delbert was in left him nearly paralyzed and with eight plastic rib replacements. Moe's back was broken; when he leaned over to tie his shoes, the pain was so sharp he would pee on himself. Benny encouraged Moe and Delbert to eat healthy and do plenty of yoga stretches and exercises, and he helped them heal to the point where they could run every day, box, scrub cars at MOVE's car wash, and do thousands of push-ups in a day.

Merle came from a very abusive home. When she was a teenager, she got pregnant twice, and both times she was forced by her parents to get backdoor abortions. The second abortion was botched, and it left her with debilitating boils and tumors inside her body. Benny gave her some dietary advice and some exercises to do; eventually her pain went away and she got better.

Some members had health issues and joined because Benny had cures for their ailments. Others had drug addictions, and Benny cleaned them up. They were using drugs as an escape from reality. But Benny breathed so much hope and love into their hearts that they didn't want to escape their new reality. Some of the women had fertility issues. Benny gave them and their husbands specific diets and exercises. Before long, babies were coming. And people came around to eat the unlimited supply of food. The reasons people joined MOVE varied widely, but each reason was respected.

Within two years, the organization expanded from a conversation Benny was having in Louise's living room to having more than fifty members. In the beginning, it was called the Movement, for the activities popular among the members, such as running dogs, washing cars, and protesting against establishments that abused animals and people. From common conversation, the group's name got shortened to MOVE, which was still fitting. MOVE's belief was rooted in the constant movement of all living things. Governmental systems created impositions on life. And if not stopped, the System would destroy all of life. MOVE's aim was to preserve life—and so to be doing good, you had to be on a move.

MOVE was run sort of like a socialist group where everyone contributed to the well-being of the overall. Benny rented a house at Thirty-Third and Pearl Streets. Don owned a house on the corner of the same street. Don's house was a three-story, six-bedroom, Victorian-styled, redbrick house. Because Don had a big house and could fit a lot of people, his house became MOVE's "headquarters." Now with a permanent location, Powelton Village became home of the mop heads, which was how neighbors affectionately referred to MOVE members, who all grew locs. MOVE members also adopted the surname Africa as a sign of unity and commitment to the teachings of Benny as John Africa.

On September 5, 1974, the group was officially and legally set up and registered with the State of Pennsylvania as "MOVE, Organization for Life." It was clear that Benny was the leader of MOVE, but he rejected the title of MOVE leader. He would say people needed to lead themselves once they had the truth. Plus, the assassinations of Dr. King, Malcolm X, and other leaders of the time made Benny paranoid about attempts on his life. So instead of allowing people to refer to him as the leader, he accepted the label the Coordinator."

Benny's writings evolved along with Benny. He was always dictating new material, and "The Analytical Book of Life" became part of a larger body of work. Called "The Guidelines," it became a foundational text for MOVE, as the Bible is for Christians.

As the Coordinator, Benny was responsible for creating strategies to confront injustices in the System. He was also a builder and carpenter, a healer, and oftentimes a referee for the hotheads who fought, and a marriage counselor for the many relationships that formed. He had a new wife, a MOVE wife—Bert. MOVE rejected the state's approval and had no interest in following rules that did not align with their mission, so MOVE members who wanted to be life partners didn't legally wed. Marriage in MOVE was simply a commitment. There was no license from the state, no wedding dress, and no wedding rings.

Gender roles in MOVE were very traditional. Benny believed that babies were supposed to be with their mothers. So a few women worked, but most didn't. And once they had children, women stayed home. Men were to protect and provide. Nobody could be gay or lesbian. Benny considered anything other than heterosexuality as antilife. In later years, some people left MOVE because of this. Benny simply saw it as part of the weeding out process.

MOVE's style of living was as unconventional as their marriages. Benny felt that as the Native Americans had their land stolen by the white man, so was water stolen from the people. He rerouted the water pipes in the house to bypass the meter and stopped paying the water bill. Raymond disconnected the phone at MOVE headquarters from its line and connected it to a local business; they still had a phone but could avoid paying the bill. Many members quit their jobs to fully commit themselves to MOVE. The organization started washing cars to raise money for food, and there was a plan to buy some land in the country so they could grow their own.

The official inner workings about who did what was organized, too. Benny gave people jobs—what he called activities—based on their proclivities. Bob Moses was book smart and legal-minded, so he was the organization's lawyer. Bert loved money, so she was the treasurer. Moe and Big Jerry were the mechanics. Louise became the minister of public relations and communications. Phil was minister of defense. Merle was the minister of administration and keeper of "The Guidelines." Marie and Consuewella were the nurses. Everyone washed cars. Everyone exercised and got as strong as they had ever been.

MOVE had a few overt missions, too. One was to set an example of respecting nature. Another was to live without paying the system for anything, or paying as little as possible. The MOVE car wash that generated $500 daily (over $2,300 in today's money), ran 365 days a year, and the tax man saw no taxes paid. Benny encouraged MOVE women to avoid hospitals if they could and learn to have their babies at home naturally.

MOVE grew so quickly because Benny offered a different perspective and a care for living things that, at the time, felt revelatory to folks. The MOVE organization predates PETA and Earth First. There were no organic health food stores back then of the kind that you see now. Benny talked about nature as the solution to people's problems and could back up his claims. This held tremendous appeal for folks who grew up struggling in the city and who had gotten the short end of the stick over and over again. For them, connecting the body, the soul, the environment, and the larger, fucked up System revealed something that felt new but obvious, once uttered. There was also a sense of rebellion, but for a greater good.

Most of the MOVE members were in their early to mid-twenties. Young and full of energy was exactly what revolution called for, Benny believed. A few members were older, though. Louise was older than Benny, and Benny's jazz buddy, Raymond, was just a few years younger. In the summer of 1974, my grandma LaVerne joined MOVE and brought all of her five children—Gail, Chuck, Dennis, and Scarlet—with her, except one: my mother.

My mother, Debbie, was the last person from Benny's blood family to join the organization. In June 1974, she and my father, Mike Sr., were part of a huge neighborhood brawl that nearly led to jail time. Mom's younger brothers—my uncles Chuck and Dennis—were not in the fight. They were just the cause of it. Their idea of fun was throwing a brick through their neighbor's window. In the fight, one of my aunts used a two-pronged BBQ fork as a weapon and began stabbing folks in the butt cheeks with it. It's a miracle no one was seriously hurt. But the cops showed up, of course. My grandma LaVerne was terrified of what would happen, knowing that three of her children were caught up in this mess. But she needn't worry. My great-uncle Benny smoothed things over with the people who wanted to press charges and then, miraculously, he smoothed things over with the cops.

My mother hadn't been avoiding joining MOVE, but she was young. Still in high school and involved in a lot of different activities. But watching Benny come to the rescue changed things. She knew it was impressive. She felt safe under his leadership, and she could feel the positive force of his influence, especially after reading a section of "The Guidelines" about education and the true love for children. She was very attracted to Benny's beliefs about the troubled state of the world's children and the steps needed to fix it. In MOVE, she felt security and hope.

My dad, on the other hand, had no interest in joining MOVE. He thought they were weird and kind of crazy. But he was madly in love with my mother, and because she'd joined and he wanted to be with her, he joined, too.

Even though Dad wasn't interested in MOVE at first, that didn't mean that he wasn't learning or benefitting from the information and examples all around him. One of the more profound examples he witnessed was the day a dog was nearly fatally shocked by a faulty wiring system. Dad was washing cars in front of MOVE headquarters, and the hose sprayed water on the porch, where some of the dogs were hanging out. One of the dogs immediately seized. People were panicking and calling out to Benny.

Benny, who usually walked around barefoot, stepped onto the porch to tend to the dog and immediately felt the current. He shouted to Conrad to remove the fuses from the electrical panel in the basement. While hugging the dog and trying to comfort him, Benny noticed my father was visibly confused about the order to shut off the electric. Benny explained, "You can't feel what me and the dog feel because you have on your shoes. Take off your shoes."

Dad did as he was told, and damn! He felt like his foot was stuck directly into an electric socket as volts of electricity surged through his body. As soon as the fuses were removed, the dog popped up with relief. Benny never reinstalled the fuses in the electrical panels. He never wanted the dogs to be hurt again.

Benny had a genuine love for all living things, and he would fight for it. That made lasting impressions on people all the time. It was reassuring, and it engendered a level of loyalty to Benny that crossed any normal boundary. He now had an army, and no one was safe from a MOVE onslaught if Benny felt that whatever they were doing was wrong or detrimental to life. Since the beginning, MOVE protested the Philadelphia Department of Education (DOE) for not properly educating children. The DOE refused to adjust its curriculum, so MOVE refused to send their children to school. MOVE constantly protested the Philadelphia Zoo and Barnum and Bailey's Ringling Brothers Circus, claiming animals were meant to be free, not born to be slaves in cages and performing tricks for an audience.

Animal abuse was a sticking point for Benny. One day at head-quarters, a group of MOVE members were watching *The Mike Douglas Show* on television when Benny saw the guest host, Richard Dawson, handcuff a monkey to a chair. The show was taped in Philadelphia. Angered by the sight of an animal being treated this way, Benny called MOVE members to attention and sent Eddie and a few others to the studio to handcuff Richard Dawson to a chair. They were able to get to him. Security was lax back then. Richard Dawson was terrified and infuriated by the act, but before he could utter a word to demand an explanation, Eddie said to him, "Now you know how the monkey felt."

MOVE protested talk shows, institutions, lawyers, religious leaders, neighbors, teachers, scientists, athletes, singers, and comedians. They protested anyone and everyone. They especially protested against police, judges, news media, and politicians. In some cases, they protested at judges' and politicians' homes and threatened to protest at their places of worship. But, no single person was protested against more than "the Cisco Kid," Frank L. Rizzo.

Chapter 4

RIZZO GETS MOVE ON A RUN

F rank Rizzo was the mayor of Philadelphia from 1972 to 1980.
He was not a fan of MOVE.

"I'm going to make Attila the Hun look like a faggot," Rizzo
notoriously said of his approach to dealing with a perceived political enemy.

Born in 1920 to Italian immigrants, Rizzo, the son of a cop, was
the owner of a true American story. He started out as a thuggish
street cop, who had only a ninth-grade education, and clawed his
way up to being a hard-nosed, take-no-shit police commissioner.
The guy was anxious to meet MOVE in the streets. He was just as
committed to his belief that Black people were inferior as Benny
was to his belief that motherfuckers like Rizzo needed to go down.
Rizzo urged white people to fight Blacks for better jobs.

Rizzo had an immense amount of support. Under his administration, Philadelphia had an unrestrained police force with a
national reputation for brutality. The US Department of Justice
even filed a civil rights lawsuit against the Philadelphia Police Department for disturbing practices, including shooting and killing
nonviolent suspects, beating people senselessly, and intimidating
peaceful citizens.

Rizzo worked to build the police budget so that he could buy
all sorts of weapons, including tanks, six-foot-tall Nazi Germany–
style steel barricades, and every type of gun imaginable: Uzis,
AK47s, Thompson submachine guns, M16s, M14s, M1s, M60s,

12-gauges, .50-caliber machine guns, 20-millimeter armor-piercing antitank guns. Rizzo turned the City of Brotherly Love into a gun show, while also stocking grenades, C4, and anything else you would need for war.

Once Rizzo got his weapons, he weeded out the police who weren't willing to use them, and he trained the remaining police to shoot first and ask questions later.

Beyond arrogant, Rizzo would hop on talk shows and radio shows and spew things like, "We are now trained and equipped to fight wars . . . this police department in Philadelphia could invade Cuba and win." And "Break their heads is right. You're dealing with criminals—barbarians. You're safer in the jungle."

Widely condemned in the Black community for his heavy-handed tactics and racist attitude, Rizzo gave his officers free rein on what he saw as troublemakers or dissidents—and minorities, of course. And this was precisely the kind of injustice and oppression MOVE opposed. As Benny and MOVE aimed more of their protests directly against law enforcement, the oppressive tactics used by the police got increasingly more violent. My mother's brother—my uncle Chuck—was only thirteen years old when police arrested him for protesting during school hours. He was easily identifiable as a MOVE kid because of his hair. Most kids that are nabbed by a truancy officer are taken home, and maybe given a fine. Because Chuck was a MOVE member, he was sentenced to ten days in jail. More and more, MOVE was vulnerable to harsher police tactics.

MOVE followed a carefully planned strategy created by Benny at police demonstrations. Threats and arrests wouldn't stop a protest. That was the strategy. "Don't be stopped. If you're right, continue to be right," Benny instructed. In response to MOVE's tactics, the cops started making trouble on the front lines, which didn't stop the organization at all. Again, if you are part of MOVE, then you were committed—and that commitment stretched far past pedestrian ideas like the wants and needs of law enforcement. Jail time and police beatings were just a part of the plan to tie up the court system, or what you might call *the cost of doing business.* MOVE members expected that coming in.

At first, MOVE's pregnant women and the breastfeeding mothers were a deterrent for police attacks, but eventually it didn't matter.

Most MOVE members were prepared for arrests and charged to the front lines when action called. Rizzo's cops successfully subdued other fringe groups like the Philly chapter of the Black Panther Party with this type of surprise and unjustified arrests. Like MOVE, the Black Panther Party wasn't a radical hate group—they wanted peace and equality and the opportunity to thrive for all, not to be harassed by police. These simple goals may seem like they should be normal now, but fighting for this was radical at the time.

In 1970, Commissioner Rizzo had members of the Black Panther Party stripped naked—down to their birthday suits—and then photographed, arrested, and publicly humiliated right in front of their headquarters, to send a message to anyone interested in aligning with their cause.

Still, MOVE proved to be a very different opponent. MOVE members felt like family. And the family's deep commitment to one another was forged by the ability to remain firm under intense pressure, which only led to more determined protests, which led to more arrests, which gave rise to even more protests.

The police response intensified to mass arrests, where every MOVE member on-site was taken into custody, including the pregnant women who weren't even in positions to be arrested. The cops played dirty. MOVE women were arrested for walking from their houses to the grocery store. MOVE women went to the public phone booth around the corner from their house to make a phone call and left the booth in handcuffs.

In May of 1976, MOVE filed a $26 million civil suit against the city of Philadelphia for the injuries and losses suffered when MOVE mothers and mothers-to-be were subjected to harsh and brutal treatment at the hands of the cops and the sheriffs.

Early MOVE member Rhonda was eight months pregnant and protesting at City Hall when sheriffs picked her up and slammed her head into a window and beat her stomach. A day later she gave birth to a stillborn baby that was covered in black-and-blue bruises. The charges against the police were dropped and the case was dismissed. MOVE had decided that the courts would never side with them, so they stopped going to the court proceedings entirely. Rizzo had MOVE on the run.

Benny aimed to get the children as far away from the confrontational atmosphere in Philadelphia as possible. He, Phil, Greg, and a few others took a trip down south to secure a mortgage on a ninety-six-acre farm in Virginia.

Phil's title was minister of defense, which meant exactly what it sounded like. He was the captain. He was as loyal to Benny as Robin was to Batman. With three of the organization's kids belonging to Phil, he was happy to search for a safe place for the children. Phil was a former hoodlum who never went anywhere without his sidearm and a pack of cigarettes. His attitude about his enemy was the same as the attitude of Rizzo's cops: Shoot first.

Benny wanted to survey the land to make sure it was what he was looking for. The men strolled up and down the rolling hills with Benny, as he laid out his criteria for what to purchase. The land needed perfect road frontage, not too secluded but also somewhat private. Benny talked about the importance of getting the children out of harm's way. Phil listened intently.

"Say, Benny," he began after a while. "Why are we running from Rizzo and the police in the first place? Why not fight firepower with firepower? I got some brothers around the way that'll knock them motherfuckers off with no hesitation. They are killing us, we should kill them back. Maybe they won't be so quick to fuck with us if some of their wives were widows."

"And what the fuck would that solve, Phil?" Benny asked with contempt. "This ain't about killing each other. This is about making a change, setting a good example for people to follow. If you want to just kill, you might as well join Rizzo and the racist cops."

As the men continued walking the land, they were enveloped by an overwhelming feeling of freedom. The clean-smelling breeze with a touch of sweet peaches in the air mesmerized them. The sky was clear of pollution and smog, and there were no buildings obstructing their view of endless nature. The grassy fields were green and lush with vegetation and had a natural spring where fresh, freezing-cold water bubbled through a pile of rocks.

"This is where our children need to be. Close to Mama. This is the definition of peace. This isn't Philly, but this is where MOVE will expand," Benny declared to Phil and the rest of the guys. "Think of a name for MOVE's sister chapter."

"Why don't we call it 'The Next MOVE'?" Greg said. "No, how about MOVE VA?"

"Nah, man, it has to be something that represents life and the direction our children are headed in," Benny responded. "Something that lets you know what this thing is about. It's got to be about the origin and the direction."

The three men surveyed the land for a few more hours. They reached the top of a steep hill, where they decided to rest and watch the sunset. As the sky was turning orange and the night breeze blew through the fields, Benny blurted out, "I got it, I got it! The Seed of Wisdom. Let's call it the Seed of Wisdom!"

Benny loved it.

The men went back to Philly. MOVE had at least thirty children. Some were babies still breastfeeding. Rhonda's son Birdie; Consuewella's daughters Tree and Netta; and Scarlet's kids Darren, Kasey, and Inchy were six or seven years old and among the oldest kids. My sister Whit and other MOVE kids, Delisha, Jamila, and Izzy, were among the younger ones.

Benny and the men gathered as many MOVE kids as their parents would allow to leave Philly to live on the farm. Not all of them went.

My mother was the minister of education. Part of her responsibility was taking care of the children. Mom made sure all the kids headed to Virginia got fed and got baths. She packed them up and watched them roll away on Big Yeller, MOVE's school bus. Mom didn't want Whit to go immediately, so she didn't send her.

Unfortunately, the farm plan fell through. When Big Yeller arrived at the farm, they were immediately rerouted. Philly police had followed Benny and the crew to Virginia. By the time Big Yeller got to the land, the sellers had received an in-person visit from the Philadelphia police and felt pressured to renege on the deal. So instead of building a new life on ninety-six sprawling acres, the dozen or so kids and three adults who supervised them had to stay at a small house on just a tenth of an acre. The house had three bedrooms and one bathroom, which didn't work properly. There was a sink but no tub at all, and the only running water was the toilet. That was how the kids washed up—with cold water only.

Because MOVE was trying to practice a natural way of living, they were trying out different ways to apply their ideas. A few examples of what this looked like, in addition to the uncombed hair, was being naked and eating all raw food. MOVE children rarely wore clothes even in the coldest of winter and in the snow. The children also ate all raw food because Benny said, "Nature gives you food raw" and "Don't no stove grow on trees." He wanted the children to be raised in as natural an environment as possible.

MOVE kids did not go to school. Benny believed that education was part of the reason the System was so advanced. He believed that the more educated people were, the more impressionable their minds were to accept the problems we face, such as pollution. "A simpler, uneducated person is harder to convince to pollute the water they got to drink," Benny used to say.

This upset a lot of people. Neighbors and non-MOVE family members called Child Welfare Services on MOVE. They believed that the children were suffering under MOVE's belief system. And they didn't think there was enough room in that small MOVE house for all those kids. When Child Services got its hands on MOVE children, the children went through invasive and rigorous examinations by court-appointed physicians. The agency claimed malnourishment and lack of cleanliness because the children spent most of their time naked. The children were separated, psychoanalyzed, probed, and given cooked food to eat.

Child Services also wanted to see MOVE children in school. This intrusion into MOVE life intensified MOVE members' passionate animosity toward the government. It gave them extra energy to fight. And slowly, Benny, Greg, and others began warming to Phil's suggestion to fight firepower with firepower. Greg got together with some of his friends and got some guns. Some MOVE members disagreed with his decision, some agreed, and some never knew he did it.

MOVE came at Rizzo harder than ever. Any place he was, MOVE would be sure to show up. If he was speaking at a press conference, Delbert might be in the crowd interrupting his speech.

"Shut the fuck up, you racist bastard!"

If Rizzo was attending a fancy dinner and opened his mouth to speak, Conrad cut in: "Hey Rizzo, why don't you stop lying to the people, you fat, filthy motherfucker?!"

MOVE confronted Rizzo and other city officials constantly

and brought their no-compromise approach with them when they did it. They did it with judges when they went to court. They protested at judges' houses if they considered the judge racist or unfair. They wanted the judges' neighbors to know who the judge really was.

MOVE members had hundreds of arrests on the books for this type of action: disturbing the peace, harassment, disorderly conduct, and the like. For MOVE, it was all in a day's work.

A lot of people in Philadelphia agreed with MOVE about Rizzo and judges, but most of them hated the way MOVE members carried out their protests and delivered their message. They used a lot of profanity. And when people objected to the use of so much foul language, MOVE cursed them out, too, for focusing on the curse words and overlooking the truth in their information.

A typical protest at the zoo would go something like this: "Say brother," a MOVE member would shout through a bullhorn to a Black man walking his son into the zoo, "why the fuck would you support a motherfucking establishment that enslaves God's creatures? I bet you are the same motherfucker that gets mad at the white man for enslaving Africans. You are a fucking hypocrite, and the reason we can't get no closer to freedom than a fucking holiday on a calendar."

You can imagine the father's reaction. Parents didn't want their children hearing that kind of language. But MOVE didn't care about anyone's sensitivity to their delivery. And when parents said they were offended by the profanity, MOVE had something for that, too.

"How the fuck could you be more offended by some words of profanity? What the fuck is more profane than slavery?"

This led to constant conflicts. MOVE went to court for disturbing the peace and other minor verbal altercations all the time. Every judge in every courtroom in City Hall was bombarded with

MOVE cases, which made it hard for the courts to hear other cases. There were hundreds of MOVE incidents to sort through. They were throwing a monkey wrench into the wheels of justice.

In court, MOVE members insisted on representing themselves rather than letting public defenders do it. They followed their own agenda regarding what was relevant in their defense, what was admissible, and who would take the lead each time. A judge hearing a case involving a typical misdemeanor arrest for disorderly conduct would have up to a dozen MOVE members in court. Some were already in custody but called as witnesses; some were spectators; and some were codefendants, all using the names John Africa for the men and Joan Africa for the women. When MOVE commandeered the proceedings to argue a case their own way, the judge often resorted to issuing contempt citations to maintain order.

Sheriffs handling courtroom security proved to be as frustrated and callous as the cops. MOVE would appeal every contempt sentence, generating additional court hearings, which would, in turn, lead to more cases as the process repeated itself, snowballing into hundreds of MOVE cases clogging up the court system. Court administrators eventually realized they were squandering significant money and resources on prosecuting what had started out as a trivial arrest, and the financial hemorrhaging showed no signs of abating. The situation called for a different approach.

To purge the logjam, judges began dismissing MOVE cases in wholesale lots, but some judges had a different agenda. Rizzo's police force started targeting MOVE members who were considered most critical to the organization.

Usually when MOVE members were put in jail, they were in for only three or four months at a time. Bob Moses, MOVE's lawyer, was usually able to argue for lesser sentences. So Rizzo's cops put Bob in jail. Conrad, Phil, and Big Jerry, the six-foot-five, three-hundred-pound ex-football player, were physically intimidating. Handcuffs couldn't fit Big Jerry's wrists. When the police arrested him, they had to use leg irons. Three men—Bob, Conrad, and Big Jerry—were arrested, tried, and sentenced to three years each. The escalation from jail sentences to real prison time was devastating for MOVE. It meant Bob Moses couldn't defend members in court, and Conrad and Big Jerry couldn't protect them from prison. No MOVE member was safe walking the street without dire consequences. That was Rizzo's intention.

Everything about MOVE got under Rizzo's skin. The unruly hair, the skin color, the naked kids, the raw food smell—but worst of all was their getting away with it in his city with no real consequences. That was about to change.

Chapter 5

THE FIRST STANDOFF

In early 1977, rumors spread of a planned police raid on MOVE's headquarters. These rumors took on a new urgency when police in Virginia raided the Seed of Wisdom house and took all MOVE children into custody. In response, MOVE prepared their Powelton headquarters for battle.

The men, led by Benny, built a wooden platform about six to eight feet off the ground, made from abandoned house lumber and railroad ties. It covered the front and side of the house and was about as wide as the sidewalk. The platform was designed so that people from the outside could see MOVE members who wanted to be seen, but it also offered concealment for those who wanted it. The platform became a pivotal physical space. It was where MOVE did everything. MOVE members shouted at the police from the platform. They exercised on the platform. They put a barrel on the platform and cooked meals from there. They even conceived some of their babies on the platform. Without question, the platform was the most communal and public spot at MOVE's Powelton headquarters. MOVE also boarded up the windows to ensure no police could enter easily. They set up around-the-clock watch posts to keep an eye out. In every way, MOVE was getting ready to make noise. Or rather, make even more noise than usual.

On May 20, 1977, dressed in fatigues and armed with baseball bats, pistols, and rifles, MOVE members gathered on the platform and spoke through a loudspeaker. They demanded an end to the violent harassment by the city and the release of Conrad Africa, Bob Moses Africa, and Jerry "Big Jerry" Africa.

Delbert spoke into the loudspeaker: "We don't believe in death-dealing guns! We believe in life! But we know the cops wouldn't be so quick to attack us if they had to face the same thing they dished out on unarmed, defenseless folk!"

Other MOVE members nodded their heads, clapped, and stomped their feet, and bumped one another's fists in agreement. Demands to free Conrad, Big Jerry, and Bob Moses continued. One after the other, MOVE members spoke into the loudspeaker to condemn Rizzo and his goons, some of whom had gathered to observe.

With the loudspeaker amplifying their voices and the platform putting them comfortably above eye level from the street, MOVE started to draw a crowd. Some were curious onlookers, and others considered themselves allies to MOVE's cause. Police came and tried to break up the crowd. Some of the people who'd gathered left before the police could usher them away. Others refused to leave and were arrested simply for being there. The people who were arrested were mostly folks from the neighborhood who'd been affected by Rizzo's racist tactics and hated him but didn't want to take things as far as MOVE always did. But looking on, it was easy for them to feel energized and full of purpose. The platform was proving its usefulness.

At the end of the day, MOVE members turned off the PA system and went inside, leaving the police unsure what to do. Much to the dismay of some of the residents in the neighborhood, building a platform around your property was not unlawful. Outspoken Black people having firearms on their own property, which everyone knew MOVE had, was not illegal. No crimes had been committed. Yet a few days later, the district attorney issued arrest warrants for every member of MOVE, including people who weren't on the platform or even at headquarters. The alleged crimes: inciting a riot and brandishing weapons. The PPD said MOVE made terroristic threats, and they noted that MOVE possessed instruments of crime—all felonies with sustained prison sentences attached. Nothing like the hand slaps they bargained for in protesting at the circus or the zoo.

MOVE was incensed. This was one of the most blatant provocations Rizzo directed toward the group yet.

Rizzo was itching to get his arrests but hesitated to have the PPD burst through MOVE's front door. He believed MOVE members had weapons and were bold enough to use them. Instead, Rizzo directed the PPD to wait and make arrests when those named in the warrants left the house. The PPD set up their own watch team on MOVE headquarters, basically daring MOVE members to be seen off the property.

Benny, Moe, and Raymond were among the MOVE members who just so happened *not* to be at headquarters for the platform incident. It wasn't uncommon for people to go away for a few days at a time. But with the arrest warrants on everybody, MOVE members not already at headquarters could not return. They would be arrested on sight. And MOVE members inside headquarters couldn't leave. They would be arrested, as well.

MOVE was essentially in a standoff with the PPD. It was unclear how long it would last.

In the early days of the standoff, negotiator Joel Todd and local activist Walt Palmer helped make some headway. The city agreed to release Conrad, Big Jerry, and Bob Moses on the condition that MOVE relocate from the Powelton Village home. Their reasoning was that the city's Licenses and Inspections agency surveyed the building and determined it to have housing code violations, like overcrowding of people and too many dogs. A small but vocal group of neighbors had been complaining for years. The city also wanted MOVE members who lived in the house to turn over their weapons.

MOVE was willing to have some members vacate the premises and said they'd find homes for the dogs. They also were willing to turn in more than a dozen firearms. But MOVE told negotiators and the PPD that they had no intention of giving up the house or abandoning their headquarters. The standoff continued.

Word got around to neighbors about what was going on. Folks realized that MOVE's resources would quickly dry up. Soon enough, police couldn't keep away the large crowds, including neighbors from the block and the surrounding area who brought supplies to MOVE headquarters by the truckload. The people that didn't like MOVE, like a crew of Black Muslims in the neighborhood and a few undercover cops, brought MOVE a crate of rotten fish and tainted meat that Delbert and Chuck kicked off the platform. Every item had to be inspected before being accepted.

The people who loved MOVE brought good food, like steaks, rice, beans, vegetables, fruit (fresh and dried), canned goods by the skid load, water, wine, juice, vitamins for the kids, reefer for the undercover smokers and sanitary pads, of course, for the women. You name it, it was donated—all in support of MOVE. This didn't surprise many MOVE members, who felt that, ultimately, they had the larger community on their side. Emboldened by the support, MOVE pressed on with the standoff. From the platform each day, they'd yell at the police about their mistreatment of people. They'd read John Africa's writings into the loudspeaker, to spread the MOVE message. They would get into personal, verbal conflicts with white police officers looking on, telling them to treat Black cops better. They'd give out fruit to children walking by, to encourage healthy eating. They exercised constantly. If the Powelton house was MOVE's church, the platform was MOVE's sanctuary. And they wanted Bob Moses, Big Jerry, and Conrad home, but they weren't going to give up their headquarters to do it.

The standoff was the first time loyalty to MOVE's mission was really tested. In accordance with Benny's teachings, all MOVE members cared for life and worked to protect people, animals, and the environment. But most people joined MOVE for more personal reasons. They agreed with MOVE's principles but something else was going on in their lives that made MOVE a soft and welcoming place to land after hardship or misfortune. MOVE members had shared beliefs, but they weren't deep enough. In Benny's absence, the organization began falling apart. Bert, Phil, and Delbert took charge and tried to keep order. But people exercised less, they ate raw food less, and they fought with each other more—both bickering and physical altercations. It became more obvious who was in MOVE because they believed deeply in the cause and who was in MOVE because it was better than some alternative—like being alone or homeless or hungry—and were at least offered righteous work to do.

A few MOVE members tried as best they could to hold the organization together in the way Benny did. But Benny's presence was so large and so respected—almost parentlike for some people—that when he was away, folks reverted back to who they were before they met him. It was like kids with the house to themselves for the weekend. Nobody knew how to act. People were hoarding resources and fighting over them. Some married men and women started cheating on one another. A couple women got pregnant and weren't sure who the fathers were.

The initial burst of support for MOVE was waning, and the reality of strained resources became a constant stressor. MOVE members were tearing up the house from the inside out just to survive. They were using slats from the walls for firewood to heat their rooms in the winter and to cook. They were using rainwater for drinking and washing clothes. Times got so tight that when the food and rations ran low, Delbert doled out food, counting cornflakes and ensuring that everybody was evenly fed.

The city was constantly looking to make life even more difficult for MOVE. They put up a six-foot-tall steel blockade to make it harder for supporters to deliver supplies. They turned off the gas and water. They discovered the phone line Raymond had rigged to a local business and cut it. They even stopped mail delivery. Rizzo was turning the block into a war zone.

MOVE members found some workarounds to deal with cabin fever. People would sneak out to go visit girlfriends or boyfriends, family, and friends. Delbert would sometimes sneak out to Dunkin Donuts. He got caught by fifteen-year-old Dennis, who was making his own store run. In a family MOVE meeting, Dennis was told to stop sneaking out, for his own safety. But without Benny's presence, Dennis didn't feel he had to respect the other members. His behavior became uncontrollable enough that the others thought he was putting the whole group in danger. Dennis didn't care. He felt that if Delbert could sneak out, he should be able to do it too.

Police officers worked overtime, operating a twenty-four-hour watch. The barricade at the intersection outside MOVE headquarters caused traffic detours. Neighboring residents within the perimeter had to show ID to get inside the barricade at different police checkpoints. If you lived on the block but didn't have identification to prove your residence, you couldn't enter.

Tensions rose as weeks and then months passed, with no end to the standoff in sight. Many negotiators and mediators sought to find a peaceful resolution. The police wanted MOVE to surrender, MOVE wanted the police to leave them alone, and neighbors eventually started to lose patience. They wanted their neighborhood back. Talks around a brokered agreement always hit a dead end when MOVE insisted that their demand for Conrad, Bob Moses, and Jerry Africa's release was nonnegotiable. The standoff also prevented MOVE plaintiffs from attending hearings for their $26 million civil suit against the city. With no one to attend the hearings, the case was dismissed.

But in May 1978, the city announced terms of an agreement that would end the yearlong standoff for good. MOVE agreed to be taken one member at a time to the police administration building, for immediate release on bail. The DA's office agreed to dispose of all pending MOVE cases within four to six weeks. A MOVE attorney would handle the court proceedings to avoid further contempt charges. The barricades and roadblocks would come down. Police would be allowed to inspect MOVE's headquarters. MOVE would relinquish their weapons. The city agreed to assist MOVE in finding other locations for them to set up their headquarters within ninety days. Additionally, the courts imposed a gag order, which allowed the city to save face about Bob Moses, Conrad, and Big Jerry's release from prison. For MOVE, this was an impressive victory. There was no bloodshed, and they had forced the city to meet their demands.

Disagreements emerged in the weeks that followed. The city insisted MOVE had to vacate the house within ninety days, regardless of whether or not they had procured an alternative site for their headquarters. The city also indicated that the Powelton house had to be razed as soon as MOVE left. MOVE strenuously objected to this demand. They were open to having another MOVE location to help solve the overcrowding concerns. But they never wanted to give up the house, let alone have it torn down.

Meanwhile, MOVE's standoff was proving productive. After three rowdy, unrelenting months of MOVE calling for the city to free Bob Moses, Big Jerry, and Conrad, the city finally relented and the men were released.

MOVE was ecstatic. Their tactics had worked. It was exhilarating, and it fueled MOVE to push for more. The terms of the agreement for the three men's release—turning over all their weapons and giving up their headquarters? MOVE refused to honor it—mostly because they ran out of time. They had to find homes for their dogs. They didn't want to have them taken by the American Society for the Prevention of Cruelty to Animals (ASPCA) and euthanized. Rizzo refused to give them an extension of time. The decision angered MOVE further. To them, Rizzo was a racist and a liar and a crook anyway, and there was no honor with crooks. They would give Rizzo nothing but a stack of guns that were inoperable.

Before Rizzo realized he had been hoodwinked, the men were released, yet the standoff continued.

By late July 1978, Rizzo decided enough was enough. He announced in a press conference that he would carry out warrants for MOVE members who broke the agreement and he'd remove the remaining members from the house, claiming housing code violations. The PPD geared up for battle. Inside the house were pregnant women, nursing babies, children, and animals. Community activists again aided MOVE and rushed the platform. They were beaten and arrested by the police, who stood at the barricades to make good on Rizzo's boast. As it turned out, Rizzo was reacting with a violent assault because of a newspaper article that reported how many tax dollars had been spent on the MOVE standoff. Police overtime topped a million dollars. A MOVE member later told me that one officer racked up so much extra money that he bought himself a boat and named it after Delbert Africa.

Still, the standoff kept going. It began to make national, then international, news.

Thousands of Philadelphians marched around City Hall in a massive protest demonstration. Internationally, Philadelphia became an embarrassment to the human rights initiatives of Jimmy Carter and United Nations ambassador Andrew Young.

On August 2, a judge ruled that MOVE had violated the order to vacate the house. He then issued arrest warrants for nearly every adult MOVE member—twenty-four people in all. MOVE members refused to leave their headquarters.

On Tuesday, August 8, 1978, hundreds of cops in flak jackets and riot helmets surrounded the Powelton house at dawn and ordered MOVE to surrender.

MOVE refused to comply. Instead, they alerted each other to prepare for the onslaught. They filled buckets with water and rags, knowing tear gas would likely be used. Men grabbed guns and positioned themselves behind stone walls and columns in the basement.

Firefighters then rolled out water cannons. The streets department used a wrecking ball and a cherry picker on the house, which tore parts of it down and smashed through the windows. The house was badly damaged. Debris everywhere. Just before 7:00 a.m., Police Commissioner Joseph O'Neill yelled through a bullhorn, "Uniformed officers will enter your home to take each of you into custody! Any resistance or use of force will be met with power!"

"We were being battered with high-powered water, and smoke was everywhere," my mother recalled later in an interview, referring to the tear gas. "I couldn't see my hands in front of my face, and I was choking. I had to feel my way up the stairs to escape the basement with my baby Whit in my arms, just so we could catch our breath. I was almost eight months pregnant." (Meaning, with me.)

Benny had taught MOVE a Never Surrender and Never Let Them Take You Alive policy. MOVE members had learned never to put themselves in a position where they were in the System's hands. Rizzo represented the System. Over and over again, MOVE had seen enough police harming them and other Black people to believe that they had a better chance staying in their house than to walk into the hellscape that was the PPD, who were on record as wanting to "break their heads."

There was a lot of commotion inside the house. Dogs barking. Water spraying everywhere from the hoses, with water rising. Men tightened their grips on their guns and yelled about the best defensive crouch to take. Women carried kids on their backs to try to keep them calm and above the water. It was chaos. As prepared as MOVE thought they were for serious conflict, now that it was in front of them, all hell was breaking loose.

Tear gas was making it impossible to breath or see. Mixed with the August heat, it created a steamy, mist-like vapor that stuck to the skin and burned. MOVE members' beliefs about the System and their faith in Benny's teachings were solid as rock, but at a certain point, it wasn't more important than a good, deep breath of fresh air. With eyes closed as tight as fights and hands reaching in front of them, one by one, MOVE members shuffled and crawled toward the light. Some folks started ripping off their tear-gas-soaked clothes, which were clinging to them. The PPD's offensive was working.

MOVE members were immediately arrested, and the last of the standoff was over.

Before everyone was arrested, Delbert was grabbed by four police officers and assaulted to within an inch of his life. It was caught on video camera, in one of the earliest depictions of police brutality that got broadcast nationally. Delbert was shot in the chest with a shotgun pellet, then knocked to the ground by the bash of a steel helmet swung by Officer Lawrence D'Ulisse and a rifle butt rammed by Officer Charles Geist. While he was on the ground covering up his face and genitals, Officer Terrance Mulvihill kicked him with a steel-toed boot so hard that Delbert lifted up off the ground. Mulvihill kicked Delbert again and again and again. Officer Joseph Zagame went airborne off one leg and came crashing down on Delbert's head with the other leg and pinned Delbert's head to the concrete. They left a nearly dead Delbert on the pile of rubble that used to be attached to MOVE headquarters, before taking him on a drive in the back of a paddy wagon. Years later, Delbert told me that they beat him all the way to the hospital. He barely survived it.

By lunchtime, all of the MOVE adults who had been in the standoff at headquarters were in police custody. When they were arraigned for court, they were surprised to learn that a cop had been killed. To this day, there is furious debate about who was responsible.

Witnesses say a man from up the street, half a block away and not affiliated with MOVE or the police, fired the first shot. The man had a mental disorder. He was arrested, questioned, fingerprinted, and released because there was no evidence that he was a MOVE member. After his release, police told him to leave Philadelphia immediately, which he did. No charges were ever filed against him.

Police said MOVE fired the first shot and that they fired back in retaliation.

The women in MOVE were in the basement with the children and were never seen with any guns. Among the men who were positioned to see what happened, some insisted that the police fired first; some accepted that MOVE probably fired, too; and others couldn't have cared less who fired first or last. For those men, the PPD's violent presence incited whatever consequences they received.

What is undisputed is that a bullet hit Officer James Ramp, killing him instantly.

For that one bullet, twelve people were arrested for the murder: my parents, Debbie and Mike Sr.; my uncle Chuck; Janine; Janet; Merle; Phil; Delbert; Eddie; Consuewella; Sandra; and DeeDee. Consuewella, Sandra, and DeeDee—down for the MOVE cause but terrified of a murder charge—told the judge they were simply supporters of MOVE and that was why they were at headquarters. They insisted they were not members. But that was not totally true. Consuewella was, in fact, a member but downplayed her affiliation to avoid the full wrath of the justice system. That left nine people from the MOVE organization accused of a police officer killing. That group became known as the MOVE 9.

The MOVE adults who weren't at the headquarters had arrest warrants out, and there was an active search to find them. Benny, Moe, Sue, Carlos, Bert, Dennis, Conrad, Frank, Raymond, Big Jerry, and Bob Moses. The children were in the custody of civil affairs cops but were soon picked up by MOVE members and relatives. A few of the children were taken to the Seed of Wisdom, but some were picked up by their non-MOVE family members and were never brought back to MOVE.

In the aftermath of the confrontation, damage to the Powelton house was so extensive that it was too unstable to leave standing. Rizzo had it torn down immediately. Ignoring that 307–309 North Thirty-Third Street had become a crime scene, police obliterated all the evidence by demolishing the house, bulldozing the property flat, and hauling away the debris. They even cut down the trees and ran it through a wood chipper.

At an afternoon press conference held later that day, Rizzo and the top city officials appeared before a prominently displayed table of weapons that they said were recovered from the house just before it was destroyed. These did not seem to be the same weapons that were actually at the house. MOVE's weapons were muddy and dirty, from the water, grime, and falling debris. The weapons Rizzo put on the table were shiny and new-looking. It became obvious to some of the media, who acknowledged it in their reporting, what kind of narrative Rizzo was trying to spin.

Rizzo told the media, in his typical flashy fashion, that he wanted to end the moratorium on Pennsylvania's death penalty. "The only way we're going to get an end to them is to get that death penalty back. Put them in an electric chair, and I'll pull the switch." He was determined to permanently get rid of MOVE.

As Rizzo spoke, video of Delbert's beating by Philadelphia police was starting to circulate widely. It provided the public with indisputable proof that blanket denials of police misconduct were outright lies.

Delbert survived his beating—barely. The video footage eventually forced the DA's office to indict three of the four officers caught on camera. The case went to trial, but it never reached the jury. Instead, in another example of how lopsided justice can be, Judge Stanley Kubaki issued a "directed verdict" at the close of testimony, acquitting the officers and allowing them to walk away as free men.

Chapter 6

BORN IN PRISON

N othing is more exciting in life and nothing is more important than a new birth.

In America, a baby is born about every eight seconds—usually
in comfortable hospital rooms or special dedicated places in their
homes surrounded by doctors, nurses, midwives, family, and friends.
Five weeks after the assault on my family's home, I was born in a
jail cell at the House of Correction (HOC) on Friday, September
15, 1978.

Mom was laying on her cot when she felt the first contraction.
Having birthed my sister Whit two years earlier, she knew this was
it. She woke up her celly. "Janine, the baby's coming."

"Are you sure?"

"Yeah, I'm sure."

MOVE women who follow the MOVE diet plan and exercise
program have a history of birthing babies pretty quickly. After
some hard pushes, a bitten off umbilical cord and a wipe down
from a warm washcloth that my mom heated with her body, I too
was on my mother's bed cradled in her arms.

HOC—located at 8001 State Road in the Holmesburg neigh-
borhood of Northeast Philadelphia, an address that I would get
to know too well—was one of five local prisons operated by the
Philadelphia prison system. The others are Riverside Correctional
Facility, Philadelphia Industrial Correctional Center, Detention
Center, and Curran-Fromhold Correctional Facility.

Built in 1874 and reconstructed in 1927, the cells were initially designed for single occupancy, in accordance with the Pennsylvania State Prison system. Although the facilities were designed to hold 1,200 inmates, they frequently housed triple its capacity, with many cells being double and, in some cases, even triple occupied. The government had no problem stacking inmates on top of each other like Saturday morning pancakes. To put that into context, try standing in one place and stretching your arms from left to right. You can simultaneously touch opposite cell walls if your wingspan is six feet or longer. Imagine three adult women jammed into that space with all of their belongings, and expected to sleep, rest, and coexist. Now imagine if one of the women were pregnant. My mother, Debbie Africa, was that pregnant woman.

Debbie Angela Davis, born Debbie Angela Sims, was a golden-brown, five-foot-four, slim, fit girl from West Philly, from a poor section commonly known as the Bottom. She was the second oldest of five kids and was known by her family as the most responsible one. Growing up, she was a straightlaced, by-the-book type of kid who never took risks. While her other siblings were finding ways to cut school, eat junk food, and hustle a couple dollars from gambling, Mom was going to school, eating her vegetables, and babysitting neighbors' kids, trying to find ways to make some money to help their mother pay the rent.

When Grandma left the house to go to work, she left Mom in charge of the house because she knew Mom would make sure her siblings ate a well-balanced meal and did their homework instead of eating doughnuts for dinner and watching television all day.

Four of Mom's uncles were military veterans who spoke about their bad experiences in the white man's Korean and Vietnam Wars. Unrest in the 1950s and 1960s took many Black men to war, prison, or early graves. From Mom's perspective, she saw two options for Black people in America: single mothers who lost their husbands to the prison system or the war machine. This reality made her uncomfortable with the idea of having children. Then came my father.

My parents met in 1969, when they were thirteen and fourteen years old. As they grew up together, they discussed ways to remove themselves from the stranglehold of the West Philly ghetto. They wanted jobs that would free them from poverty. They had dreams and goals, and they were willing to work to achieve them. Mom got a job at an insurance company and Dad did the unthinkable. At age sixteen, he enlisted in the United States Marine Corps.

Mom was desperate to escape the vicious cycle of death and destruction, and she was willing to do nearly anything to change the trajectory of her life. MOVE had been helping her to do that. Now she had a double cell.

In a double cell, the two people sharing it were in such tight quarters that only one person could be off their bunk at a time. There wasn't enough empty space for both people to stretch or exercise simultaneously without smashing into each other. And forget about any kind of privacy. The toilets were exposed right at the cell door, where anyone inside and outside your dwelling can easily see, hear, and smell whatever you're doing.

The cells were so disgustingly humid during the summer that it would take a pair of lace underwear two to three days to dry. I've often heard prisoners and ex-prisoners talk about how they would sit on their toilets and use a cup to scoop water out of the toilet tank and pour it over their heads until the evening. They do that from the morning when it gets scorching until the evening when it gets cooler.

My mother often told me about how things were so much worse during the winter, when the water in the faucet trickled out at about thirty-three degrees, while it was two degrees outside.

The water would be so cold it hurt, but the women had no other options.

The bulk of the inmates were kept in the general population. Still, like many prisons, HOC had a vicious hole, full of pitch-black cells that hardly housed one person—and were reserved for inmates who required extra discipline. The hole at HOC was oppressive, segregated, and dirty. The isolation cells were separate from the rest of the population and used so seldomly that the administration didn't have keys for the bars anymore, so they had to install new locks. My mother spent three years in an isolation cell.

Cell walls were full of old, lead-based paint that had curled up on the walls and hardened into stiff, flaky scales. The first turn of the knob on the faucet released a thick black sludge instead of water. In order to take a drink, Mom had to run the water for minutes at a time to give the pipes time to clear out the smell of chlorine and goose shit. These were the conditions for her last month carrying me.

My mom had delivered my sister Whit two years beforehand, with just my dad present. Home birth was the MOVE way. Mom wasn't going to do it any differently with me, no matter where she was. So when she went into labor, she didn't alert the prison guards. Mom didn't trust doctors anyway, especially not prison doctors. She didn't want a nurse to cut the cord or an obstetrician to smack my butt to make sure I cried. Just MOVE family who anxiously waited to greet me on my arrival. She had trust in the other MOVE inmates who were locked in their cells right on the same jail block. She quietly grinded her teeth and grunted through the labor pains.

Merle sang to cover up the sounds of any noises from my cries once I arrived. The women around my mom didn't want the guards to hear me. Merle was a novice singer but a pretty good one, and people loved to hear her singing old tunes from the 1950s and

1960s. This was her perfect opportunity to belt out one of her favorites. She sang "Maybe" by the Chantels until I got quiet. Merle, who'd had two backdoor abortions that she deeply regretted, often talked about how she wished she had protected her babies instead of killing them. At the moment of my birth, she felt like "this was a chance to protect an innocent life."

DeeDee stood guard and kept her eyes peeled for any intrusions from officials and inmates. Consuewella was like my nurse. Never afraid to get her hands dirty, she jumped into action. Consuewella cleaned up the mess from my delivery, chopped up the afterbirth into little pieces and flushed it down the toilet. Mom lay on her cot and wrapped me up in a blanket after she washed me up with the same water from the faucet that poured black sludge before it ran sort of clear.

I was born on a day Mom was scheduled to be in court for the MOVE 9's preliminary proceedings. All nine codefendants were supposed to be there. The charge was a conspiracy to commit murder in the shooting death of a police officer, but those proceedings would have to wait. The day was all about me.

Shortly after I entered the world, Mom tore a page off of a notepad, jotted some words down, folded the paper, and gave it to Janet as she passed Mom's cell and headed to court. "Make sure this gets to Mike," my mother said, slipping the folded piece of paper into Janet's hand.

My father, Michael Keith Davis, grew up the youngest of eight. His parents were Georgian migrants who left the south because, as his father said, he "wasn't going to allow white folks to treat his kids the way they treated him." Dad's mother had a brother who disappeared when he was a young teenager, never to be seen again. The family suspects that the Klan killed him and hid his body, which was not unheard of at the time and was immortalized in the plot of *Mississippi Burning*. Only there were no white FBI agents looking for my great-uncle, like in the movie.

My paternal grandfather, James, taught my father the value of hard, honest work. If you worked hard, you deserved the benefits of your labor, he liked to say. My paternal grandmother was willing to share her earnings from her nursing job with her children as long as they responsibly used the funds to bring in more resources. Coming from a strong Black family home with a secure upbring, Dad wasn't like most of the people who joined MOVE. And he never adapted to living primitively around rats, dozens of dogs, windowless houses, or cops surveilling his every move. My father was turned off by much of the activities in MOVE. He was there only for my mother. He loved her and wasn't going to leave her anywhere without him. This made it more infuriating for him when he learned from Janet that his only son was born in a jail cell.

Janet was one of at least five women in MOVE who were less than five feet tall. What she lacked in height she usually made up for in sheer tenacity, like Louise.

She rolled up in the courtroom like she owned the joint, spotted my father, and placed the letter in the palm of his hand. He opened it, eyed the words, and teared up.

"So, Mike, she had the baby," Janet told him. "It's a boy. I saw him. He's healthy and strong, and his first name is Michael, after his father who is also healthy."

Dad looked proud but angry. Janet gave him a congratulatory hug. Then she turned her attention to the judge, Charles P. Mirarchi Jr.

"Debbie Africa just gave birth," Janet told the judge. "She's holding her beautiful baby boy right now."

"Debbie Africa should be in court," Judge Mirarchi shot back. "I don't know what kind of games you all are playing, but this is not the place."

"Debbie Africa just had a baby!" Janet repeated, this time shifting the energy to the media. Janet wanted every journalist to write it down, put it on the record, and report on it.

"I'm telling you, reporters Mumia Abu-Jamal, Linn Washington, E. Steven Collins! I'm telling you, stenographer! And I want all the spectators to write it down! Debbie Africa had a baby!"

Mumia Abu-Jamal, then a radio reporter, listened intently. As a member of the Black Panther Party (BPP) from the age of sixteen, he was very familiar with unjust court proceedings. He was personally stalked by FBI director J. Edgar Hoover. As minister of communication, Mumia wrote articles for the BPP newspaper and distributed them around Philadelphia. His role with the Panthers got him put on the FBI's counterintelligence program watch list, called COINTELPRO. One day while out shopping with his pregnant wife, Hoover saw Mumia crossing a street and took the time to do the wink-and-gun gesture—he winked at Mumia and pointed the gun at Mumia's wife's pregnant belly.

In courtrooms, Mumia had seen Black women fighting to be heard and getting their mouths stuffed to muffle their voices. So nothing he was seeing in the courtroom that day with MOVE surprised him.

Judge Mirarchi motioned for the prison guard. "I need to hear from the matron."

(Years later, when I asked Janet why she let the cat out of the bag about my arrival, she said she wanted to make sure my birth was on the record, so that the court could never deny my existence. It wasn't unusual for MOVE babies not to have birth certificates, Social Security cards, or even medical records. For Janet, having my birth legally recorded would help protect me from any concealed malfeasance by prison guards.)

Janet twisted her lip and eyed the judge. "I said Debbie Africa just had a baby boy!"

"Enough!" Judge Mirarchi snapped. "If you continue, I'll have you removed from this court without any hesitation!"

"He is strong! He is healthy!" Janet continued. She was looking at the reporters. "He's downstairs in the cell right now. Write it down! I want y'all to know that the baby is there. I saw him. Other inmates saw him move. He is alive! Women have seen him. I'm making it clear right now that if anything happens to this baby, he existed!"

Armed bailiffs and court ordered police officers rushed to Janet and removed her from the courtroom.

My dad's fury at the whole ordeal boiled over. He started yelling to the judge, "You call this law?! You call this law?!" He was escorted out, just as Janet was.

The courtroom erupted into chaos.

When Janet was returned to her cell, my mother was being taken out of jail. Luckily for me, the matrons had returned to the prison and saw that what Janet said was true. They rushed Mom and me out of the prison because they felt that a baby in a jail cell was an insurance liability. At first they tried to bring us out with a couple of white men that my aunt Gail didn't trust. "Wait," she said, as she stopped the head matron, Lieutenant Speech. "We don't know them two men. They look like two racist butchers. My sister and my new nephew ain't going nowhere with them."

Gail's staunch resistance forced the guards to allow her to hand-pick a guard who would take my mom and me to the hospital. Prison officials didn't want a problem out of MOVE, especially concerning a baby. But if they did, Gail was prepared to give them one.

Janet, still being Janet, accompanied my mother as she exited the jail—making sure all the people in the sixty-three cells got a good look at me as I passed. They were all witnesses.

Chapter 7

JOHN AFRICA ON THE RUN

With the MOVE 9 in jail, Rizzo was only partly satisfied. Benny was still free, along with many of his most trusted comrades and ardent supporters—all of whom were wanted for arrest. Rizzo was determined to bring in the MOVE members who were still at large and to convict the MOVE 9 who were behind bars. He wanted MOVE destroyed and was determined to get reinforcements for support. He called in the big dogs: the Federal Bureau of Investigation (FBI) and the Bureau of Alcohol, Tobacco, and Firearms (ATF).

The first thing the Feds did was read the playbook of Rizzo's idol, FBI director J. Edgar Hoover. He was the mastermind of COINTELPRO, a notorious counterintelligence program that targeted—among many groups—the most influential Black political organizations of the time, along with those organizations' leaders and members.

From the literal COINTELPRO handbook: "First things first, find out about any members that have a crime hanging over their heads and take advantage. Any misappropriation of funds needs to be exposed. Take full advantage of any and all weaknesses."

It wasn't shocking that some MOVE members had criminal records that the ATF could exploit. And Don Glassey was maybe a drug smuggler. These federal ATF investigations ran independently, but in total parallel with the ongoing Philadelphia police action against MOVE. Confidential informants, or CIs, were working to implicate MOVE in a bomb-making and gun-running scheme that led to the indictments of several people, including Benny and Moe. Those two were still underground. The PPD and the Feds had no idea where they were. They were indicted anyway.

It took a little doing and at least two years' worth of coercing, but the FBI and ATF found their confidential informant within MOVE. The plan was simple, though the execution wasn't: The CI had to convince as many MOVE members as possible to acquire guns and other weapons, using sources the CI suggested. Then when MOVE members were caught red-handed by the authorities, point to John Africa as the brain behind the operation.

Up to this point, only MOVE members knew Benny was John Africa, because no one was ever called John Africa. Everybody in MOVE called Benny "Benny" to his face. But when it came to MOVE work, everybody *referred* to Benny as John Africa. Even Benny, when writing and talking about MOVE, referenced John Africa in the third person. "The MOVE organization is committed to destroying the System," Benny might say. "John Africa has given MOVE the commitment to stone the System into the ground." That was how it always was. Benny never acknowledged himself as John Africa. Instead, he said John Africa spoke through him.

Further, MOVE members often called one another by different names, to keep outsiders guessing about MOVE's goings-on. MOVE didn't like folks in their business, until they themselves wanted you to know. So at any given time, one MOVE member could be referred to by three or four different nicknames. For example, my name is Michael. I go by Mike. But while growing up in MOVE, I was also called Makita, Kita, and Pooga, and when interviewed by the *Philadelphia Inquirer*, I told them my name was Jack. This was typical. We gave officials fake names because they didn't need to know our real ones. That meant authorities pinning down which MOVE member was John Africa was going to require help from the inside. Rizzo had that inside help. And he knew that nothing would be better at trial than a criminal informant from inside MOVE, as a star witness against the organization.

The CI got to work right away.

Using their position in the organization and their intellect, the CI was able to convince a few MOVE members that Benny wanted to buy nuclear weapons, then blow up the ice caps at the North Pole to flood the entire earth. The absurdity of this claim is off the charts. MOVE's strongest belief was always that all life should be preserved and protected. But the CI knew who in MOVE was so dedicated to doing what Benny wanted that their love and trust for Benny could be used to the FBI's advantage. The CI also knew who was well-meaning but an idiot.

Will Smith was not one of the idiots. A six-foot-three ex-football player, Will had a voice that sounded more like it belonged to a lion in the Sahara than to a man in Philly. Will wanted to keep doing MOVE business the way they'd been doing it. "Benny said do it this way so this is the way we are going to do it," Will told the CI, when approached about the weapons and the ridiculous ice caps story.

A few other MOVE members believed the story, though. The CI had convinced them to work against Benny. Now the CI was trying to convince Will to join, too.

"I know what Benny said," the CI told Will, "but when you were not around, he changed his mind and said we need to get more guns. He said the System will try to kill us and we need to defend ourselves. Plus having guns is not illegal."

Will was having none of what the CI was slanging. "I don't care about legal or illegal, I care about what's right. And as far as I'm concerned, Benny knows what's right. You don't."

Benny had commanded Will's full, unadulterated respect. People assumed Will was strong because of his size and booming voice, and that strong people couldn't be depressed. But Will struggled with depression all his life. He had been to therapist after therapist and found no answer to his problems. He deeply resented his inability to shake free of his depression.

When Benny came into his life, Will felt like he finally had the solution to his problems. Benny's jovial persona was so infectious that people around him took on his mood. So Will spent as much time around Benny as he could. And when he wasn't around Benny, he had the next best thing: Benny's words. Will carried "The Guidelines" in an army-green knapsack everywhere he went. He never wanted to be anywhere without Benny or Benny's teachings as John Africa.

It was working well. Will didn't feel depressed anymore. He was so enthusiastic about his newfound happiness that he was willing to do anything for Benny. Including stand up for him and for MOVE as an organization in court, no matter the consequences. When MOVE members had to face judges, Will's voice could be heard roaring John Africa quotes in the courtroom. His voice blasted over the sounds of the commotion that usually followed when a judge would sentence a MOVE member for assaulting a police officer when the group was really just defending themselves at various protests.

"You judges are confusing God's way of self-defense with your way of legal destruction!" Will would shout. "Because you are confused about the power of right! The purpose of defense! The power of righteousness is man's God-given right that must not be tampered with! This is God law!"

The police dog's barking and the judge's gavel knocking would be drowned out by Will's powerful voice as he repeatedly yelled, "The power of truth is final!"

Being bound, gagged, and held in contempt never broke Will's loyalty to Benny. Will was emblematic of the kind of members

MOVE had—dedicated, relentless defenders who felt grateful to Benny because he had improved, or even saved, their lives. He had helped many of them cast out their personal demons. They would never give up John Africa's identity or do anything to harm MOVE.

Rizzo and the CI that his team deployed knew the scale of the task at hand.

By late summer 1978, MOVE was in retreat mode. The headquarters had been demolished, the MOVE 9 were indicted and soon to go on trial, some MOVE members had lost contact with their children (from when their relatives took them after the confrontation), and remaining MOVE members were wanted for arrest. MOVE as an organization was on the ropes. Benny—aka John Africa—had not been seen in many months. About a dozen other MOVE members also had disappeared. Most of them were not on the platform at headquarters when the other members were screaming into the loudspeaker "Free Bob Africa! Free Jerry Africa! Free Conrad Africa!" Some of them were not present for any part of MOVE's standoff against the PPD. Yet they all had arrest warrants out for them. And they were presumed to be armed and dangerous, with likely connections to MOVE sympathizers who had followed MOVE in the news or were allies. The feds began a nationwide search for them all, complete with wanted news stories and posters on display at post offices in the area.

When Benny first realized he and a few other MOVE members needed to get out of town or risk felony arrest, he packed only enough stuff that would fit in his army-green duffle bag and gathered his crew. It was just him, Moe, and BayWolf. They were too smart to travel by car, bus, or train because they knew the stations would be heavily guarded. So they got on what Benny called their iron horses—what most people call bicycles—and rolled out. They were unsure where they would be going but knew it would be in an unexpected direction and they would be together. Excellent nutrition and fitness habits had prepared them for their journey. They knew they could ride for a long time. And bikes would allow them to be agile and to hide and retreat easily, if needed.

If you've ever seen the 1980s middleweight fighter Tommy Hearns, you've seen Moe Africa. He was tall, slim, dark brown skinned, and had a laid-back disposition until it was time to fight. BayWolf was average height for a man, about five foot eight, with a slim, athletic build and kinky, black starter locs.

Because MOVE had members living in Virginia, where they were raising MOVE kids in the MOVE way, Benny figured heading south would put them straight in the path of the Feds. So he and the fleeing MOVE members headed north on their bicycles.

Riding a bike is fun. But not for eight to twelve hours at a time while you are on the run from the federal government.

The mountains and roads in upstate Pennsylvania had hills that lasted for miles at a time. Moe and BayWolf had ten-speed racing bikes, which were modern back then. Benny's bike, his iron horse, was a 1950s one-speed, which must've made the journey insufferable.

Years prior, when things were much more peaceful, MOVE members would go for bike rides together all the time. The people with the nicer bikes always wanted to show off to the others. Moe, who was financially doing all right, always had bikes with the newer, fancier, more improved features. He worked in the center of Philadelphia's downtown area as a draftsman for an architectural firm. He had money in the bank and owned a duplex; he lived in one unit and rented out the other. Moe always drove a new car, and his wife always had new clothes and an expensive stroller to push their babies around in.

Moe's bike was new and fast, with all the bells and whistles.

Most MOVE members in the 1970s were teenagers or in their early twenties, and loved trading their bikes back and forth. Everyone liked Moe's bike. Sue's bike was really fancy and updated, too. It was easier to ride up hills because of the ten gears, and it had smooth tires and a comfortable seat. Benny's one-speed bike was heavy and stiff. Back in Philly, Bert used to have a bike that looked pretty with its floral-decorated paint, but it was really a piece of shit. It wasn't as strong as it was shiny, and when Big Jerry sat on it for a ride once, the rims bent, and by the time he got from one end of the block to the other, the bike had shrunk by twelve inches. Everyone laughed at the totaling of Bert's bike except for Bert. She didn't say a word but her giant, grape-size tears said it all. Benny tried to make her feel better, but he was still laughing. "Don't cry, Bert. It's still rideable."

While Benny, Moe, and BayWolf were on that ride from the Feds, their passage was made even more arduous by repetitive starting and stopping. It was already tough enough to ride a bike up and down mountains for hours at a time, but Benny made it tougher. Whenever the men came across a dead animal on the road, Benny made them stop and lay their bikes down, then pick up the animal and place it in the tall grass, bushes, or anyplace he felt it could rest in peace without a human putting it in a plastic trash bag or in the back of a trash truck. The men encountered rabbits, raccoons, squirrels, and turtles. They even discovered a few dead deer, which they dragged out of the road by their antlers and laid respectfully in the bushes. It didn't matter that they were being sought by federal agents. Benny believed that all life was important. If you saw a person in the road, you'd pick them up, and help get them to their final destination. That was how he felt about the animals—big or small. It didn't matter if it was a beaver, a duck, some small, unidentifiable rodent, or a moose. Benny was filled with love for all life and all living things.

Moe and BayWolf had become burned out from all the dead animals, from all the hills, from pedaling for miles and miles, and from avoiding traffic and detection. But not Benny. Benny soared up hill after hill on his one-speed iron horse as if he were shot out of a rocket. Nonstop pedaling. And when he'd reach the top, he'd pause, glance at the huffing and wheezing men behind him, dip into his bag, pull out his canteen, and take a long swig.

Once, as Moe and BayWolf caught up with him, a strong gust of wind hailed, pushing them.

"Did you feel that?" Benny said, with a laugh. "That's Mama patting y'all on the back for doing a good job."

Appreciating the comment, the men rode on with pride through the backcountry roads of upstate Pennsylvania. Nighttime brought in cool weather, making the morning dew soak everything under it. Benny was attuned to the weather patterns enough to understand where the group needed to sleep under the trees to avoid getting wet.

On their journey through mountains and around winding turns and up and down what seemed like endless hills, the group was fortunate to come across farms that contained all kinds of fruit and vegetables, including blueberries, corn, strawberries, apples, squash, grapes, and more. The men could eat until they were full. Raw food was the diet of choice for MOVE, anyway, so finding food on farmland was perfect for them. After filling their bellies, they would fill in the spaces of their duffle bags with the food and continue on.

During the fourth day of the ride, a storm was heading in, and they spent the night in a barn on someone's property. They did not know who the property owner was and did not get permission. They crept in at night after sunset and crept out in the morning before sunrise.

A couple days later on their journey, Benny spotted a long,

winding driveway, and Moe and BayWolf followed him down it. They came across a house that looked occupied. They knocked on the door, and nobody answered. They checked the doorknob, and it was unlocked. They went in. No one was home. The cabinets were full of food. The beds were made up and neat. It was like "Goldilocks and the Three Bears," but with trespassing fugitives.

The mostly white-populated rural hills of Pennsylvania were not the safest place for the men to be, but exhaustion from their constant riding forced them to live even more dangerously than they were already living. Sleeping with one eye open felt better than sleeping in a windy thunderstorm.

The men were careful not to disturb too much in the house. But after one night was so comfortable, it turned into two nights and then three. Not wanting to press their luck too much, after the third day, they packed their bags up and headed out. Just as they were rolling down the winding driveway from the house and onto the main road, a van headed up the driveway. Whoever lived there was returning home from their travels. It was a close call.

The men continued on as Benny preached how Mama was looking out for them. He believed she was bestowing on them incredible intuition as a reward for their commitment to appreciating and advocating for all life. How else would they have known exactly when to leave that house?

Benny had this internal connection to what he saw as God and as Mama, or Mother Nature. He believed that as long as you were doing what was working out for you, then protection would come. That became a staple phrase in MOVE: "Do your work." It could be a command, a demand or request, a threat, or whatever. *Do your work* could be used in any context. But usually, it was a way to say that you were not supposed to do something or that you were supposed to do something else. Or whatever else Benny wanted it to mean. When things were going well, you must be doing your work. When things were going rancid, you must not be doing your work. That was how Benny saw it, so that was how it was.

They kept riding. Benny felt like they must be doing something right because things kept working out for them. They escaped this or got through that, and the van at that house came just as they were leaving. "We must be doing our work," Benny would've said.

The trio continued eluding the authorities, and they never get caught sleeping in different people's houses and barns. Benny took it as confirmation that he—and by extension MOVE—was literally on the right path and doing his work. By the time the men made it through the rural back roads of New York State up to Watertown in mid-August, and then onto Massena, they'd biked about six hundred miles over about a month's time. In Watertown, New York, they stopped at a local diner for replenishment and saw on television the headlines about Elvis Presley's death. They didn't stay in Watertown long. Feeling unwelcome in the all-white area, the men hopped back on their bikes and decided to head a little farther south.

Finally, Benny, Moe, and BayWolf landed in Utica, New York. Their bicycle journey had come to an end. Utica might have had the same funny vibe the other towns had, but people were so upset over the death of their King, Elvis Presley, that when Benny and the crew arrived, people were too distracted from mourning his death. It felt better than all the eyes that immediately landed on them in Watertown. Exhausted, the men decided to make Utica their home for a few months to regroup and strategize.

Needing money, the group got jobs. Benny landed a job as an interior decorator, of all things. One wealthy couple was so impressed with his work that they wanted to put him on the payroll full-time. Having a skilled handyman who could build furniture, cabinets, and bookshelves, hang wallpaper, paint, plumb, and do just about every other project a house needed to function properly meant that the couple didn't have to hire as many other workers.

I've seen some of Benny's crafts. Sturdy, practical, and lasting. In fact, I still have a piece or two of his work that was passed down to me in my home.

Benny's job abruptly ended when the couple was watching the news and a "Wanted Fugitives" commercial came on. I'm not sure if Benny saw himself on TV that night or not, but I know he didn't stick around or take the chance of being recognized. At any given time the government could have located him and lowered the boom on him.

Like the post offices in Philly, the post offices in Utica hung bulletins that read, "Look out for these fugitives." MOVE members were described as armed and dangerous. Their hair made them easily recognizable. Moe and BayWolf cut theirs, but Benny kept his, usually hiding or tucking his under his hoodie or a trucker hat.

As the winter began to set in, Benny, Moe, and BayWolf knew they couldn't stay in one place for too long. Plus they felt that they were still not a safe enough distance from Philadelphia. They wanted to keep on moving.

Winters in upstate New York were brutally cold, and thirty to forty inches of snow wasn't unusual. That made riding bikes out of the question. Instead, Moe took a bus from Utica to what he considered the perfect city for a group of traveling Black people looking for refuge—a city that was part of the Underground Railroad: Rochester, New York.

Once he got to Rochester, Moe immediately scouted out the area to see if there was a particular location that gave off a good vibe for Black people. Nightfall came quickly. Moe needed to settle in. Not wanting to spend any money on a hotel, he walked over to the homeless district in downtown Rochester and found just what he was looking for. Moe talked to the homeless people there, asked lots of questions, listened to what they were saying, and paid attention to the crude shelters they created for themselves.

Once he was satisfied that he had enough information, Moe made his way to an appliance store, where he got himself a refrigerator box from the scrap pile.

Moe took that box back to the homeless section and set himself up for the night. When he woke up in the morning, he was surprised to see the box covered in snow because he had been so warm throughout the night. Later that day, he went to a real estate office and got a listing for apartment rentals. He saw a place he liked and he put a deposit on it. Then bought a bus ticket back to Utica to join back up with his MOVE brothers. When he returned, he saw that Benny had bought a school bus reminiscent of Big Yeller.

The old, 1950s Volkswagen bus was just like Benny's iron horse. It had seen better days. It had so much rust damage that the floor mats were the only thing separating their feet from the asphalt. They loaded their bikes onto the bus, and Moe drove it through a blizzard.

By car, with an average driver behind the wheel, Utica is about two hours east of Rochester. Moe was a pretty slow driver in general. Driving through a blizzard made the trip take much longer, which was terrible for Moe because the biggest hole in the floor of the bus was directly under the clutch and brake pedal. By the time the bus stopped at their new home on Flint Street, Moe's toes and feet were purple. Fortunately for Moe, Benny and BayWolf got him in the house and warmed him up before his feet were permanently damaged. It was a good thing they were done driving for a while, too, because as soon as they stopped, the bus's front wheels fell off the axle.

Benny sent for more members to join him once he, Moe and BayWolf settled in for a few weeks. To keep authorities off their tails, Moe had arranged for his sisters, who had no affiliation with MOVE, to pass messages to MOVE members. Moe would travel to other cities, like New York and Washington, DC, and make phone calls directly to his family and MOVE supporters. He didn't feel safe doing that from Utica. Benny sent notes and instructions to people he figured would be sure to inform others about what to do next. One by one, Rochester was becoming more populated with an underground version of the MOVE organization. Big Jerry, Bob, and Conrad, who were released with the gag order, were among the first to arrive. But many others came, too.

Big Jerry, Moe, and Conrad worked on the bus and did a good enough job to get it rolling again. They also began servicing vehicles for their neighbors. In just a few weeks, they generated enough money to buy an abandoned gas station and create a steady income stream. To legitimize their earnings and disguise themselves further, some of the more recognizable figures in MOVE finagled government IDs with alias names. Frank became Nick. Benny was Bill. Moe became Jimmy Slant. Big Jerry became Ernie. Bert became Toni Barron. Sue became Maria Zarka. Carlos Perez became Franco Zarka. Dennis became Dan Dabny. Benny's jazz buddy Raymond became C.P., after the initials of jazz legend Charlie Parker.

Over time, the Rochester MOVE family included Benny, Frank, Bob Moses, BayWolf, Moe, Mary, Sue, Carlos, Dennis, Big Jerry, Raymond, Conrad, and Benny's MOVE wife, Bert. They bought up to seven houses, two gas stations, and a restaurant, and were planning to buy more. The real estate company was happy to see them every few months with cash in hand, ready to purchase their next property.

They also spread Benny's teachings about treating life with respect, especially to people who used to fight dogs for sport. They were employing and empowering Black people in the area and "boosting the economy," according to the owner of the real estate agency.

In later years, the Rochester crew only ever spoke of their experience there with fondness. The city was fantastic to them, mainly because of how MOVE members carried themselves and did so much for the community. Even though they lived hard, they loved and appreciated what they took away from living so closely together. It reminded them of the Powelton headquarters that had been destroyed. They felt like they were doing the work of God.

Chapter 8

VIRGINIA

After I was secretly born in the House of Correction in 1978, the prison guards eventually realized what had happened. Stunned, they called for a doctor, and my mom and I were taken to a nearby hospital. Mom knew she couldn't keep me. Not in prison and not with murder charges hanging over her head. She folded me tightly into a hospital blanket and handed me over to her mother, LaVerne, and her aunt Louise. LaVerne and Louise took me to the Seed of Wisdom house in Virginia, which Benny, Phil, and others had set up the year before, in 1977. This was where they wanted to raise MOVE children—out of the city, in the fresh air, near nature, and away from the prying eyes of people who questioned MOVE's methods. By 1981, when I was two and a half years old, a lot had happened in my short life. A lot had happened for the other MOVE kids, too.

Rhonda and Don Glassey's ex-girlfriend Marie took care of us in Virginia. Rhonda had shiny skin with freckles, like a spotty banana, with the biggest, beautiful smile that anyone had ever seen. Although beautiful, she was very short-tempered and had a mouth that could spit out curses, as if dirty language whitened her teeth.

Marie was big and strong, like an NFL linebacker. Together, they were the "big people" in the house. The adults we listened to. Scarlet was there, too, at times. I remember Rhonda's voice a lot from back then. She often seemed gloomy and down, maybe because years earlier she'd lost a pregnancy after a brutal physical altercation with sheriffs at City Hall. Rhonda always listened to Billie Holiday, "Lady Sings the Blues" kind of songs. At least until Chaka Khan came on the radio. When she did, she became like an extra on *Soul Train*.

There were a lot of kids. I was one of the smaller, younger ones. Darren, Birdie, Tree, Netta, Delisha, Little Phil, Allen, Lena, and Melissa—they were the bigger, older kids. They were mostly between four and seven years old.

Whit, Taylor, Violet, Lenny, and I were among the little kids—all under three. All of us had dreadlocks except for Lena, who was half white but looked all white. I wasn't quite sure why her hair didn't look like ours. But I knew it was different. The rest of us avoided combs at all costs and also shared a similar-almond brown skin tone. Lena had really pale skin and light eyes. I never saw the adults comb her hair, but it still never loc'd like ours did.

Darren, Birdie, and Melissa's dreadlocks were the longest. Mine were Afro styled and bushed out in different places, while the rest of the bunch's hairstyles fell anywhere in between.

Darren and Birdie were like the leaders of the kids. They often competed with each other for the top spot. If Darren had a sweet potato, Birdie had a sweeter one. If Birdie could crack walnuts with his teeth, Darren could crack Brazil nuts. If Darren ran five miles, Birdie ran six miles. We, as the other kids, cast our votes by choosing to listen or side with one or the other because we loved Darren and Birdie and didn't know who we wanted leading us. I often chose Darren because he was the best fighter. But their competitiveness with each other was relentless.

I remember one day the adults gave us a whole watermelon to share. Darren declared, "I want the heart." The younger kids respected Darren enough to let him have the heart of the watermelon. But not Birdie, who grabbed the heart, stuffed it in his mouth, and flicked the juice from his fingers into Darren's face. Darren picked up the rest of the melon and slammed it over Birdie's head. Birdie chased him out to the back alley and the two boys had an all-out brawl. Five minutes after the fight, they were playing together. That was how it was. We kids were allowed to roam, to play, and sometimes to work out our disagreements with a fight.

The Seed of Wisdom property was supposed to be the start of MOVE branching out from Philly. Benny wanted a beautiful, ninety-six-acre farm nearby, but MOVE only got as far as purchasing the rickety three-bedroom, one-bathroom, single-family house that me and other MOVE kids called home. Despite its appearance, that place held so much love, but I'm sure for the adults it wasn't easy to live without all the amenities it lacked.

The house was always clean but bare, with no cosmetic touches whatsoever. We didn't have heat, hot water, bed frames, mattresses, or electricity. The walls had old, peeling, 1950s wallpaper. The floors were splintery, dark-colored pine boards. There were far too many of us to have our own rooms, and there was no formal structure to how the rooms were organized for sleeping. So most of us slept in sleeping bags on the floor in whatever room the adult we wanted—that we felt the most comfortable around—was in. I always stayed near Scarlet. Being close to her made me feel safe. Even when things got shifted around sometimes, I still found a way to make sure my makeshift bed—which was really a sleeping bag—was next to Scarlet's.

In the very early days of MOVE, Benny wanted to limit any feelings of insecurity if a child's parents weren't around, because they were often either in jail or hiding underground. So we were taught never to call our mom's Mom. Benny saw MOVE as one family unit, and he was clear about this with everybody. To Benny, when you categorize families with titles, you create divisions and cause prejudicial practices. Benny wanted no such divisions or hierarchies in parenting. Simple as that. As a result, all the MOVE children called all the MOVE adults by their names. Benny was this way with his own father.

My mom told me of the time when Benny's father, my great-grandfather Fred, was staying with his daughter, my grandma La-Verne. Benny would come to the house, ringing the doorbell and knocking simultaneously. He would talk fast and demand that the kids clean up the house, make sure they help, and not be lazy. And then Benny would go to his father and say, "Hey, Fred, how are you doing? How are you doing, old man? You look like you've been drinking. Have you been drinking? Have you been drinking that wine? You've been drinking that wine?" And then he'd come, pick him up, and start swinging him around.

Fred would complain but be laughing the whole time. "Benny, put me down! Boy, put me down!"

And Benny would be laughing himself. "Shut up, old man. Shut up, old man, before I knock you out. I'll knock you out, old man. Shut up."

Then Benny took his father to the basement. He opened the door and threatened to throw him down the steps if he didn't behave himself in my grandmother's home. He'd say stuff like, "Boy, I'll throw you down these goddamn steps if you don't behave yourself." That's how Benny talked to his father. And then he'd add, "You better not be messing with these kids, either."

Finally calm, Fred would say back, "Benny, these boys, they come around this house, they ain't got no manners. Michael, Jimmy, and whoever else is coming around here to see these girls, they come into this house and act like the house ain't got no roof. They come in with their hats on their heads."

And Benny would be, "Aw Fred, Fred, why were you messing with them kids? You know them kids ain't doing nothing wrong. Leave them kids alone."

That was how Benny talked to his father. So in MOVE, it carried over. It was the same. Loving and fun, but everybody was supposed to be equal. It didn't matter that three of the children were Scarlet's, two were Marie's, and one was Rhonda's. None of the children called their mothers Mom. Your first name was how you were referred to, as part of MOVE life.

At the Seed of Wisdom house, we quickly fell into a routine that began with us popping up bright and early to eat apples, onions, sweet potatoes, tomatoes, carrots, bananas, spinach, garlic, oranges, and hot peppers. When new fruit came back in season, I got to enjoy the watermelons, peaches, and plums. Black grapes were like candy for me. The sweetness delivered a magical experience. I also really liked peanuts.

On a daily basis, the adults exercised. We were supposed to care of our bodies and remain strong—that was instilled in me for longer than I can remember. The women who cared for us exercised what seemed like all day and every day. They did pushups, pull-ups, sit-ups, brick lifts, and stretching. They ran a lot. We saw the adults exercising all the time, and we exercised, too. Sometimes they told us to, but sometimes we did it without prodding. While the adults were exercising, we'd be either exercising with them or we'd be playing games that we made up, singing songs, and listening to stories. The older kids would tell the younger kids about what it was like when they were in police custody, or when the psychiatrists would examine them and ask them a million questions. We would be mesmerized by these stories.

Taylor seemed like he was just as strong as the adults. He could do so many push-ups that even if we knew how to count, we would have lost count. I tried to follow in his shadow but lacked the strength to do very many. I struggled to do ten.

"Keep working on your push-ups every day, Kita. You'll get strong," Taylor would say.

After the workouts, we were free to play games like tag and hide-and-go seek in the yard. The grass was taller than me, allowing me to hide easily. Some days these games went on all day. Rain days were special because we got to have fun jumping into the puddles, laughing, and splashing muddy water on everybody. After the rain, we had fun shaking wet tree branches over anyone who was still dry. When the storms didn't let up, we escaped to the big yellow school bus parked in the yard. The bus must've been broken down, because it never moved anywhere. We played in it all the time, climbing over and hiding under the seats, running up and down the aisle, and messing with the windows.

Our days seemed like a television show—especially because we had only the simplest things and drew insurmountable joy from singing, racing, telling stories, and making fun of each other, which was usually my favorite part of the day. Overall, we pretty much had fun and constantly explored, taking on exciting new adventures every day, even though we mostly stayed in the house or outside around the property. Drifting away from the property was a big no-no, mainly because of the perverts. We were constantly instructed to stay away from perverts.

"Don't look at, talk to, or go near any perverts!" Rhonda would demand.

Who were the perverts? Anybody who was not in MOVE was a pervert, be it man, woman, or child. Even the occasional visitor like this guy named Hank who used to come by to see Rhonda. We kids would call him a pervert to his face. Rhonda eventually asked us to stop. She said that he spent enough time around us to be considered a friend. He had food that was different from the food we ate. His food was cooked. I remember him eating fish and rice for dinner, and the following day mixing cold leftover rice with sugar and milk and having that for breakfast. I guess that was a Virginia farmer thing.

Hank saw how we lived and must have had some questions and sympathy for us, because the smell of the cooked food he was bringing to the house was most definitely enticing. It didn't sit well with Hank when the adults insisted that we kids couldn't eat cooked food, even though he could see that we desperately wanted some. So if any of us were crying or upset about something, he'd wait until we were out of Rhonda, Marie, and Scarlet's view, give us a taste, and say, "Don't tell." We never did.

The cops were beyond perverts. We didn't call them perverts, even though we knew they were. We just called them cops. Some of the bigger kids, especially Allen and Taylor, seemed worried about the cops coming to take us away, just as they did with my parents. The oldest kids like Tree and Netta had been taken by the cops before. I didn't know exactly what the cops would do if they came for us, but I can't remember not thinking that their uniforms made them look like very scary people.

Being so far away from MOVE headquarters in Philly and now living in an unfamiliar environment made it challenging for the group of us in Virginia to move around or for the adults caring for us to really go anywhere. Having more than a dozen kids joined at the hip wherever you went made it even harder.

For Rhonda, Marie, and Scarlet, it was extremely tough. They were frustrated. Rhonda was in her early twenties. She and Marie wanted to go out. They wanted to have fun. There were young men in the neighborhood they wanted to talk to. There were restaurants. They wanted to have friends and have a good time. But instead of having a life of freedom, they were stuck taking care of kids who didn't belong to them and were part of a revolution they were getting tired of being involved in. They were over following MOVE rules. But they felt like they were in a bind. They didn't want to leave the kids, fearing what would happen if they left. They also still felt some commitment to Benny. He was easy to believe in. They trusted that under his leadership, things would work out.

It was the most uncomfortable time for some of us in our lives then. With limited resources, the three women had to talk their neighbors into shopping for us. One man who lived up the street went to the spring to get our water. Another man who lived down the road went to the store to get our raw food. Not only did people in the community get our food and water, but they usually paid for it, too. They felt badly about all the kids in the house and wanted to help.

The day before the cops showed up seemed like any other day for me. It was late winter going into early spring 1981, and I was almost three years old. For the big kids, something was off. The day went on without much laughing or joking with them. Later while playing in the backyard, Darren, Birdie, and Tree told us to make Hershey Kiss shapes out of the mud and put them on the windowsill. They said if we ever got away from the cops and came back home, we could recognize our house by the mud shapes we left on the sill.

The very next day at the crack of dawn, sirens came from all directions. Red, blue, and yellowish lights spun around the walls as I opened my eyes. I was terrified. Before I knew it, cops burst into the room, yelling and screaming and ordering everybody to stay down. They grabbed me right off the floor, out of my sleeping bag. Some of the kids had already escaped and made it outside the house. On the way out the doors, my eyes scanned and frantically searched for Rhonda.

I didn't see her. We kids were put in a police van and locked inside. I looked out the window and could see Darren running from the cops. He was locked in a police car at some point, too, but somehow he'd escaped. He was hard to catch, but he was still just a kid. I can admit now how traumatizing it was to watch his recapture. On the one hand, I wanted to see Darren successfully elude the police. On the other hand, I wanted him to be with me wherever I was going. Darren's presence made me feel less scared and less alone.

Once we were all in the van, we rode for a while. I don't remember how long, but when we stopped and the doors opened, the police made us get out and go into a dilapidated building where we saw two nuns. I had never seen nuns before. They looked like penguins to me. Every time one of the kids walked past them, they said, "Bless you, child." Their tone rang of a faraway holiness that we grimy-looking kids had little capacity to reach. The nuns looked at us like kids in need of saving. It was terrifying.

The nuns seemed agitated while they hurried us down some steps and into a basement. We were left alone for a while. There was still no sign of Rhonda, Marie, or Scarlet. I clung to Darren.

When the nuns returned, they took one kid at a time and walked us up from the basement. Frightened by what would happen to us, we all hid behind a hot water tank. Even the bigger kids seemed helpless. We all cried and grabbed onto the railing when it was our turn to be taken away. We didn't understand what was happening. All these perverts and nobody from MOVE.

When it was my turn, the nuns took me into a kitchen, sat me in a chair, and tried to comb my natural dreadlocks straight. I resisted because it hurt so much. Each stroke ripped a clump of hair out of my scalp. When it was Taylor's turn, he screamed and fought so hard he knocked over what sounded like metal chairs and maybe a kitchen table. The nuns gave up on him quickly and sent him back down to the basement.

When we saw Darren again, his head was patchy and bleeding. It was half Afro and half dreadlocks. The next day, the door opened again, and a nun stood at the top of the steps for what we thought was about to be round two. She spoke with a sweet voice from the top of the stairs, saying, "Come on, guys. Come on out. Come on out, you guys." Darren was only about nine years old at the time but spoke for us all. "Fuck you! Get away from us, you fucking pervert!" Darren had paid attention to how MOVE adults talked to police.

"Come on, you guys. You got to come out," the nun insisted.

"Fuck you, pervert!" Darren yelled again. "You fucking pervert! Fuck you! We ain't going nowhere with you!"

Another day or two passed like this. There was no sign of the MOVE women. It felt like we'd been there forever. We were too scared from the hair-combing incident to trust the nuns when they tried to bring us food. The nuns cooked us foods most kids would like: pancakes, eggs, and bacon. We refused to eat any of it. The nuns didn't understand us. Noticing our already lean bodies, I think they were getting scared that we were malnourished and would starve. So they dragged us out of the basement and tried to force us to eat. Taylor stubbornly continued to resist. Exasperated, the nuns grabbed his head, pried his mouth open, and shoved a chocolate candy bar inside it while he kicked and screamed. There was more chocolate on his face than in his mouth. The nuns re-alized they were getting nowhere with us, but they could tell that Darren had influence. He was like a leader. They figured if they could get Darren to eat, we'd follow. First, they had to win his trust.

They called Darren up from the basement and promised him they would be nice. They offered him any food he wanted. By this point, Darren was hungry enough to eat whatever they put in front of him. He caved and picked bacon, a food he remembered from before his family joined MOVE. After a while, he was on his way down the steps with food for the rest of us. Birdie still refused to eat. Some of us followed Birdie's example. Taylor would eat only a banana because it was raw. The rest of us ate from the plate

Darren brought down, and we ate everything on it. We were too hungry to care whether the food was cooked, raw, or otherwise.

After eleven days with the nuns, at what I now know was an orphanage, we heard the sounds of someone knocking on the door. The adults had been released from jail and had come to get us. We were overwhelmed with joy when we heard Rhonda's and Marie's voices. We ran up the stairs straight to them. Rhonda looked at our condition and immediately started screaming at the nuns. "You bitch! You fucking bitch! Look at these kids! You call yourselves women of God? What the fuck is godly about what y'all did to these kids?!"

While Rhonda was yelling, Marie was leading us out of the house. The nuns tried to plead their case, claiming they were just trying to clean us up, but Rhonda was hammering her with so many *shut the fuck up*s and *fuck you bitch*es that the nuns couldn't verbalize a complete sentence.

Suddenly we could hear police sirens. A neighbor had heard the commotion and called the cops. Panic set in among the kids. Step by step, we inched across the open lawn with Marie. I was trying to stay attached to her, never wanting to be separated from her again.

Seeing our reactions, in a calm voice, Marie said, "It's okay, I got you. Darren, Tree, Birdie, you see that U-Haul truck parked on the other side of the fence? Hank is right there waiting for all of us to take us home. I know y'all are ready to get out of this place. Go 'head, run as fast as you can. Don't look back at this place. Don't stop until you get there. When you reach the truck, get inside. Help the smaller kids get in, and then you wait for Rhonda and me."

We kids barely waited for Marie to finish talking. We flew as fast as we could.

Halfway across the lawn, Violet was shouting, "Faster, run faster!."

Everybody sprinted toward the truck. Little feet were running, stumbling, falling, and getting back up. Birdie was pulling Whit.

Taylor, Little Phil, and Lenny were kicking up dust. Marie carried me from the house to the truck.

Just as we all made it to the U-Haul, the skies opened up, and the rain began to fall so hard it sounded like hail. When Hank hit the gas, the tires spun in the mud. Rhonda and Marie jumped out of the truck from the front seat and pushed. They were pushing anxiously, trying to rock the car back and forth free. "Push, Marie, push!" Rhonda urged.

The truck launched forward. Rhonda and Marie, covered in mud from the spinning wheels, scrambled back into the truck, and we blazed down the street as fast as the 1970s U-Haul truck could fly, which was not that fast.

It was dark and hot in the back of the truck. We breathed on each other as we slid around on the floor. We were slippery from the rain, and some of the kids had wet themselves.

For the next few hours, we rode. We rode the entire way on one tank of gas. I was trembling the whole way. It was pitch-black. I couldn't see who I was sitting next to. My hands and fingers were shaking uncontrollably. I couldn't help but worry that it wasn't over. We finally arrived at Thirty-Ninth and Reno Streets in West Philadelphia, where LaVerne was awaiting our arrival. The two-story house had a redbrick exterior that was painted brown. Inside, it was neat and clean but bare. Three bedrooms and one bathroom. Very little, if any, furniture. We slept four or five kids to a room, with one adult in each room.

But first LaVerne and my aunt Scarlet made sure we got baths and food to eat. When they took our clothes off of us, they gasped in horror. We were skin and bones, with scabs on our heads where the nuns had tried to comb our hair. I had a severe rash that stretched from my navel to my thighs. Taking a bath was excruciatingly painful. Changing bandages that were sticking to my skin was even worse. If not for my trust in LaVerne, I'm not sure I would've been able to bear the pain. But her gentle touch and sweet, consoling voice let me know that I was safe and gave me comfort.

Benny and the Rochester crew got word about our return home to Philly, and Moe snuck into town to make sure we were alright. Moe came by to bring us food. He brought us peanuts and apples, tomatoes, oranges, and multiple types of roots, pears, and grapes. I dug in and ate and ate. And even after my stomach was completely full, I continued to eat. I ate so much that that night my bowels released in the bed while I was sleeping, and I didn't know it. I was happy to return to what felt like our everyday, peaceful life. Home with family and the kind of food we ate. We still had to be wary of the perverts and the cops, but at least for now, we were back home safe. This is my first memory of Philadelphia. It was terrifying but still a good one.

On Reno Street, as is common in Philly, the houses were row homes. There seemed to be a lot more people than in Virginia and they were in much closer proximity to everything. Me and the other kids weren't used to this. After a few weeks, and once we'd healed and settled in, LaVerne took all the kids aside and gave us a long lecture. She said, "We are family. We are MOVE. We are guided by the wisdom of the Coordinator. The outside world is not a part of MOVE. The outside world is different from MOVE. We all protect each other. We don't hurt anyone. But if anyone outside of this house, outside of this family, tries to hurt you, you fight them. You fight them hard.

"People will say nasty things to you on the street, and that's all right. They can say whatever they want. But if they want to fight you, you tear their asses up. If they threaten you, you tear their asses up. You don't let anyone hurt you. You don't let anyone hurt your brothers and sisters. Out on the street, don't fight each other. Y'all might fight in this house but don't fight each other on the street."

LaVerne scanned our faces to make sure we were getting what she was saying. Then she continued.

"And if anybody messes with your brothers and sisters, fight together and help each other. If one of you gets in a fight, all of y'all get in it. If they grab you, grab their fingers, bend them back, and try to break it off. Fight hard and fight wild like the cats do. Scratch, punch, kick, bite them if you have to, and bite them hard. If you can get away, get away, and run from the fight if you have to. But run slowly. Try to pace yourself, so you don't get too tired. While you're fighting, though, make a lot of noise. Scream and holler like the way the dogs do when they fight. If you can find a stick, a brick, a bottle, fight with that and strike them. If you see people that can help you, you scream for them to help you. We are family. We protect each other, and we stay together."

I listened intently and knew she meant business.

Chapter 9

JOHN AFRICA VS. THE FBI

MOVE spent three years in Rochester. During that time, they became beloved and appreciated by most of the neighbors because, in addition to real estate, gas station, and restaurant businesses, with each snowfall, MOVE members got up to shovel and clear both sides of the street, the paths on the sidewalk, and all the driveways and garage areas on the block. Everywhere snow fell, MOVE shoveled it, and they cleaned off and dug cars out as well. Keep in mind that it snows more in Rochester than it rains in Seattle. So by the time they'd finish clearing the snow and getting a couple of hours of sleep, they'd be back outside to clear more snow. Neighbors appreciated a chance to sleep in and not having to do anything snow related.

MOVE also took care of the neighborhood dogs. Benny would send Carlos and others to go to the store to get them fresh meat. He didn't believe in feeding dogs Alpo or Science Diet or whatever stuff comes in the bag on the shelf in the supermarket. MOVE members fed the dogs what dogs naturally eat. That meant chicken. That meant cow. Benny would be cutting up and butchering meat for the dogs. Steak, hamburger, neck bones, turkey tails, fish heads, raw beef, and even horsemeat. MOVE's Rochester neighbors didn't mind. It saved them money and their dogs were happy to eat good food.

For dogs on chains, Benny and others would go around, hop over fences, unchain the dogs, and let them run around in the backyard. A lot of the neighbors were inhumane to their dogs. They'd just put them outside and keep them there. It'd be cold and icy in the wintertime. The dogs would be freezing, shivering. That was not the MOVE way. It was common for MOVE to offer to build doghouses for the dogs that didn't have backyard shelter.

"Look, my boys and I are carpenters," Benny would say to the neighbors. "At no cost to you we can build you a doghouse for your pooch."

"Whatever y'all want to do," the neighbors would usually respond.

Benny and others in MOVE would gather wood from scrap yards and abandoned houses, and use what they could salvage. Then they'd build doghouses. The neighbors didn't have to pay for parts or labor or anything, so they were happy about the arrangement. Well, most of them.

There was one incident where a neighbor was not so happy. He was a church preacher. This preacher was proud and didn't want anybody building doghouses or feeding his dog. He didn't want anybody telling him what to feed his dog or how to care for him or to add water to his bowl. Every time the water froze, MOVE would pick at it with ice picks and uncover the water. This pissed the preacher off.

"Look, this is my dog. This is my property," the preacher told Benny, spitting with anger. "Could you stay away from my dog? Stay away from my property!"

"What the fuck is the problem?" Benny replied, "We are taking care of the dog. We ain't asking you to do it. From what I can see, you ain't doing it. You a fat motherfucker but you want the dog to be skinny."

"Fuck you!" the preacher shot back. "This is my dog!"

Benny was a man who worked out constantly, had extremely powerful hands, and rode a bike across states. If he wanted to be a violent man, it would have been easy for him to put that preacher's head through a slab of concrete. However, he chose to try to reason with him.

"Look man, the dog needs real meat. He is going to be out here sleeping in this cold Rochester weather. He doesn't need to be balled and curled up, or shivering." Benny knew he was making sense and the preacher's resistance infuriated him. "He needs a fucking doghouse. You got a house. Why don't the dog have one?"

The preacher was silent.

"What the fuck is wrong with the dog having a house that you don't even have to provide?" Benny continued. "Don't you like having a place, and what makes you more important than the dog? If you don't want to sleep on the goddamn ground outside in the cold weather, what the fuck makes you think the dog wants to sleep in the cold weather? And you, a preacher, call yourself a man of God. What the fuck is godly about that shit? You are acting like a goddamn devil."

The preacher had been listening and pondering at first. But Benny had crossed the line. That man of God finally lost his cool. He walked away from Benny midspeech, returned with a rifle, and aimed it at Benny.

"Get away from my dog and get away from my house," the preacher demanded.

"Shoot me, motherfucker! Shoot me! Shoot me! You so motherfucking bad, you got that goddamn gun in your hand, you're going to end my life, go ahead." Benny laughed. "Shoot me, motherfucker!"

The preacher didn't move.

"You ain't going to shoot me, are you? You're going to pull that motherfucking gun on me, but you ain't gonna do shit with it, are you?"

The preacher maintained his aim. A passerby rushed to a pay phone and called the cops and, of course, Benny got arrested.

"What's your name?" the arresting officer asked.

"My name is Lee Vincent Phart," Benny lied, rearranging his government name.

"All right, Lee. Come on," the cop said as they locked Benny up.

It was not a great idea for Benny to get arrested while he was on the run from the Feds. But it worked out as a test to see if the Rochester police were on to MOVE or not. They didn't seem to be at the time because they simply took him down to the station, then let him go with a warning. "Just stay away from this man and his dog," the cop told him.

Benny got lucky but he didn't see it as luck. To Benny, it was Mama looking out for him because he was doing his work.

During the three years Benny and other MOVE members were hiding out in New York State—first in Utica, then in Rochester—they were living out in the open but were mostly inconspicuous. Then Clarence, a long-time MOVE member, showed up out of the blue. Benny was suspicious of Clarence right away. He pulled Bert, Sue, and Carlos aside and said, "Don't talk to that mother-fucker." Benny thought that Clarence might be wired. He didn't have any concrete evidence, but his hunch was so strong that he warned the others.

"Clarence is a cop," Benny said more forcefully.

I don't think Benny actually thought Clarence was an under-cover police officer or federal agent. That was just how he talked. He thought Clarence was working with the cops.

"Whaaaaaat?" Sue asked. "You think so? Really?!"

"Goddamn right I think so. Sue, he's a cop."

Not even a month later, every MOVE member in Rochester was arrested. Nobody knew if Clarence was the reason, but there were strong suspicions. Inexplicably, the Feds surveilled the group long enough to learn everyone's daily routines. They set up a sur-prise early-morning raid, and dozens of agents swarmed all their homes. When the Feds surrounded Benny, he looked at them and said sarcastically, "We were expecting y'all last week. What took you so long?"

Very few negative incidents happened with the family in Rochester. That was why neighbors were shocked when fifty federal agents and twenty-five local police officers rushed out of Benny's, Moe's, and all the other MOVE members' houses around the city and brought them out in handcuffs. To the neighbors in Rochester, these folks were their friends, and some were their lovers. They followed the paddy wagon to the police station.

Many members had cut their hair in Rochester, so they didn't look like their original mug shots. The papers showed the before and after pictures of MOVE members with headlines that read "Like Night and Day." It shocked the whole town. People in Rochester couldn't believe their friends were dangerous people the police said they were.

While they were in Rochester, and long before Clarence's sudden return, BayWolf and Bob Moses decided to leave Rochester. So when the Feds showed up to capture everybody, BayWolf and Bob Moses were already gone. I heard they crossed the southern border into Mexico and remained in hiding until the statute of limitations expired on the 1977 rioting charges connected to the incident on the MOVE platform.

Everyone who remained in Rochester was arrested and transported to Philly. Except for Benny and Moe, they were all facing state charges with up to ten years in prison. For some reason, Bert, Dennis, and Carlos were tried together. Everyone else—Sue, Conrad, Raymond, Frank, and Big Jerry—was tried individually. Benny and Moe were facing much more serious allegations. They were charged with a bomb-making, gun-running scheme, in addition to the 1977 rioting charges. These were federal charges, and it meant they had to be held in a federal prison. Because they were arrested in New York, they had to be held in a New York jail. As a result, Benny and Moe had to commute for court from New York City to Philadelphia every day with armed US marshals.

Criminal charges came swiftly, in May 1981. So did the trial. By the end of June, Benny and Moe's case in the federal courthouse in Philadelphia had become known citywide as "John Africa versus the System." And it was an exciting trial, not only because the two defendants acted as their own attorneys, but because MOVE members had always eluded long, serious prison time. The police had been dealing with MOVE for almost ten frustrating years. And now they had the head of the group and his main lieutenant in handcuffs.

Benny didn't seem worried at all. He had no faith that the US justice system could hold him with their laws. He had ultimate faith in Mama and was guided by MOVE's beliefs and principles— what he called MOVE law. Benny believed MOVE law would protect him and his fellow MOVE members as long as they put the principal first in everything they did. MOVE law was truth unbroken, unblemished, and continuous. Every part was connected to another part and was consistent.

Benny would say, "A trustworthy example is a consistent example. You don't have to question whether the sun will rise tomorrow. You just expect it. Because the sun has been there as long as you can remember, as long as your mother can remember, and long as every mother and grandmother and great-grandmother can remember. This is why people trust MOVE."

MOVE was consistent. Benny was consistent. He showed so much concern for other people's well-being that everyone knew he really cared. He was like this to everybody—*everybody*—even to the cops who arrested him. Even the perverts he warned MOVE kids to avoid. Benny was always consistent in his actions and his goals. That bred trust. And trust made people believe.

While Benny and Moe were on trial, Benny got a chance to put his beliefs about the power of trust and consistency to the test. It started with a flat tire on the highway.

Every day of their trial, Benny and Moe had to drive two hours from New York City to Philly, and back. One day on the drive down, the car they were riding in had a blowout. The US marshals escorting the men didn't know how to change the tire. This happened at a time when people didn't have cell phones, and walkie-talkies had a limited range. AAA, or the American Automobile Association, wasn't as well-known as it is now and even if it was, they would've had to wait hours for rescue. Things were really different back then. If you ran out of gas on the highway, you had to walk to a gas station. If you had a flat tire, you had to walk to a pay phone, find a tow truck company in a widely distributed, thick telephone directory called the Yellow Pages, call a tow truck, and wait for help to arrive. Or if you were desperate enough and not too scared, you might wave down a driver passing by and hope they would help you without hurting you.

Basically, if you got a flat tire in 1981 on the highway or on a back country road and didn't have a spare, you could be there all day or even part of the next day. So there Benny and Moe were with their marshal escorts, on the highway with a flat tire. Cars and trucks were just whizzing by them at high speeds, and no one stopped to help. Benny, who hated having to make this long drive every trial day, grew annoyed and began to chastise the marshals. "Man, this is fucked up. This is a very fucked up situation."

One of the marshals looked puzzled.

"We sitting on this motherfucking highway with all of this traffic, all these fast-moving vehicles, these fast-moving trucks, sitting here ready to get fucking killed because y'all motherfuckers rather ride us up and down a goddam highway than just make provisions so that we don't have to ride up and down this highway," Benny argued. "I don't understand why you let the government treat you this way. I don't understand what the fuck the problem is. You got a wife at home, don't you? You got kids at home, don't you? All right, so what happens if you get killed on this fucking highway because you too goddamn spineless to stand up to these mother-fuckers and tell them that this ain't necessary? We don't have to do this shit like this.

"You put your kids and your wife's lives in danger because if something happened to you, what the fuck do you think is going to happen to them?" Benny went on. "Man, I'm not saying this to you to be disrespectful. I'm saying this to you so that you can learn to respect yourself. Are you mad at me because you think I'm being disrespectful? Motherfucker, you are being disrespectful to yourself and everybody else."

He then explained that Moe could change the tire and that if they took off his cuffs, Moe could knock it right out.

The marshals just looked at each other. "I don't know about taking off his cuffs."

"Look, we are in this goddamn car. We ain't going nowhere, and we ain't gonna do nothing. Just give him the goddamn tire iron, and he'll do it," Benny replied.

Reluctantly, the marshals took the cuffs off Moe, and Moe changed the tire. Then, as promised, Moe got back in the car.

Once they were back in the car, Benny goes, "Look, this is the last time I'm taking this ride. It's unnecessary, and it's unsafe. So when you get back to the courthouse, you tell them that that's it. We ain't doing that no more, and don't just tell them that I said we ain't doing it no more. You tell them *you* said we ain't doing it no more. That's it. You tell them for your own self that you ain't doing it no more either."

When they returned to the courthouse, Benny told Judge Clifford Scott Green flatly, "I ain't doing that.

"We don't have a jail in the federal courthouse that can house you. We would honor your request. But we don't have a jail," Judge Green responded.

"What do you need a jail for? We ain't going nowhere," Benny said. "Look, one of them rooms, offices or something, we don't need much. Just put us in one of the rooms. Get us some food, blankets, pillows, and that's all we need."

Surprisingly, Judge Green said, "Okay, due to these unusual circumstances, I'll allow you to stay here."

The marshals started bringing Benny and Moe food to eat like canned goods, SpaghettiOs, packs of Oodles of Noodles. But MOVE members ate mostly raw and natural foods.

"What the fuck is this?" Benny asked, "No really, what the fuck is this shit?"

Benny started examining the packages and reading the unpronounceable ingredients.

"Man, I'm not eating this shit. You're trying to poison me?!" Benny said, "This ain't what I eat."

"Well, this is the food we got," the marshal said with a sigh. "It's this or nothing."

"You going to have to figure out something because I'm not eating this," Benny replied. "I'm on trial for my life, and I need the energy to fight and defend myself in this trial. I need energy, and what's going to give me energy is the food that I eat. I need my diet."

"Well, what is your diet?" the marshal asked.

"My diet is sweet potatoes, and I need bananas and pineapples, some fruit. I need substance. I need real food, man!"

They went back and forth about it for a while, then the marshal contacted Judge Green on the matter.

"Okay, give him what he needs," the judge said, agreeing with Benny again.

The marshals went to the natural food co-op market that Benny had been a member of since the early 1970s and brought back the food.

There's a picture of Benny holding a box of fruit and a pineapple. He had come out of the courthouse during the trial, without handcuffs, and gone to the car to retrieve the food. Benny turned to look at the photographer just as he snapped the picture, and then returned to the courthouse.

The people trusted him. Wassulick, the federal agent who caught and apprehended him, would not wear his gun around Benny. People felt comfortable around him. Perhaps Wassulick felt that as well. Not only did he take off his gun around Benny, but he also had John Africa quotes taped to his office desk.

During the preliminary hearings and jury selection for Benny and Moe's trial, Benny had to question some people to determine who would be jurors. He would interview different people, ask them who they were, where they were from, and all about their backgrounds.

Mark Durant and Will Carr, were serious, Cornell- and Harvard-trained prosecutors. Durant was undefeated and had never lost a case prior. When Benny would see Durant in court, he'd go over to them, wrap his long arms around both prosecutors' necks in embracement, and say, "Hey man, you think you are going to win this case? Do you think you are going to win this case? You ain't going to win this case. I'm innocent. I'm going home. You ain't going to find me guilty. I'm going home."

Benny and Moe were representing themselves. Because Moe had no legal sense at all, he relied on Benny for everything. The courts assigned a public defender, John Snite, to the case. Mr. Snite was respectful and did not interfere with Benny taking the lead, and he assisted only when asked, which was seldom. Benny wrote the opening statement and Moe read it:

"I'm not going to object to these ridiculous proceedings because I object to this entire system. So to interject with parts of this procedure would compromise my integrity because I object to the entire thing, the entire proceeding. So y'all go ahead and do what you must and I'm going to get some sleep."

Benny folded his arms on the defendants' table, put his head down, and dozed off. Day after day he slept. He slept through much of the prosecution's case. He slept through cross-examinations and through whole testimonies. He said it was easy to sleep because the fluorescent lights in the courtroom hurt his eyes. A few moments roused Benny, though.

There was one particular moment in the courtroom where the prosecutor had one more witness—his star witness and ace in the hole—and the most unexpected informant of them all: Don Glassey, MOVE's first white MOVE member. Nobody saw it coming, not even Benny.

Don had gotten busted for drug trafficking in the early 1970s before he joined MOVE, and the Feds were holding it over his head. "You are a soft white boy," they told him. "You won't last a year in prison." So Don agreed to flip. He was the last person Benny expected to be walking to the witness stand for the prosecution. Over quivering lips and trembling hands, Don pointed at Benny and testified, "He had guns, bombs and all kinds of weapons."

Benny paid Don's testimony no mind as the Feds brought in shopping carts full of explosives, bombs, and guns. Then the prosecutor said, "Well, we don't have to bring all of it in, just enough to give the jury an understanding of what we have here."

"What? You ain't going to bring it all in?" Benny told the court. "You don't want to show them all the evidence? No, don't bring some of that shit in here. Bring all that shit in here. Bring it all in. Bring every shopping cart you got in the hallway. Roll that shit in here so the people can see what you trying to say I was involved in."

And so they did, filling the courtroom with weapons and explosives. Benny stayed focused on what was happening in the courtroom, but the betrayal of Don hit him especially hard.

Midway through the trial Delbert was called as a witness to talk about what he knew about Benny and what he knew about the System that was accusing Benny. He spoke about the raid on the Seed of Wisdom house in Virginia, which police had carried out a few days earlier. On the stand Delbert told the jury, "MOVE people had historically been treated horribly since MOVE had our first demonstration at the Bronx Zoo. Our children have never received any compassion from the police or Rizzo's fat nasty ass. In fact, down in Virginia, sadistic nuns that the police took our kids to, after they raided our house, put our MOVE women in jail, and combed the kids' dreadlocks out of their scalps. They beat our kids and pushed them down basement steps when they wouldn't cooperate with them. They stuffed chocolate candy bars in their mouths because the kids wouldn't eat from them because the kids don't know them, and don't trust them, and they broke—"

"Stop! Stop!" Benny yelled. He couldn't take hearing it anymore. He didn't want to hear about how we suffered.

Delbert paused for a moment, then continued. "MOVE people are always harassed and brutalized by police and officials. Right now, Sue and Bert Africa are recovering from wounds from their arrests in Rochester, and Bert is with child. Our kids ain't been turned back over to us. Until we get better treatment and all the kids are back healthy and safe, we're going on a hunger strike. All our kids got to be back."

Benny nodded silently in agreement from his seat at the defendant's table.

Going on a hunger strike in 1981 was a big deal publicly because just a month earlier, in May 1981, Bobby Sands, who was a controversial member and leader in the Provisional Irish Republican Army (IRA), died on a hunger strike while imprisoned at HM Prison Maze in Northern Ireland. Depending on whom you talk to, Sands was either a revolutionary or a terrorist. What's not debatable is that Sands's hunger strike and subsequent death brought renewed attention to hunger strikes as a method for imprisoned people to be heard. So MOVE followed suit. Everybody in MOVE who was in prison—the twelve people captured in Rochester and the MOVE 9—went on a collective hunger strike.

Benny gave no sign of taking a bite and he didn't miss a day in court, though he continued to sleep through much of the proceedings. This frustrated the prosecution. But the trial continued on.

MOVE's hunger strike ended twenty-six days later, after Scarlet and Marie rolled up on the nuns and took the kids home. During this period, my dad called LaVerne every day and asked about me, Whit, and the other kids. He was desperate for us to be back with family.

"Michael, we got the kids back," LaVerne finally was able to tell him, with relief.

The rush of emotion my dad felt took the energy out of his body. A wall he was near caught his fall and he slid down it, with the phone still attached to his ear.

Meanwhile in court, when it was Benny and Moe's turn to call witnesses, they called to the stand everybody that they'd missed during the time they were gone and wanted to see. Their trial questions weren't about the case at all. Instead, they used it as an opportunity to have reunions with people they hadn't seen since they'd fled Philly four years earlier. Judge Green allowed this and the prosecutors didn't object. I can only imagine how the jury reacted.

After nearly two months of long testimonies and statements from witnesses, it was time for closing arguments.

Judge Green turned to Benny and Moe. "Gentlemen, this is closing statements. Do you have anything to say?"

"Do I have something to say?" Benny responded, "Yeah, I got something to say."

He stood and wiped his eyes, post-slumber, and began:

"People ain't going to condemn the MOVE organization as being a bunch of kill-crazed, bloodthirsty murderers when it's the government spilling blood, killing life out of greed. But the government is attempting to indict me for spilling blood, burning flesh, and killing life by saying I was making bombs. I ain't going to spend a lot of time talking about this bomb making a frame-up. My innocence is proven with every innocence of energy you breathe, every drop of innocence you drink, every morsel of innocence you eat. The very message you are hearing is me. My righteousness is represented throughout this information. So now, if the government is still looking for an excuse to hold onto this foolish, inorganic bomb-making accusation, the government will have to look outside this letter relying on their familiar reference of hallucination because the government ain't going to find no excuses here. Relying on the government's theories, opinions, and ideas, relying on everything that allows for an excuse. I don't need no bombs. But if you want to call life a bomb, I've got the most giant bomb existing. It's already made, and the MOVE organization is constantly dropping it, bombarding the system with the truth. As for these scientific bombs, the FBI's charging me for deriving? I ain't going to make no bomb. Bombs backfire on the people that create them and all those that believe in them, because bombs are explosive, destructive, and corruptive. But wisdom is informing, and when you put what is right to a person, you ain't in danger of getting what's wrong back. This is the difference between what I use as my defense—my bomb, and what the government uses as their so-called defense—their bombs."

Benny continued for about forty-five minutes, telling the court all the ways in which he had nothing to do with the destructive System. He was about building, he said, not destroying.

From the day of arrest on May 13, 1981, till the closing argument was read the trial lasted a little over two months. The jury deliberated for about two weeks before finally coming to a unanimous verdict.

"How do you find the defendants?" Judge Green asked the jury.

"Not guilty."

The courtroom erupted in cheers.

Some people were stunned when the jury came back with the not guilty verdict. But not Benny. The not guilty verdict was just another way of Mama telling him he was doing his work. To Benny, it reinforced that he and MOVE were on the right course and that MOVE law would always prevail. As MOVE supporters and spectators were cheering, Benny leaned into the mic and said his famous quote, "The power of truth is final!" then left the courtroom.

Outside the courthouse, a local news reporter approached Benny with an extended microphone. News had broken all over town that MOVE's John Africa had won. "Mr. Africa, what did you feel when the verdict was read?" the reporter asked.

"Nothing. I was asleep."

Another reporter asked him, "Was it hard? Was it a tough case?"

"Tough? That was easy," Benny said with a laugh. "I whipped them."

A third reporter asked, "What are you going to do now with the MOVE cult?"

Benny had a ready answer. He knew how the news had been portraying MOVE, and he was happy to clarify. "It's not a cult. It's an organization."

During the trial, people in the city of Philadelphia saw Benny for who he was. The remarkable thing about it was that people had been hearing about him, about this man who could run as fast as a dog and ride a bike up a seven-mile mountain with nonstop, constant peddling. People had listened to all these different stories about this person who could connect with others on a personal level, and who had started to become a legend. But by July 16, 1981, the whole city got a glimpse at the teachings of MOVE and who Benny really was.

During the trial, people could see that Benny wasn't talking about the System needing to be destroyed just for himself or for Black people or for any particular race of people or for animals. He felt the System needed to be destroyed for the good of all life, including the authorities trying to put him behind bars. Folks could see the truth in that.

One of the most powerful moments of the trial was during the hunger strike. Benny was clear about the kinds of food he would eat, and Judge Green accommodated him. Benny felt a personal gratitude toward the judge; it showed that just because a person is a judge, they're not automatically compromised. He wrote Judge Green a personal letter and thanked him. Because writing gave Benny a headache, he dictated to Moe what to write. Benny took the time and made the effort to thank the judge for being a fair person with him.

Many people believe that revolutionaries are all "Fuck the police and judges and politicians too." Usually that's the case, but here that would not have made sense. The System was the enemy. And people who upheld the System were protecting the enemies.

This act of gratitude towards a legal authority was a side of MOVE that outsiders, and even some MOVE members, had never seen before. This was what Benny called the strategic revolution, or what other people call catching more flies with honey.

Meanwhile, Carlos, who was on trial for the 1977 riot charge, was not so fortunate. He received a guilty verdict five months after Benny and Moe were acquitted. After the prosecutor recommended three years as his sentence, Carlos screamed angrily, "That's all you got? Give me what you got!" He couldn't fathom why he was found guilty and Benny and Moe weren't. He blamed his lawyer. He couldn't believe what was happening.

"Two more?" Judge Kendall H. Shoyer calmly asked. "I can give you more if you want more."

Carlos was enraged. "Give me more than that! Is that all you got, motherfucker? Please give me more! My lawyer already sold me out. As a matter of fact, I want more years!"

Benny and Moe's acquittal of all their charges made the MOVE members still in prison feel invincible, like they had been living with and were being led by a god. They knew Benny was a wise man, but his unlikely not guilty verdict made it seem like Benny could walk on water or part the Red Sea. In their minds, MOVE was the truth and MOVE's followers couldn't be conquered. Carlos felt that way as much as anybody else. He had seen how MOVE thrived in Rochester until Clarence and Don ratted them out.

So Carlos's conviction came as a shock to him. He looked right at that judge and proudly said of his prison sentence, "I don't give a fuck how much time you give me!"

Carlos slammed his hands on the desk, popped up, and punched his lawyer in the face, knocking him out cold. Then he ran toward the bench to charge the judge. The sheriffs grabbed him, but they couldn't stop him. Two or three sheriffs, a couple of guards, and the judge were scrambling away. The guards cracked him in the head with nightsticks. Chairs were flying everywhere, and somehow Carlos was still headed for the judge on the bench.

Judge Shoyer was a significantly older man, and Carlos was still very young and in shape, eating raw food every day for years. He was strong as a gorilla and got as close to the judge as he could. Carlos could feel the hairs on the judge's neck before sheriffs grabbed him and subdued him. Then they took him to jail.

Instead of three years, Carlos ended up getting twelve to fifteen years.

Less than two weeks after Benny and Moe were acquitted in July 1981, it was the MOVE 9's turn to receive their sentence. Theirs was the longest, costliest criminal proceeding in Philadelphia history at the time. The nine defendants—my mother, Debbie; my father, Michael; my uncle Chuck; Janet; Janine; Merle; Phil; Delbert; and Eddie—were each given a court-appointed lawyer, but like Benny, they chose to represent themselves. With a thorough working knowledge of the court routine, they seized every opportunity to challenge anything the judge had to say. They would need every break they could get.

The MOVE 9 were on trial for the death of an on-duty police officer. That unleashed a lynch mob mentality for which MOVE served as a scapegoat, irrespective of guilt or innocence. Years of suspicions, hostilities, and insults between MOVE and the cops surfaced when they faced each other in court.

Finally, nearly three years after their arrest, the nine codefendants were found guilty of third-degree murder, conspiracy, multiple counts of attempted murder, and aggravated assault. On August 4, my mom's birthday, each defendant was given a sentence of thirty years minimum and one hundred years maximum. Sandra, DeeDee, and Consuewella had been present in the house on August 8, 1978, the day the crime happened, yet Sandra and DeeDee were never seriously charged. Consuewella refused to disavow MOVE; she was tried separately and sentenced to sixteen to twenty-three years.

In total, for the death of Officer James Ramp, MOVE members were sentenced to 923 years.

Chapter 10

THE PRISON RIOT

Several days after the MOVE 9 were convicted and sentenced, the trial judge, Edwin Malmed, was a guest on a local talk radio show. Journalist Mumia Abu-Jamal called in and asked the judge if he knew who shot and killed Officer James Ramp. The judge replied, "I have absolutely no idea," and said that because MOVE members wanted to be tried as a family, he convicted them as a family. The nine codefendants protested that they were convicted only because of their unwavering allegiance to MOVE rather than any complicity in the death of a policeman.

With nineteen members sent off to long-term prison terms, MOVE's profile in Philadelphia shrank considerably. A handful of members like Louise, LaVerne, and Pam continued to do the organization's work, but it wasn't the same. They held rallies on the vacant lot where MOVE headquarters had been. It wasn't much, but it did help attract a few new members who became pivotal in leading MOVE forward: Teresa and Ramona Africa.

But inside the prisons, the battles continued. Just as they confronted police on the streets, MOVE members also faced the guards in prison. The way they dealt with uncooperative neighbors was the same way they handled other prisoners. MOVE members exercised relentlessly and flexed their muscle whenever challenged or threatened, using the same approach LaVerne taught us as kids: if one of you is in a fight, you all fight.

Racism in Philadelphia was overt during this time. MOVE's

popularity didn't stop officers or officials from outwardly displaying their bigotry toward them, especially behind bars.

Segregation was in full effect at Huntingdon State Prison, where my dad was sent. Playing on the same sports team and high-fiving each other on the basketball court in the yard didn't mean you got to eat with each other in the mess hall. Whites ate on one side of the room, and every other race ate on the other. Prison officials even announced chow time for people based on race. Whites ate at 11 a.m. Everybody else ate at 12 noon. Same with dinner, commissary deliveries, and hospital emergencies.

This was a far cry from the way things were at Holmesburg County Jail, where all the MOVE 9 men were held for the three years between their arrests and convictions. Holmesburg was a short bus ride from Philly. Easily accessible for visits from family members. That meant my father got to see his mom, his MOVE family, and his relatives pretty regularly. Huntingdon was a five-hour car ride deep in the Klan valley section of Pennsylvania. Pennsylvania is notoriously racist with nicknames to match its reputation—PennsylTUCKY, PennsylBAMA, PennsylKLANia.

My father's introduction to Huntingdon was on par with the description Bob Moses, one of the MOVE members released in 1977, gave from his stint there:

"They had me locked in a glass cage cell like Hannibal Lecter for twenty-four hours a day, naked. No clothes, nothing to read, no television, nothing to write with, nothing. I was completely alone for days at a time, just me and the cinder block walls. It was even hard for me to know what time or day it was. The only visitors I got were from the cockroaches, which was a dreadful sight at first, but after being completely alone and not knowing how long this would last, the cockroaches became a welcome sight. Because even though they were disgusting to me at first, the idea that they were the only life I could see made me see them differently. The food was good except it was mixed with snot from the guard's nostrils and phlegm from their chests. On the first day they slid-served some junk under my cell door. I slid it back. The next day they slid some more junk, I slid it back. By the third time they slid it, I was so hungry I just started eating. As I was gobbling it down, I realized it was the same tray of food from the first day. Another time the food looked like every guard on duty's hock spit was on the tray. It was a terrible experience. I couldn't wait to get out of there."

When my father got to Huntingdon, the glass cage had been disassembled but the other tactics were still highly active. The isolation in the cell was on full tilt, the word "nigger" was in full use by inmates and guards. Dad stayed out of trouble mostly, but when it came to protecting his beliefs, like not cutting his hair, refusing to give blood, demanding to be let into the general population, and demanding more time for recreation, he stood his ground. This landed him time in the hole at first, but eventually he garnered respect from inmates and staff, and they eased up on the harsh treatment. At least one guard got to the point of writing letters to the Department of Corrections in support of my father, asking that he be released from prison. But long before that support letter was written there was a lot of resistance.

The resistance came to a head on December 3, 1981, when the MOVE 9 were called back to court for their appeals. All the men were doing their time in separate prisons across the state. The women were clustered together in the one state prison Pennsylvania had at the time for women. But all the MOVE 9 were having similar experiences. They had had enough of correction officers' antics. MOVE handled conflict with the guards the same way they dealt with people on the street—with hands squared, wrapped, and ready to brawl.

It started with the MOVE women. Bert, Benny's wife, was being moved back and forth from jail to court. In the holding cells, other women who were also being transported to and from were smoking like chimneys, and the smoke made Bert sick. Cigarettes were a hot commodity in prison because most people smoked, and they were bartered like money. Bert said the smoke bothered her lungs, and she refused to come to court. Judge Kendall H. Shoyer, the same judge that Carlos attacked, ordered her to go to court anyway, and when she refused, she was physically forced by correctional officers. When Bert resisted, all the other MOVE women got involved in her defense. They yelled obscenities, got into a pushing-and-shoving match with the guards, and then were forcefully taken to the restricting housing unit, or the RHU, where they were isolated from the rest of the population and from one another. The RHU had a long, dark hallway in a separate building about two miles away from the main prison. The inmates called it the house on the hill because it was a house on a hill. From the outside it was a stone building that looked abandoned. It had six small concrete cells on each side of the unit. Each cell had a small, rectangular vent that you could open about a half inch. The bed was nailed to the floor and was topped with a thin mattress that shed lint like a long-haired collie. The door was heavy and so tight to the jamb and the floor that a piece of paper couldn't slide under it. That was one of two doors locking the women in—the second was a set of bars.

When Sue was granted a phone call, she called home and told Benny what had happened. Benny instructed Moe to expose the harsh treatment to the public. Benny didn't like doing media stuff himself. So Moe got on local radio—on 1340 AM with Philadelphia broadcast legend Georgie Woods—and told listeners that correctional officers had attacked MOVE women. When the MOVE men heard this, they followed the MOVE rules: if one of you fights, you all fight. Separated by prisons or not, the rule still applied. The tactic they'd act out barely needed explaining: the MOVE family would attack every head guard they came across until the MOVE women were treated better and sent back to the prison's general population.

Phil was the first one to attack in Holmesburg. He saw a guard coming down the prison hall and said, "Hey, motherfucker! What the fuck are you going do about your brother guards attacking my MOVE sisters?!"

"Africa, go back to your cell."

Boom! Phil's overhand right exploded onto the guard's jawline, knocking him clear across the floor. Immediately Phil was covered in guards, knocked unconscious, and thrown back into his cell. MOVE had eight members at Holmesburg. The five men from the MOVE 9—Delbert, Phil, Chuck, Eddie, and my dad, Michael—plus Carlos, Frank and Dennis, who'd gotten arrested in Rochester. Three other men in Holmesburg—Count, Scooty, and Kareem—became close supporters of MOVE while being jailed near them. Together, all the men except for Frank decided to stand together and wage a confrontation against the guards. Frank stayed out of it so he could report the outcome to Benny. They all got in one cell and refused to come out until their demands were met. After that, all hell broke loose.

Twenty-four correctional officers suited up for battle. All but two of them were Black. One was Puerto Rican and one was the white captain. Their weapons looked more like they were entering into a street fight than a prison riot. They had flak jackets, helmets, shields, ice picks, jagged edge, broken-off mop wringers, night sticks, baseball bats, fire hoses. They were ready for a serious fight.

MOVE knew the drill. Phil gave a speech anyway:

"They will come in here with the water, but it is from our God. The life they turned into technology and used to make those weapons, we are going to take them *from* them and use it *on* them. Fight like your life depends on it because it does. Fight like these motherfuckers just beat your wife because they did. Fuck this System and anybody that protects it."

The guards came marching in military formation down the cellblock. Other inmates in the jail knew what was coming, and screamed and spat at the guards as they passed their cells. "Let me out, motherfucker! You want to fight MOVE? You are going to have to fight me, too! I'll fight you!" Suddenly inmates not even in MOVE wanted to stand with MOVE and fight.

The guards ignored the chaos as they marched on. They got to MOVE's cell and stopped. Carlos, Dennis, Delbert, and Phil were in the front, ready for battle. MOVE members and prison guards stared at each other without making a sound. And then suddenly, "Fire! Get them niggers!" the white captain yelled.

The guards parted, and the fire hose blasted Dennis in the chest. He was unmoved and spread his arms wide and yelled, "Long live John Africa, motherfucker!"

The water wasn't working to back the men up. The guards couldn't reach the prisoners from where they were, so they were forced to open the cell bars. Just as one guard got close to the open cell, Phil pulled him in, threw him on the floor, and slammed the cell bars closed. The prison guard was trapped. He backed up to the cell's wall and braced himself, knowing the MOVE men would beat him to a pulp, which they did. They beat that guard unconscious. Recognizing what was happening, the other guards tried to get in to rescue their partner. When they finally did, they, too, were pulled inside and given the same beatdown.

Kicks, punches to the face, knocking folks out, trying to push past, knock past, knock through the vests the guards were wearing—it was pandemonium. Some MOVE men took the shields off the guards and protected themselves. This continued until the cell was full of people and the bars could not be forced shut anymore, which made everybody spill out into the hallway. By that point, Dennis was bleeding badly from his hand, where he had been stabbed with an ice pick. Carlos had a hunk of meat hanging from over his eye from where he had been bashed with a broken-off mop wringer.

Delbert got slammed over the head with the baseball bat as the men scrambled in the hallway to regain their position. He tried to stop the blows with his forearm and did, just in time to hear the bone crack. Phil was on the ground with four guards whaling on him with bats and nightsticks. Carlos jumped on top of him to give him some relief and instantly regretted it. The MOVE men were finally outnumbered, outweaponed, and out of gas. More guards came in, and the men were all handcuffed and forced to their feet, as the guards made a gauntlet. Each MOVE man was pushed through it and received a gang-style beating along the way. Chuck tried to run through as quickly as possible, but every guard wanted to ensure they got their licks in.

No area of the body was spared from the heavy blows. Eyes, ears, knees, and back, and at the end of the gauntlet was the final guard who had a special torture method. He forced each man back down on his knees with his legs wide and his arms handcuffed behind him. The guard took an underhanded swing of a baseball bat and yelled, "No more MOVE babies for you, motherfucker!" The last guard hit the men in the crotch as hard as he could, then watched the men crumble to the floor. They were wet with blood, sweat, and exhaustion, and beaten like wild animals.

The MOVE men were still ready to fight. But in a step of pure cruelty, the guards stood over the men and pulled out box cutters. They told the men to stay still, as if any of them had energy left to move. The guard grabbed the men's prison jumpsuits and cut every inch of fabric off each man's body. They were stripped naked and thrown shivering through the December cold air into the back of a police van.

After four hours, the men arrived at a hospital that was only a five-minute drive away. Doctors surveyed their injuries. My dad's testicles had swelled to the size of two grapefruits. Chuck had ten broken fingers. Scooty had a gash in his forehead that, forty stitches and forty years later, still hasn't fully healed. Scooty was on the front page the next day in the local newspapers, displaying his wounds with the headline, "24 Hurt in MOVE Melee." Kareem, who was in the Black Liberation Army, was in the cell with Phil, beaten but happy that he was standing by his MOVE brothers.

No charges were filed against MOVE, Kareem, Count, Scooty, or the guards. And once this fight was over and all the imprisoned men were released from the hospital, everyone was back to being scattered throughout seven different prisons across the state. Some of the men never saw each other again.

Chapter 11

RUMBLINGS OF DEFIANCE

Back on the outside, an acquitted Benny, fresh out of jail, needed a place to stay. His sister Louise insisted he stay with her in her extra bedroom. Louise loved her house and thought it would be the perfect oasis for her brother to rest after running and fighting for so long. Her house's address was 6221 Osage Avenue.

Originally built in 1925 with the newest and highest-grade building materials, it was still immaculate when Louise purchased it in the early 1960s. It was a classic Philadelphia row house. Three bedrooms, two bathrooms, maybe 1,800 square feet. Brown brick exterior and two stories with a basement and garage accessible only from the back of the house, facing an alley. It had soft, royal blue carpet, newly painted walls, and the latest Sears Roebuck appliances in the eat-in kitchen. Louise had climbed her way into West Philly's Black middle class. She was so proud of her house, and proud that she could offer her brother a comfortable place to stay.

The day Benny arrived on Osage Avenue, MOVE members and supporters, old and new, were there to welcome him. Most MOVE members were in prison, so their young kids, newly arrived in Philly from Virginia, were on hand to greet Benny. "Long live John Africa!" everyone cheered. It seemed they never left.

From the minute Benny set foot in Louise's beautiful home, a slew of people, dogs, cats, bees, birds, squirrels, and other animals followed him. Louise would come home from a long working day. From the corner, she could see the squirrels and birds in front of her house, eating a pile of cracked corn and mixed nuts that Benny put out for them.

When she came into her house, she was devastated to see Benny and a bunch of kids having a water fight in her living room, on what used to be her pristine carpets. At any given time, fifteen MOVE kids lived in, spent the night at, or visited Louise's home. There were so many kids in and out of Osage Avenue it looked like a day care center.

On days when Louise came home to a quiet house, it was usually because the kids were in the basement, tearing it up with their play. Benny regularly met with MOVE people on the main floor about MOVE business, the future, the past, which members were committed and which ones weren't. Benny could see the dismay all over Louise's face. Most times, she'd come into the house without saying a word, walk up the stairs to her bedroom, and close the door.

Her expectation of Benny at her house obviously did not fit the reality of his presence. She thought her brother was going to use his larger platform and court victory to move his movement forward and take advantage of all the eyes watching him. She assumed he'd be busy doing news interviews, television appearances, and radio. She did not expect him to become more reclusive from the public or more extreme within MOVE. But Benny did both.

At its founding in 1972, MOVE was not religious in the conventional sense. Benny didn't think the world's great religions were natural. He said, "You never saw animals looking for a church, a mosque, a synagogue, or a temple." To Benny, the purpose of religion was to reconnect you to God because you realized you'd been disconnected. And if you are connected to God, you don't need religion. Just like you don't need a crutch when you have strong legs.

So MOVE was deeply religious, but the religion was life. Instead of praying to a God that you couldn't see or hear, Benny said to pray to your brother, who can help answer the prayer. MOVE prayed with their actions. If you're hungry, find food and eat. Don't simply say words about it.

After Benny beat the Feds, he truly believed that he was unstoppable. That the laws of the government could not win against him. That Mama, or Mother Nature, was on his and MOVE's side. This intensified a religious component to the organization that had always existed but never to the degree of invincibility. MOVE was evolving as more than an organization committed to sustaining and protecting all life. Benny was emerging as more than a revolutionary or a proponent of MOVE's radical belief system. For the first time, his leadership was taking on spiritual guru—type vibes. Benny saw his work within MOVE, combined with his perceived invincibility, as godlike. He encouraged this thinking. Some MOVE members believed Benny had uncommon, otherworldly abilities, and some strongly did not.

Louise didn't see any of this coming. Benny was just her brother who had bold ideas about valuing life that she'd come to agree with. Other MOVE members were surprised, too, but they trusted Benny more than anything. He'd earned that from them. Plus, they themselves felt emboldened by Benny's court win. They, too, believed Mama was on MOVE's side.

No one took the privilege of Benny's presence or his teachings more seriously than Louise's son, my second cousin Frank. Frank tried to make as complete a disconnect from the System, from within the System, as he could. He'd walk or run if he had to travel somewhere instead of riding in a car. If he needed new clothes, he'd borrow them, take someone else's clothes, or buy them from a thrift store instead of buying them new from a department store. His fierce discipline around eating only raw, natural food and never, ever, eating anything else—no matter how miniscule—was commendable but also so strict and unforgiving as to be unusual.

Everybody tried to follow MOVE law, but it was common for members to dabble in non-MOVE-related activities. Even Benny chewed gum and ate rice and boiled potatoes sometimes, which was not raw food. Every other member followed MOVE law about 60 to 70 percent of the time. Frank tried to follow it 100 percent, to be as much like Benny as he could, and in some cases, Frank surpassed him.

He recognized that Benny was really strong, so he started emulating him in other ways, too. Frank started walking like Benny. He started talking like him. He started dressing like him. Have you ever seen a man that's been around someone or watched them so closely for so long that they begin to look alike? Think about Kobe Bryant chewing his gum with hands on his hips just like Michael Jordan. If Benny was Jordan, then Frank was Kobe. He followed the movements, habits, and teachings of Benny closely, reverently, and with total adoration. When imprisoned MOVE members called the Osage Avenue house to speak to Benny, they could actually be talking with Frank without knowing it. That was how similar Frank started to sound compared to Benny. Before long, Frank was an impressive mimic of everything he heard Benny say, saw him do, and what he believed.

For example, Benny often walked around barefoot, even in the wintertime and in the snow, to keep his feet conditioned and strong. Frank did the same.

If Benny felt a cold coming on, he'd eat raw onions and raw garlic like it was candy. So did Frank.

Benny hated the smell and taste of ketchup. He said it made his stomach hurt. Once Frank learned that, he didn't allow people to bring ketchup in the house when Benny was there.

Frank was copying Benny so closely that he began to lose sight of himself. At first it was a little cute, endearing, and even funny at times. But eventually it became annoying. Louise called him out.

"Frank, I know you love your uncle, but you can still love him and be yourself."

"I don't want to be myself. I want to be like Uncle Benny. When I'm myself, I'm weak, uncoordinated. But when I think about Uncle Benny, I'm strong and safe."

Louise looked at her son. "Frank, do you think Delbert is strong? Do you think Dennis is strong? Do you think Mike and Debbie are strong? They survived the attacks from Rizzo, and they are still strong and in fact much stronger. You can be strong without trading yourself for it."

Frank was undeterred. "Ma, you like who you are. I don't like who I am. I want to be like Uncle Benny."

Frank started to believe that Louise was trying to come between him and his beloved uncle, and he didn't like it. He began to feel resentment toward his mother. Louise let the matter drop but the damage was already done. She loved her son but didn't like who he was becoming.

MOVE had become too much for Louise, as well. She had agreed with MOVE's practices since its beginning, but now things were out of control and only getting worse. The naked kids bothered her. Them being naked in the winter bothered her worse. The stringent diet was a serious problem. The lack of education, the absence of structure, the ever-growing chaos with neighbors.

Louise began to rebel and speak out more and more. Most people in MOVE were in awe of Benny or intimidated by his knowledge and presence, so they wouldn't dare say anything against him, even if they disagreed. Louise was his older sister, and although she loved, respected, and admired her brother, she did not allow him to walk all over her. Louise's doubts were like cracks in the organization that grew into giant fractures, which split MOVE wide open.

Chapter 12

MUTINY I

N ow is when I remember a lot clearer. It's 1983.
I was about five years old and living at my grandmother LaVerne's house on Reno Street. She'd taken responsibility for raising my sister Whit and me, and always assured my mother that we'd be okay. Me and some other kids were in the living room playing with a tennis ball. LaVerne was sitting on the couch with an annoyed look on her face. A black rotary telephone on an end table beside the sofa was ringing off the hook. LaVerne had positioned herself at the perfect distance on the couch from the phone, where she could bend her elbow to lift the receiver up and put it back down to hang it up. I could hear voices I knew on the other end yelling, cursing, and threatening.

"LaVerne, who is that on the phone?" I asked.

Never changing the expression on her face or moving an inch, she said with a curt and dismissive tone, "Nobody."

The phone kept ringing, she'd lift it up, and we'd hear the frantic yelling and berating from familiar voices.

One time, a voice said, "You traitor! How dare you violate the Coordinator, you violating bitch?"

LaVerne immediately hung up.

The phone rang again. Same thing. LaVerne picked up the phone—"Mama coming for your ass, you fucking traitor!"—and she slammed it back down.

The phone rang again. "You called the cops on Frank? You fucking System-loving motherfucker!"

This went on and on and on.

It wasn't hard to recognize the voices. I knew who they were but I had never heard them like this. It was like seeing a familiar face in an unfamiliar place. You recognize them immediately, but it takes your brain a moment to process who they are because you don't expect to see them in that space. I had heard MOVE members' voices yelling at people all my life but never at each other in this way. They were saying things to LaVerne that were typically reserved for System people, like the police.

"You think you can do better without Benny, you fucking tramp? You think your lifestyle is superior to MOVE? Your son is a faggot because of your lifestyle! Your daughter is a whore because of your way of thinking!"

LaVerne maintained her composure. She'd pick up the phone and put it back down.

This went on nonstop all day and all night, tag-teaming phone calls from imprisoned MOVE members like Sue. Frank and Conrad called for days at a time, at all hours. Two o'clock and four o'clock in the morning. It was like they didn't sleep. I'd wake up in the morning to go to the bathroom, and the phone was still ringing, and LaVerne was still sitting on the couch in that same spot picking up the phone and hanging it up. Eventually LaVerne took the phone off the hook and tucked it under the couch cushion. I don't know why she didn't do that sooner.

It took a lot of work for LaVerne to make a phone call. As soon as she'd put the phone back on the hook and to get a dial tone, the phone would ring, and it would be the harassers again. She had to time it just right. She had to pick up the phone at the same time they were hanging up the phone and start dialing before their call came through. This went on for what seemed like months.

This period was such a complicated mess. Leading up to all the harassment LaVerne received, Frank, Benny's mimic, became very important. Benny considered Frank to be the most loyal member of MOVE because Frank's dedication and commitment to Benny was so outstanding. Benny wanted to reward it. He said that Frank deserved to be "crowned" with the highest honor that a MOVE member could reach. All original members had titles Benny gave them: minister of confrontation, minister of education, minister of defense, minister of communication, minister of information, and so on. Their responsibilities were unwritten, but it was clear how they functioned.

> Minister of confrontation: one who demonstrates a willingness to confront anyone who opposes MOVE
>
> Minister of defense: one who demonstrates a willingness to defend MOVE members and John Africa
>
> Minister of education: one who demonstrates a willingness to educate people within the organization about MOVE law
>
> Minister of information: one who demonstrates a willingness to inform close supporters and the community about MOVE law
>
> Minister of communication: one who demonstrates a willingness to communicate MOVE's position to the media

The titles were pretty standard, but they were also coveted. It meant that you had Benny's deep respect and trust. And it spread the leadership responsibilities across the organization, which was what Benny advocated. From the beginning, he never wanted MOVE to have one single leader. Even after his acquittal, when Benny became a public figurehead for MOVE, he said he still didn't want MOVE's internal operations to be run by one person. He said he wanted only to do his job as coordinator and help things run smoothly. But he also wanted to be considered the leader without being called that.

Everybody understood what it meant to receive a title from Benny. The highest title he ever bestowed was to Frank. Benny made him MOVE's naturalist minister.

The naturalist minister had to be able to demonstrate all the other ministers' roles, but also follow a very challenging diet that was at least 80 percent raw food and exercise rigorously. I'd heard from several MOVE members that Frank could run a mile nonstop at full speed. In the entire fifty-year history of the MOVE organization, Frank Africa was the only naturalist minister. It was such a high bar to clear. Frank ate raw sweet potatoes, raw peanuts, raw potatoes, raw eggs, raw fish, raw chicken. He even ate raw beef. This diet gave him unbelievable strength and fitness. When he first joined MOVE, Frank was the slowest runner; he could only do a few pushups, and he had no skill in boxing. But by the time he left Rochester, he was leading the pack in most of these categories.

Benny was so flattered and impressed with Frank's transformation that he started using Frank as the example for how a true MOVE member was supposed to be. Most members didn't see it that way, especially the men. They felt that Frank was a suck-up. They didn't feel they had to kowtow to anyone. Neither did the women. While they all loved Benny and believed in his abilities, they wanted MOVE law to be less prohibitive. They wanted to eat cooked or processed foods occasionally; some wanted to play the field and have sex with as many people as they could. Sometimes they wanted to smoke cigarettes, drink liquor, and get high. Some folks had trouble letting go of who they were and who they wanted to be. They believed in MOVE, but completely submitting oneself to someone else's way of thinking could be too much for anybody. Except for Frank.

Frank said he submitted so willingly because he believed Benny's teachings, that using Mama as his guide made him a better man. In his mind, he was clear that MOVE law would correct whatever faults he had, and because Benny was the author of MOVE law, Frank followed Benny and the law to the letter.

With Benny's loud stamp of approval and the new title of naturalist minister, Frank's ego swelled out of control. He started to believe he could do no wrong. Frank also knew that Benny wanted to use Louise's Osage Avenue house as a new headquarters for MOVE. The house was becoming more and more like a MOVE house and less and less like Louise's house. Benny and Louise were locking horns constantly. And Frank the Mimic resented his mother for daring to defy Benny. He was looking for a reason to confront her, and he got his chance when Louise disobeyed a direct order.

Early one morning, Frank burst into Louise's bedroom, yelling and screaming about watermelons and LaVerne. He and LaVerne had had a massive argument on the telephone, and Frank was fuming about it.

MOVE's primary source of income in the summertime was watermelon sales. They purchased the melons in bulk from a food distribution center and used Scarlet's old Chevy van (usually driven by LaVerne), to transport them to Osage Avenue. Then MOVE members would haul melons around the neighborhood, using wagons that some of the guys had built from scrap wood.

Frank wanted to make sure MOVE made money that day. But Scarlet and some of the women from Reno Street had other plans for the van. They were headed to the casinos in Atlantic City for the day. Frank was beside himself and let LaVerne know it.

"LaVerne," Frank began, trying to keep his composure, "you know we use the van to buy melons. This is how we buy food for us and the kids."

"Frank, I told you, I can't give you the van today. You'll be okay for one day."

Frank went to say something else, but LaVerne wasn't having it. "Frank, do you hear the sound on the other end of your phone?" she said flatly.

"What sound?" Frank asked.

Then a dial tone. LaVerne had hung up on him.

Frank was shaking with rage. He felt beyond disrespected. He paced for a bit, then marched into Louise's bedroom. Louise was still sleeping, but Frank's loud entrance and booming voice startled her awake.

"Ma! Ma! Wake up!"

Louise squinted her eyes open and looked at her son with confusion.

Frank was all worked up. "LaVerne hung up on me, Ma!"

"What?" Louise replied, still disoriented.

"She hung up. Ma, wake up and call LaVerne to talk to me."

Louise was still confused but could hear and see Frank's aggravation. She sat and scooted to the edge of her bed. "Frank, what is going on?"

"I told LaVerne we needed to use the van to buy watermelons, and she told me we couldn't because she's using it to go to the casino. The casino! Fuck Atlantic City! We need the van."

He marched in and out of Louise's room. Finally, he marched back in and totally lost his shit. "Ma, she hung up on me! She hung up! Call that bitch and tell her to talk to me!"

Louise couldn't believe how her son was acting. "Frank, if you were talking to her the way you're talking to me, I would hang up on you, too."

Frank paused his pacing and stared intensely at his mother. "You would talk that way to your son? To the naturalist minister?"

Louise was happy to repeat herself so that there was no lapse in clarity. "If you yelled at LaVerne," she began slowly, "the way you're yelling now, I don't blame LaVerne for hanging up on you. I would have hung up on you, too."

She continued, "If you can't make LaVerne give you the van, I can't make LaVerne give you the van." Louise was frustrated and done with this conversation. Frank had woken her up for this, and she couldn't see how it had anything to do with her.

Frank got quiet. He sat next to his mother on the bed and put his forehead up against hers. Then he asked her again, softly, "Ma, are you gonna call LaVerne for me?"

"No."

And that was all it took. All of Frank's frustrations about folks not following MOVE law, his mother not accepting Benny's god-like status, her impertinence about Frank as a man came to a head. His anger and frustration boiled over. Without warning, Frank punched Louise hard in the side of her head.

Frank's wife, Teresa, who was standing at the doorway, screamed, "Frank, what are you doing?! What are you doing? That's your mother! Frank! *Frank!*"

Louise was screaming and grasping at her son's arms as he set up for his next punch, which landed in the same spot as the first one. Next, Frank wrapped his hands around Louise's neck and squeezed. Then he grabbed a pillow and covered her face with it.

Teresa screamed for Benny, who ran in and yelled at Frank to stop. Frank finally did, but the damage was done—between mother and son and, critically, within MOVE.

Right away, opinions were divided. Frank started out in MOVE as a gentle person who wouldn't hurt a soul. Many MOVE members who were in prison had trouble believing he had done this horrible thing to his own mother. Others felt that Benny should have done to Frank what Frank did to Louise.

My grandmother LaVerne took Louise's side immediately. That led to all the harassing phone calls I saw.

Many other close members took Louise's side without hesitation, as well. To them, she was a defenseless woman who only stood four feet, eleven inches tall and weighed one hundred pounds soaking wet. And she was assaulted by a five-nine, 160-pound, muscle-bound man. People like Delbert felt that there could be no good reason for any man to beat up his own mother. Delbert and some other MOVE men wanted a piece of Frank.

But others felt differently.

Frank's wife, Teresa, took Louise's side at first.

Verbally, Benny took Louise's side, but the way he treated Frank told a different tale. Frank was in no real way punished, and Benny never made him apologize. In fact, because Benny and Frank were so simpatico and because Benny championed Frank so passionately as naturalist minister, it was hard for people to believe that Benny wasn't somehow involved in this episode. That led to Frank's beating of Louise becoming more a gauge of a MOVE member's commitment to and belief in Benny than a judgment about the beating itself.

Many MOVE members took a position based on how they felt about the people involved, regardless of the facts of the incident. Anyone who took Louise's side became a target of verbal abuse to those who took Frank's side. People closer to Frank took his side. They didn't even need to hear an explanation. Their minds were made up before they heard the full story. Some people *still* have not listened to the whole story and don't want to hear it, for fear that they may have to admit Frank was wrong. For example,

Sue totally dismissed what happened and even wrote Louise hate mail for putting Frank in a position to receive criticism. Similarly, Carlos didn't like what he heard about Frank, but he still took Frank's side. He said, "If Frank did that, he must've had a good reason for it."

MOVE members who stood by Frank were locked into their beliefs about MOVE. They might admit that Frank went too far, but Frank's devotion and discipline to upholding MOVE's ideals trumped everything. No person was bigger than MOVE. No person's mistake was, either.

Though mother and son, Louise and Frank represented two sides of a power struggle within MOVE that had been simmering for years and was finally coming to a head. Everybody in the organization still supported the goals of the organization. They protested for the release of the MOVE 9, they sent money to imprisoned members' commissaries, they took care of one another's children, they believed in their commitment to preserving and protecting life. What Louise and Frank didn't see eye to eye on was Benny's evolution into a godlike figure. Benny saw himself that way. And so Frank saw Benny that way. Louise didn't, and that enraged Benny and Frank.

Louise received constant harassment, after Frank beat her. In letters from imprisoned MOVE members, they blamed her for her own assault because she questioned Benny and undermined his authority by telling other MOVE members, like newbie Ramona, that Benny wasn't God.

Disgusted, angry, and hurt, Louise went to pick up some of her belongings from her house on Osage Avenue. Scarlet and LaVerne accompanied her for moral support.

Benny had basically taken Louise's house over, so she was mostly sleeping at LaVerne's place on Reno Street, before eventually renting an apartment a mile away in a building called Chestnut Arms.

But that day, full of fury because of what Louise had endured, Scarlet and LaVerne took the opportunity to give Frank a piece of their minds.

"Frank, you hit Louise, but you wouldn't do that to Delbert, you pussy!" Scarlet yelled at Frank from the car window as they rolled toward the house. "You hit a woman, but you won't fuck with the MOVE men, you coward! Wait till I tell the MOVE men in the prison what your punk ass did, you fucking bitch!"

By this time, the fighting between the Louise supporters and the Frank supporters had caused MOVE to lose sight of its original mission. Disagreements were always a problem in the organization, but this was next-level. The MOVE 9 and other MOVE prisoners were writing one another hate mail and circulating it from imprisoned members to other imprisoned members, back out onto the street, and then back to prison again. Letters were coming home from jail as fast as the mail carrier could deliver the mail. The organization seemed out of control.

MOVE members had been trained in governmental confrontation, verbal confrontation, hand-to-hand combat, and weapons training. To know and see MOVE fight with police, neighbors, and other System people was scary enough. But to see my family using their training and experience on one another was scary on another level.

The mood in our house on Reno Street felt like an ongoing tragedy. It wasn't as bad as a death in a family, but I could feel my family breaking up, and everybody was powerless to stop it. Mostly the children would stick close to one another for comfort. Sometimes we'd huddle together and sit in silence, surrounded by chaos and yelling and ringing phones.

Even though MOVE members were fighting one another, MOVE was still fighting in the courts to free the MOVE prisoners. This bigger fight against the System temporarily brought everybody in MOVE together.

When LaVerne had to go to court, she would have supporters watch me and the other kids. One day while at Pam's house, when I was about five years old, I saw a patchwork blanket that someone had made. I don't know who. The names of the MOVE children were stitched on it. Although none of us kids were in school, LaVerne had been teaching us some fundamental life skills, like how to spell our names and memorize our addresses and phone numbers.

I scanned the blanket, looking at the names: Tree, Netta, Tomaso, Delisha, and so on. I didn't see my name. I flipped the blanket over and still couldn't find my name. I didn't see my sister Whit's name. I didn't see Darren's name. I felt so many emotions while staring at the blanket, first confused, then angry, then really hurt. I wondered why Benny would allow the divisions among the adults to trickle down to the kids. I was just a small child and loved everybody in my MOVE family. I didn't want to become separated from Frank, Marie, or anybody else. It felt like a massive injustice was being dealt to the kids. There was little or no compassion for us. The adults got to choose a side based on their feelings, but we kids were assigned a side. I hadn't argued with anyone, so for my name to be left off the blanket made me feel like under Benny's leadership, whoever made the blanket had cast me out of MOVE.

I wasn't the only person who noticed. It was also clear to Scarlet. She was done with MOVE life. She was tired of confrontations, sleeping on the floor, eating raw food, fighting the police, and going to jail. The cocktail of it all became beyond exhausting, and the risk wasn't worth the reward. She wanted a different kind of life.

After visiting Pam's house, seeing the blanket, and feeling that mix of emotions, the other kids and I returned to our house on Reno Street the following morning. Scarlet didn't know about the blanket incident but she didn't need to. When she saw us, she offered us something we had never formally had before: breakfast. As kids in MOVE, we ate whenever we were hungry. There were no set mealtimes. But this day, Scarlet told us we were going to eat something cooked—or rather processed—and not raw and natural. She put a box of cornflakes on the table. There were maybe six or seven of us gathered around it, grinning at each other. Normally we ate raw sweet potatoes or raw spinach coated in vegetable oil as our first meal of the day. Cornflakes was something different. We were very excited.

Darren poured the cereal and reached for the sugar. It was obvious he'd had cornflakes before and knew what to do.

Not wanting to go too far away from MOVE law too fast, Scarlet told Darren, "Hey, skip the sugar."

Darren poured the milk into our bowls, and I ate cereal for the very first time. It felt extraordinary eating processed food without having to sneak it. With these loosened rules, it was becoming obvious whose side we in the Reno Street house were on, whether we chose it or not. A flood of new possibilities seemed to wander into the house after that, as if people had been holding back from doing things they'd wanted to do for years.

Scarlet talked to us as we ate our cereal. "There's gonna be some changes around here. What y'all want for dinner? Fried chicken or spaghetti and meatballs?"

I had yet to learn what either one tasted like. Darren had a life before MOVE, so I let him choose. He chose spaghetti and meatballs. The floodgates were open. Scarlet called Sears Roebuck, JCPenney, Macy's, and every other department store she could think of and applied for credit cards.

The first thing she bought was a mattress for herself, which got delivered to our house. While the food was cooking on the stove, she called Belmont Elementary School to enroll Darren, her son.

We kids had a good time eating regular American grub and cutting up. The realization of what was happening hadn't fully hit us yet. But then it did. Scarlet pulled a chair from the kitchen and told Darren to sit in it.

"Kita," she said to me, using my MOVE nickname, "go get me the scissors from my room on the dresser."

I ran upstairs, got the scissors, and brought them to her.

"Go into the kitchen and get the broom and a trash bag," she told me.

When I came out of the kitchen, I was stunned at what I saw. Scarlet was cutting off Darren's locs. Piece by piece, loc by loc, the scissors effortlessly sliced through his hair. He was sitting in a yellow kitchen chair in the dining room, with a towel wrapped around his neck to catch the hair. Scarlet was cutting and discarding his locs with disgust. Darren sat still and seemed to be a little down about it. Each time five or six locs were cut, he'd pick one up and stare at it before dropping it to the floor. All the kids got a haircut except for me and Whit. Our parents were still in MOVE, and even though Scarlet wasn't, she continued to respect our parents' wishes. I was too young to understand what this really meant.

Then ding, the food was done. I had a mountain of spaghetti with piping hot red sauce and three giant meatballs on my plate. I didn't know how to eat it. I had never used a fork before. Usually, when I ate spaghetti, it was hard pasta, and I would use my saliva to fuse several pieces together and then eat it like a carrot. But this was something else. Scarlet walked me through it, demonstrating how to twirl a tangle of noodles onto my fork and how to cut the meatball. When I ate it, I couldn't believe how good it tasted. Scarlet watched in sheer delight at how happy she made us. She was giddy and couldn't stop laughing at her newfound freedom.

As Darren's mother, Scarlet could make big decisions only for him. But she wanted all of us to be able to do what normal kids did. When a family friend offered Darren a bike, she happily accepted it. When kids in the neighborhood were going to school, she wanted us all to go too.

Meanwhile, four miles away at Louise's house on Osage Avenue, where Frank's loyalists congregated, it was business as usual: conflict, turmoil, and unrest. The MOVE kids over there were getting increasingly weary of the MOVE life. Multiple times they tried to run away and find LaVerne on Reno Street. They had spent so many years with her that they didn't remember their birth mothers and fathers anymore. Netta hadn't seen her mom, Consuewella, since she was about three or four years old, and she was now about eleven or twelve. The last time Little Phil saw his parents, he was only about four. MOVE policy forbade the kids from visiting their parents in prison. We didn't call anybody Mom and Dad or know which adult we belonged to. But that was about to change, at least for the Reno Street kids.

With the new inclusion of a "normal" lifestyle, Scarlet was done hearing her own children calling her Scarlet. Darren was her oldest, the leader. "Darren, I want y'all to start calling me Mom."

"Okay," Darren said, smiling brightly. He was thrilled about it. His three siblings followed.

Seeing this, I tried it, too. Scarlet asked me to do something and I said, "Okay, Mom."

Scarlet hit me with a line that shattered my heart and still makes me tremble when I think about it: "I'm not your mother."

I ignored her response and tried to unhear her. *She couldn't be talking to me*, I thought. I tried again.

But this time, Scarlet was annoyed: "Kita, I'm not your mother."

LaVerne, looking on, interrupted. She understood what was happening and knew what kids needed. In a soft, sweet, gentle voice, she said to all the kids, "I want y'all to call me Grandma."

I stared blankly and didn't move or say a word. I feared getting rejected again. This was making me wonder who my mother was. Nobody had ever told me, and I had never asked.

LaVerne saw my hesitation and singled me out. She put her hand under my chin, tilted my head up and looked right at me. "You, too. I'm your grandmother. I'm your mother's mother."

This was revelatory to me. Still shocked by Scarlet's remark, I didn't have the mental capacity to appreciate fully what LaVerne was doing for me. I was trembling with questions.

My mother has a mother?

Who is my mother?

Where is she?

While all this happened for me at Reno Street, the inner strife within MOVE grew. For the people who had been wanting out, the controversy around Frank beating Louise provided an easy opportunity. For people who believed in the original mission, this was the moment to prove their commitment and do everything in their power to take MOVE to the next level. Some people like Bert seemed to renew their commitment to MOVE. But others, like Marie, packed their bags, grabbed their kids in the middle of the night, and left, never to be seen again.

The unity and our unbreakable bond made us so powerful as a group. But now, with two pillars of the organization at odds with each other, the line was drawn, and *Whose side are you on?* was the common question.

The phone rang, and I heard a different voice. It was Benny saying, "LaVerne, what's going on, Suga?"

Grandma slammed down the phone. Benny got the same treatment as all the others. The breakup felt like a wound in the family that would never heal.

Chapter 13

MUTINY II

The internal feud had died down a little.

The calls had stopped, and people could at least see each other without violent hostility. You could still feel a grudge and a little tension when MOVE members aligned with Frank came from the Osage Avenue house to see members staying at the Reno Street house. Osage and Reno became the two main factions within MOVE, and members discussed them that way. It wasn't always clear if visits between the two houses were for peacemaking or spying. I remember Rhonda coming from Osage to see if a re-union could be rekindled. She left our house on what seemed like a positive note. Things seemed like they might get better.

A couple weeks later, I was upstairs playing when I heard the front door open. I listened to the sound of many little feet coming into the house. I peeked downstairs. It was the Osage kids—Birdie, Delisha, Phil, Netta, Tree, Tomaso—and some new kid named Jay whom I had never met. I ran downstairs and greeted them. They looked sad. All of their tiny faces were wrapped in quiet anger and they looked a little defeated. We kids had only seen each other on and off for the past two years, but we'd been listening to the adults bash each other that whole time. Now the Osage kids were at our house out of the blue, and they had their guards up.

Darren sat on his new bike and exchanged pleasantries with them while giving them the scoop on the new lives we were living.

"We eat cooked food daily," Darren told them. "Sometimes Scarlet gives us candy. I got this bike, and I ride it every day. I go to school, I got friends. We get toys for our birthdays!"

Darren wasn't bragging, really. He was just excited to tell them the new things we were doing.

Listening to Darren further angered the Osage kids. They were still quiet, just looking at each other, shaking their heads. After a few hours, Big Jerry came to pick them up, and they left.

I didn't talk to them, so I didn't know what they were doing at our house. Darren later told me why they were there.

"On a routine shopping trip at the Italian market, Scarlet ran into a MOVE supporter named Kareem. Kareem had been part of the prison riot with the MOVE men at Holmesburg. He was accompanied by one of MOVE's newest and most passionate members, Ramona. Ramona was first introduced to MOVE a few years earlier while she was a student at Temple University Law School. She was headed to City Hall to watch a court case with her class, when Pam Africa caught sight of the group and approached them.

"What's your name?" Pam asked them.

Ramona spoke right up. "I'm Ramona Johnson."

"Well, Ramona, you want to be a lawyer? You need to go check out the MOVE 9 trials and see what America's idea of justice really looks like. Nine people are being railroaded for a crime they did not commit."

Ramona did, in fact, check out the trials. In the seven years since, she'd become Benny's right hand, especially with communications. Her formal education and exceptional organizing skills were proving pivotal. She was also fiercely dedicated to Benny's agenda and methods.

Not done with the feud and wanting to prove her loyalty to Benny, Ramona said something disrespectful to Scarlet when they ran into each other at the Italian market.

"Why are you shopping at the produce market?" Ramona said with a snarky voice. "You left MOVE. Why are you buying raw food?"

Scarlet was always ready for a fight. "Eat shit through a straw, you dumb bitch."

They yelled and argued for a few minutes until the commotion got the attention of shop owners, who called the police. When the police arrived, Ramona and Kareem were arrested for making a ruckus. The worst part about this story was that the Osage kids were with Ramona at the time of the arrest, so the cops were going to call social services to take them.

Having seen what happened the last time MOVE children ended up in the hands of the state, Scarlet wouldn't let that happen again. So she brought them home with her to Reno Street.

After seeing how much fun we seemed to be having outside the MOVE lifestyle, the Osage kids rebelled hard and constantly. When they returned to Osage Avenue, they packed some sweet potatoes and peanuts in a shopping bag and ran away from home. They were caught quickly because supporters recognized them by their hair and knew MOVE didn't let the kids out without adult supervision. When the Osage kids returned home, a few of them found scissors and cut their own locs off.

Over the coming days, they ran away again and again. They were always caught, but after the final attempt, they had to deal with Frank, who singled out Birdie as the strongest and most influential of the kids. Birdie had dark brown skin, the longest locs of all the kids, and a widow's peak that you couldn't see until he cut his hair.

"Let me tell y'all something. Before I let y'all leave MOVE and become my enemy, I'll kill you myself!" Frank screamed.

At first, Birdie was scared of disobeying Frank. But after countless lectures where he was hearing this same jargon repeatedly,

Birdie was over it. He was nearly a teenager. He started to feel braver and more defiant with the adults, and with the other kids, too. And Frank? Birdie started to think of Frank as a wannabe Benny and therefore not worthy of much respect. Frank's threats started to feel hollow.

Birdie was so upset about things at Osage that he told Benny he wanted to visit LaVerne's house on Reno Street. Surprisingly, Benny allowed it. I think he was ready to make peace, even if LaVerne wasn't ready yet.

When Birdie came into the house, he was obviously agitated. Loudly and angrily, he said, "LaVerne, I'm hungry!"

Typically, the children didn't go inside the refrigerator or the cabinets where food was stored. At some MOVE houses, the cabinets and fridges had padlocks on the doors to prevent the kids from raiding them. The adults were in charge of what we ate, even when we started eating cooked and processed foods. But LaVerne didn't blink. "What do you want to eat, Birdie?" she asked.

"An egg," he answered.

"How many do you want?"

"Two."

"Okay, go ahead and get 'em."

I don't know what Birdie was thinking right then, but he went from agitation to outright anger. I could see the look on his face.

"What's wrong with you?" I asked. I was far too young to really understand Birdie's frustrations.

"Shut up!" Birdie spat out. He pushed past me.

I followed him around, listening to his brown bell-bottom corduroys swishing as he walked, pacing the living room like a wild, caged animal, grunting and breathing heavily. He cracked one of his eggs open with his tooth and sipped it through the shell as he walked to the backyard.

What is wrong with him? I wondered.

I kept following Birdie, just watching and wondering. He went over to the drain next to the house's downspout and stared down it. Sucking on his egg and just staring. Then all of a sudden, he threw both eggs down the drain, shoved me out of the way, and stormed back into the house. After a while, Conrad came to pick him up. As they walked out the door, Conrad eyed Birdie and asked sarcastically, "Are you satisfied?"

Birdie didn't say anything to us, not even goodbye. He just left.

Confused, I asked LaVerne, "Why is Birdie acting so mad?"

"He's frustrated. He's hurt," she said.

Back at Osage, everything came to a head after the kids' final runaway attempt. Frank, Moe, and Conrad had a meeting with them and asked them why they were so unhappy. The biggest complaint the kids had was MOVE's restrictive diet. They saw how people outside their homes got to eat. They felt slighted and envious.

Frank was annoyed and insulted to hear this. He felt that because they were basically born and raised in MOVE, they were clean and therefore didn't have the temptation for cooked food that the older members had. They had no food addictions to overcome.

"I wish I could've started from where y'all started with MOVE law," Frank preached angrily. "If you want to eat cooked food, do it outside. Don't bring that lifestyle shit in here."

That was not the response the kids were hoping for.

After Frank's rant, he sat around visibly upset for hours. He suggested the stove be removed from the house, and Benny allowed it. He was not going to budge on his stance about cooked food, and he wanted the kids to know it.

I didn't understand it then, but Birdie's demand to visit our house was to get some relief from Osage. When he said he was hungry, he probably expected LaVerne to give him cooked food because that's what we ate sometimes. But Birdie's mother, Rhonda, was still in MOVE and had not authorized LaVerne to give her son cooked food. LaVerne wasn't going to go against Rhonda's wishes. It was the same decision Scarlet made when she cut Darren's hair and put him in school but didn't cut my hair or send me to school. She wasn't going to go against my parents' preferences for me. The unwritten rule was, I couldn't do anything that wasn't in the MOVE lifestyle unless my parents, who were both in prison, approved it. That rule was broken at times but not often.

It created some heartbreaking moments for me growing up.

When Scarlet took her kids to Disney World, I wasn't allowed to go because, to my parents, there wasn't anything amusing about a roller coaster that could fly off the tracks and kill everyone on it. They said I didn't need that kind of amusement. So I missed out on a great trip to Disney World.

When a trip to a Philadelphia 76ers game came up, I couldn't go because my parents said large, uncontrollable crowds were dangerous. I was so disappointed. I loved basketball.

In time, Scarlet got fed up with trying to live her own life with her own kids on the one hand and follow the rules of MOVE with me and Whit on the other. She started allowing me do things outside of MOVE law and telling me not to tell my parents, like with the spaghetti. I didn't want to lie to my parents, but I guess that first taste of spaghetti and meatballs made my occasional lies by omission more appealing than telling the truth.

I settled into life on Reno Street with my grandmother LaVerne, my aunts Scarlet and Gail, and another aunt named Rochelle. They were the four adults looking after seven kids: Darren, Inchy, Whit, myself, Mocky, Rock, and Steven. When the newest and youngest of our crew, Mack, was born, that made eight. None of the women were in MOVE anymore, but Scarlet was the one living all the way live. Not just amusement parks, but candy, new clothes, makeup, jewelry, boyfriends, furniture, color television. Nothing was off-limits for her, except for drugs and too much alcohol.

Benny didn't allow prison visits for the kids, but LaVerne broke that rule, too. I was still confused about my mother's identity but never spoke about it to anyone. It just stayed on my mind. I don't remember wondering about my father as much. I think I was trying to understand what the word "father" meant. After all, I was being raised by all women. Men were around only peripherally. But one day that changed.

LaVerne woke me and the other kids up really early on this particular day. It was still dark outside.

"Get dressed," she said, as I rolled over and plucked cold out of my eyes.

We were all groggy and confused, stumbling around and bumping into each other in the dark on our way to the bathroom, trying to get clean quickly. We had only a tub. No shower.

LaVerne was bathing us three kids at a time. First all the girls: Whit, Inchy, and Mock. Then the youngest boys: me, Rock and Steven. Darren would bathe himself after us. LaVerne put our clothes on and spit shined our faces. Then we headed to pick up Louise from her new apartment at Chestnut Arms. After Frank beat her, she never lived at Osage again.

Louise had bought LaVerne a gray 1978 Oldsmobile Cutlass Supreme. This was one of those old, wide cars that eleven people could fit in, if most were kids. This was before laws were enacted that required everyone to have their own seat belts and kids to be in secured car seats. We all piled in, sitting on laps, singing songs, excited about taking a long drive. It was always a fun time when a lot of people in our family were doing any kind of activity together, especially when Louise came with us because she was a natural entertainer.

Louise liked to tell us stories about the old days. About herself as a little girl or movies she liked to watch, like the old, 1930s Tarzan movies and *The Wizard of Oz*.

"Back in those days I loved to roller-skate," Louise would begin, turning toward the back seat to face us. "The skates were different than they are today. Today's skates are made like a shoe, when your feet grow you have to get a new pair. The skates we had were adjustable and you had to have the key to adjust them. I loved my skates so much I didn't let anybody ride them. I used to sleep with the key around my neck so no one could take 'em without me knowing. That was back in the old days when products were made to last."

We hung on every word.

Louise was born in the 1920s, so even though we were riding in a 1970s model car and the current year was around 1983, to her we were riding in a practically new model car. When she gave LaVerne the keys to it, she raved about its modern features, like how "there's a button on the dashboard that could pop the trunk."

Louise helped us pass the time with her stories, but of course, with seven kids in one car, we asked the same two questions repeatedly: "Where are we going?" and "Are we there yet?"

We kept asking these questions as we drove over mountains and hills, and along backcountry roads. As we passed by massive trees covered in leaves and ivy, then by farms and animals. We saw a lot of animals—cows, horses, chickens, sheep, deer. We even saw a black bear at the bottom of a hill once. The stars in the early-early-morning sky were endless. They seemed so close I felt like I could reach out and touch one. We got lost, stopped for directions, got back on track, and got lost again. This was before the days of GPS, cell phones, and navigation systems. Our map was a giant old, wrinkled book under the driver's seat called *Road Atlas*.

After hours of travel, we arrived at a giant, medieval-castle-looking redbrick building. I couldn't read yet, but today I know the big sign out front read Huntingdon State Prison.

Upon entering, we were greeted by a military-looking white man sitting behind a big desk. "Name and number!" He didn't even look up at us.

"Michael Africa," LaVerne replied, her voice even.

"I don't have an Africa. Name and number," the man said again.

"Michael Africa."

"I don't have an Africa."

LaVerne was keeping her cool, but she was getting annoyed at the prison guard's behavior. She'd driven a long way with a bunch of kids for this.

"AM4973," LaVerne said.

"Davis!"

LaVerne rolled her eyes and mumbled under her breath, "Racist motherfucker."

A loud bang of metal on metal came from the far side of the room.

"IDs!" the guard yelled out.

LaVerne and Louise handed over their identifications. All the adults had to sign in before being allowed inside. The guard verified the IDs, tossed them back to LaVerne and Louise, and shouted to another guard who was manning the door to let us enter the prison gate. "Front!"

We walked through a heavy steel door that was buzzed open remotely. Then we came to a big room shaped like a giant cricket paddle, with tables and chairs along the handle, and big round tables and chairs in the paddle area, where we sat and waited. Lots of people were coming and going. Some wore uniforms like the desk guard, some wore brown jumpsuits, and some wore regular street clothes. After a moment, I saw a man with locs walk in from a far door. Most of the people I knew had locs, so I assumed he was one of us. He walked up to LaVerne, hugged her, and thanked her for coming to visit. He embraced the others one by one. I was surprised at how familiar and friendly the women were with him. I had no idea who he was, so it puzzled me that everyone else was so comfortable with him.

Then he turned his attention to me as he sat down, smiling and staring at me. "What's your name?" he asked.

"Kita," I said.

"Yeah, that's your nickname. That's not your real name. What's your real name?"

I shrugged my shoulders. I knew myself by only one name.

"Your real name is Michael."

I just looked at this man, thinking, *Um, my name is Kita.*

"Do you know what my name is?" the man asked me.

I shook my head.

He smiled again. "My name is Michael, too. Do you know why we have the same name?"

I shook my head. He leaned in closer to me.

"We have the same name because I'm your father. You're my son."

It's hard to describe what this was like for me. I knew it was important. Having the same name made it even more special.

The room fell still. And then slowly—as if in slow motion—I smiled big. I mean *big.* I reached out my little arms and wrapped them around my dad's neck so tightly. His beard tickled my face. I closed my eyes and instantly felt connected, like a void that I didn't even know was there was being filled. It was amazing.

"Dad," I said, and it didn't even feel weird, "can you sneak home with us?"

"I wish I could, son, but no."

"Sure, you can. When we leave here, we will go out the door that we came in. Just come with us when we walk out."

Dad chuckled. "Let's go get some snacks, Mike." No one had ever called me Mike before.

He took me around the room to the vending machines to get water and something to nibble on. The machines were filled with terrible cold sandwiches that I wasn't technically supposed to be eating, as a MOVE child. But luckily the machine also had fruit and bags of roasted nuts. Dad spotted an inmate whose prison job was to take photographs during visiting hours, and we took pictures together. Then he proudly introduced me to his friends.

"Yeah man, this is my son."

I never grinned so hard. I was full of pride and joy.

Before long, it was time to say goodbye. We left without my dad. I didn't feel sad when we left because LaVerne told me he was in prison for taking a stand against injustice. That was how people in MOVE really saw it. On the back of envelopes that MOVE members wrote to and from prison, they wrote, "Remember, the fight the MOVE organization is waging on the streets, in the courts, and in the jails is for your sons and daughters too." MOVE included that so that anybody handling the letter—guards, mail carriers, or anyone else—would know what MOVE was and know its purpose. LaVerne was explaining this to me and the rest of the children on the long car ride home while Scarlet was rolling her eyes, uninterested in hearing anything positive about MOVE. She assured me of how strong my father was for taking the stand he took. I felt much pride and motivation, like I was ready for the world.

As LaVerne talked, I was replaying the scenes from our prison visit in my head. It was magical. Dad knew exactly what to say in every situation. I saw him get respect from every person in the jail, including the guards.

When we got back to Philly, we dropped Louise off at her apartment first. She instructed me to follow her as she ran in to grab three Tarzan movies that she'd dubbed for me all onto one VCR tape: *Tarzan Finds a Son!*, *Tarzan's Secret Treasure*, and *Tarzan Escapes*. While explaining to me what was on the tape, she saw the blinking light of her answering machine. She pressed play.

"Louise, I'mma kill you bitch! You called the cops on Frank! You're a traitor!" She quickly pushed stop. The robotic male voice of the answering machine said, "You have one hundred and twenty-seven messages. The tape is full. Please change the tape."

Louise's mood changed. She knew it was a good chance that every one of those 127 messages were hateful rants from MOVE members intent on keeping the Osage versus Reno conflict alive.

Chapter 14

LIFE WITH MY PARENTS IN PRISON

I was getting comfortable in my new life. The simplest things brought me the most incredible fulfillment and fun. When your life is filled with mud, an occasional Hershey's Kiss, and waiting for the changing seasons to get new fruit or new weather, it doesn't take much to make you happy. And that was how it was for me. I didn't have many material possessions, but neither did anybody else I knew. What I had was my family. I remember asking for toys to play with. An adult would always respond, *If you want to play, play with your brothers and sisters.* When we tried to play with kids in the neighborhood, the reaction from the adults was *No, don't play with them. You have each other.* That made the kids in MOVE a very, very tight crew.

We did everything together. We ate together, we played together, we rested together, we fought together—against System kids and one another. We laughed and cried together.

With the divisions between the adults escalating, I missed the Osage kids terribly. Not that there wasn't plenty happening at Reno to keep my mind occupied.

Scarlet had enrolled her kids in school. She was trying not to live according to MOVE law anymore. She was living how she wanted and raising her kids how she wanted, too. They'd come home after the school day ended and tell Whit and me all about it.

"The teacher is nice, and the other kids know how to draw and color. And they go on field trips to farms and camping."

ncent Lopez Leaphart, whom his family called Benny and whom the world knew as Jol
rica, coming out of a courthouse. He was on trial for making and brandishing weapon
d he refused to eat jailhouse food. Here, he is retrieving fruit that the judge stretched t

WE CALLED OURSELVES "THE MOVEMENT" FOR ONLY A SHORT TIME. IT WAS THEN DECIDED TO SHORTEN IT TO MOVE.

MOVE IS NOT AN ACRONYM, IT SIMPLY MEANS ACTIVITY, AND ACCURATELY DESCRIBES THE ORGANIZATION, FROM RUNNING DOGS, TO RUNNING OURSELVES, TO WASHING CARS, TO DEMONSTRATING, TO ALL OF THE ACTIVITIES ENGAGED IN BY MOVE MEMBERS. THUS, THE BEGINNING OF THE MOVE ORGANIZATION.

UP TO THIS POINT WE HAD BEEN REFERRING TO THE WRITING OF JOHN AFRICA AS "THE BOOK", AND REFERRING TO JOHN AFRICA AS "THE AUTHOR". THIS TOO WAS CHANGED. THE BOOK WAS NOW REFERRED TO AS THE GUIDELINES. THE AUTHOR, ALSO BEING THE FOUNDER OF MOVE, WAS NOW REFERRED TO AS THE COORDINATOR. OUR CHILDREN WERE NOW GETTING INVOLVED, ACTIVELY TAKING PART IN MOVE ACTIVITIES.

HAVING EXPLAINED WHAT THE WORD MOVE MEANS, IT FOLLOWS THAT PEOPLE WOULD WANT TO KNOW WHAT THE ORGANIZATION STANDS FOR — WHAT IT IS ABOUT — THAT IS, IN ADDITION TO THE ACTIVITY OF RUNNING DOGS, RUNNING OURSELVES, ETC.

Original handwritten writings of the MOVE organization's core beliefs, as dictated by John Africa to his sister Louise. These writings helped to introduce MOVE to the Philadelphia community.

THE MOVE ORGANIZATION IS ABOUT REVOLUTION — TOTAL REVOLUTION! REVOLUTION MEANS CHANGE. A CHANGE FOR EXAMPLE FROM POLLUTED AIR, TO A LACK OF POLLUTION IN THE AIR — A CHANGE FROM WATER THAT IS DIRTY, UNCLEAR, STAGNANT, TO WATER THAT IS CLEAN, CLEAR, MOVING — A CHANGE FROM OPPRESSION TO THE COMPLETE LACK OF OPPRESSION. JOHN AFRICA TELLS US —

"YOU CAN BREATHE THE AIR WITHOUT POLLUTION, BUT YOU CANNOT BREATHE POLLUTION WITHOUT THE AIR" — HE TELLS US ALSO THAT... "IF THERE HAD EVER BEEN A REVOLUTION, THERE WOULD BE NO NEED FOR ONE NOW." IT APPLIED THEN, AND IT APPLIES NOW.

THESE DAYS, IN ADDITION TO OUR INITIAL DEMONSTRATIONS, WE WERE DOING RADIO SHOWS, FREQUENTLY READING FROM OUR GUIDELINES AT A LOCAL CHURCH IN PHILADELPHIA, AS WELL AS READING FROM THEM ON VARIOUS STREET CORNERS.

THE NEWS MEDIA HAD ALREADY BEGUN TO WRITE UNFAVORABLE THINGS ABOUT US. IT WAS NEVER ACCURATE — RATHER IT WAS ALWAYS SLANTED, TAKEN OUT OF CONTEXT, DISTORTED IN SUCH A WAY THAT OUR PURPOSE WAS MIS-REPRESENTED AND THEREFORE MISUNDERSTOOD. THIS KIND OF UNFAIR, BIASED, AND PREJUDICIAL NEWS COVERAGE WAS TO PLAGUE US THRU-OUT THE ENTIRE HISTORY OF

MOVE was constantly at odds with the city of Philadelphia. They had different tactics for interacting with authorities, whether it was holding court on the infamous platform at MOVE headquarters on Powelton Avenue, negotiating with the city through their attorney, or protesting in the street.

Top and bottom right: Special Collections Research Center, Temple University Libraries, Philadelphia, PA

HEAR OF THE CONTINUED JAILING RAILROADING AND OPPRESSION THAT HAS HAPPENED AND IS STILL HAPPENING AT MOVE TRIALS

Frank Rizzo was mayor of Philadelphia from 1972 until 1980. He was known for overt racism and brutality against Black people. It was under his administration and his police department that most of the violent assaults on MOVE occurred.

Special Collections Research Center, Temple University Libraries, Philadelphia, PA

Phil Africa and Mike Africa Sr. were among the MOVE members indicted for the murder of Officer James Ramp in 1978. Here, they are being escorted by Philadelphia sheriffs into court.

Merle Africa and Janet Africa were two other people indicted for Officer Ramp's death. Nine MOVE members were indicted and convicted. They became known as the MOVE 9. *Special Collections Research Center, Temple University Libraries, Philadelphia, PA*

The siege on MOVE by Philadelphia police led to the beating of, subsequent arrest of, and protest by MOVE members who viewed the assault on MOVE as excessive and unlawful.

Special Collections Research Center, Temple University Libraries, Philadelphia, PA

My big sister Whit and me. Whit had been sad talking on the phone to our dad. He asked me to make her laugh. My grandmother LaVerne caught the moment.

This was my first time meeting my dad. I remember the moment he said to me, "You're my son." I was so excited. He was my hero from day one.

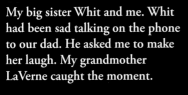

MOVE kids (*from left to right*): Rock, Inchy, Darren (*in back*), Tomaso (*in front*), Whit, and me. We were standing in front of the house on Reno Street.

MOVE kids were largely raised together and parented communally. We spent a lot of time at Cobbs Creek Park in Philadelphia. This is where we played, swam, and learned about nature.

Under police orders, a helicopter dropped a bomb on MOVE headquarters on May 13, 1985, shocking the nation. The blaze consumed three city blocks, destroyed sixty-one homes, left more than two hundred and fifty people homeless, and killed eleven MOVE members, five of whom were children. Only two people survived. *Special Collections Research Center, Temple University Libraries, Philadelphia, PA*

John Africa

Frank and Teresa Africa

Rhonda Africa

Conrad Africa

Raymond Africa

Netta Africa, Tree Africa, and Birdie Africa, with other children, giving an On a Move salute.

Tomaso Africa

Phil Africa Jr.

Delisha Africa

Ramona Africa

Wilson Goode (*right*), who was mayor of Philadelphia from 1984 until 1992. He later apologized for his role in the bombing and recommended that the city formally apologize as well to help with the healing process. Here, Goode is with Ed Rendell (*left*), then district attorney. Rendell later beat Frank Rizzo to become mayor of Philadelphia, serving from 1992 to 2000.

From left to right: Wilson Goode; Brigadier General Leo Brooks, whom Goode brought over from the Pentagon and who was managing director of Philadelphia at the time of the bombing; William Richmond, who was fire commissioner and agreed to let the fire burn; and Gregore Sambor, police commissioner at the time of the bombing, who suggested letting the fire burn.

CITY OF PHILADELPHIA

DIRECTOR OF HOUSING

JULIA O. ROBINSON
1234 Market Street
Seventh Floor
Philadelphia, PA 19107
686-9750

July 12, 1985

Ms. Louise James
3943 Reno Street
Philadelphia, PA 19104

Re: 6221 Osage Avenue

Dear Ms. James:

I am writing to advise you to disregard the letter which you received from me dated June 28, 1985, which offered to restore title in your property to you.

While the City does not intend to extend the offer stated in the June 28, 1985 letter, please be assured that you will be compensated for the value of your property, which was condemned by the Redevelopment Authority of the City of Philadelphia.

I regret any misunderstanding that may have been caused by the previous correspondence which was sent to you inadvertently.

Sincerely,

Julia O. Robinson
Director of Housing

JOR/CMP

To add insult to injury, after bombing and burning down the MOVE house on Osage Avenue, the city used eminent domain to take the property.

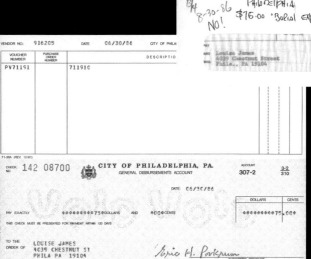

To cover the burial expenses for John Africa, the city mailed his sister Louise Africa a small check. Louise refused to cash it. She was insulted by the gesture.

The MOVE 9 men (*clockwise from top left*), Delbert Africa, Eddie Africa, Mike Africa Sr., Phil Africa (*holding Bird*), and Chuck Africa, in Holmesburg County Jail in 1981.

The MOVE 9 women (*from left to right*): Janine Africa, Janet Africa, Debbie Africa, and Merle Africa. This photo was taken before they all went to prison in 1978.

Moe (*left*) visiting Chuck (*right*) in prison.

My mom, Debbie Africa, in Muncy State Correctional Institution, circa 1988.

My dad, Mike Africa Sr., in Huntingdon State Correctional Institution, circa 1982.

MOVE partnered with other protest organizations, such as the International Concerned Family and Friends of Mumia Abu-Jamal and the International Leonard Peltier Defense Committee, during the original Occupy Wall Street protest to free Mumia and other political prisoners.

This is a protest at the Philadelphia district attorney's office to free the MOVE 9. I'm holding the mic. I was about sixteen years old here.

My family and I visited my mom at Cambridge Springs State Correctional Institution as often as we could. *From left to right*: my son Alex; my wife, Robin; my sons Tommy and Koby; my daughter, Alia; my mom, Debbie Africa; and me.

We visited my dad as often as possible, too, at Graterford State Correctional Institution. *Standing, from left to right*: Tommy, Koby, Alex, me, and my dad. Robin and Alia are sitting.

My mom was released from prison in June 2018. My dad was released four months later. This photo captures the first time they saw each other at home, after forty years apart. During those decades, they only ever got to see each other at their trials and at court proceedings. They could only communicate through letters and messages through family and friends. *Tommy Oliver*

They got married six months later. I walked my mom down the aisle. *Tommy Oliver*

"Please," I begged Scarlet, "can I go to school?" It seemed like so much fun.

"No, Kita," she told me. "Your parents don't want you in school."

Learning that Scarlet was not my mother made a big impression on me. And it lingered.

I still had not asked who my mother was, and nobody had said it outright. But Scarlet and LaVerne saw how much meeting my dad meant to me. For my dad, I think my visit confirmed something he didn't really have to see to know. And after we'd met, there was not a crumb of doubt left: I needed to know my real parents. They had the enormous task of trying to impart MOVE principles on me and my sister Whit from prison. There was only so much they could do from behind bars. That was particularly difficult because I didn't understand why the rules were different for me, or who was calling the shots. Somebody must've gotten word to my mom about how I was feeling. She had been following Benny's no-prison-visitation policy for MOVE children and refused to let me visit her. Then things changed.

At Christmas that year, Muncy State Prison, the prison Mom was in, had a holiday packages program where the inmates could send gifts home to their loved ones. There were many items to choose from, including candy, shoes, toys, basketballs, footballs, and clothes. My mother sent me and Whit one big package. We were MOVE kids, so it was filled with assorted fruits and nuts.

I gobbled the fruit down quickly. While I was stuffing my face with grapes, apples and pears, Whit was unfolding a blanket. I was mesmerized at the sight of it. It was a multicolored patchwork. Pink fabric was wrapped around the edges of the blanket.

I frantically dug through my package to see if I had one, too. Gail was already unfolding it, commenting on how nice it was. Mine was identical to Whit's except it was a little smaller with blue edges instead of pink. Both of them had our names sewn in the corner. I loved my blanket immediately. It became my security blanket. I carried it around everywhere I went. I dragged it around the house, across the dirty floor. I took it to the park, on car rides, and on bus trips. I carried it around so much that LaVerne started calling me Linus, after the blanket-toting kid from the *Peanuts* comic strip. Like Whit's, my blanket was a patchwork masterpiece. I learned later on that both our blankets were made out of all the MOVE 9 women's old clothing.

Around the same time, I began to suspect that my mother was indeed Debbie. It was the way Scarlet had responded to me calling her Mom and the way people were talking about this Debbie person around me. It was starting to click in my head. Looking back, I don't think it was a secret so much as everyone assumed I already knew.

Maybe seven or eight months later, LaVerne again woke up the household in the wee hours of the morning. Again, we all piled up in that old gray Oldsmobile and picked up Louise. Again, Louise entertained us with legendary stories from the front seat. I had no idea where we were going, and it didn't occur to me to ask.

Louise, driving, treated the hilly roads like roller coasters. It was autumn, and the Pennsylvania mountains were what every spectacular, colorful postcard hopes to look like. The leaves on the trees were red, green, and yellow. I remember coming to the top of the Appalachian Mountains and everyone in the car gasping with amazement at the landscape. Louise drove down the hill like it was the Great American Scream Machine at Six Flags Great Adventure and said, "Y'all see how beautiful Mama is? Y'all see how beautiful Mama is?! A painter might try to paint a picture of that mountain range. But after seeing that his painting can't compare to the real beauty of Mama, he'll throw his painting in the trash."

We all agreed. The beauty was unforgettable.

After hours of driving, we reached a building that was capped with a giant, shiny, golden-colored dome. It was the same process as before. Exchanging IDs, ornery guards, signing in and waiting. I didn't know what to expect sitting in the visiting room, but I was a nervous wreck. By this point, I had figured out why we were there. My only previous prison visit that I remembered had been to meet my dad. Moms and dads go together.

On the surface, I tried to remain calm and appear poised. But inside, my heart was racing. I couldn't stop my knee from jackhammering up and down.

I saw a door open. It took only a split second before each inmate walked in, one by one. But it felt like forever.

From my chair, I scanned the faces and judged the women as they entered the room. I had one thought in mind: *I hope my mom is pretty*. The first woman came out. She was short and pudgy. I didn't think she was my mom. The second one came out. She was really tall like a basketball player, but she did not match my mental image. The third one came out, and she was white. Definitely not my mom.

The next woman strolled in. She had beautiful locs and brown skin. I thought that could be her, but she ran to a different family. The suspense was killing me.

The door stayed closed for a few minutes.

I could not stop my knees from bouncing. Being strong is one of the most common demands made on all MOVE members. If you want to eat cooked food but know you shouldn't, be strong and resist the temptation. If you want to rest and skip your one thousand daily push-ups, be strong and do your work. If you're missing someone you haven't seen in a while, be strong because you'll see them soon. Remembering this, I relaxed and leaned back in my chair.

After a few minutes, the door opened again. A woman with honey-brown-colored skin came walking through. Sunlight piercing through a window in the visiting room was reflected off her forehead. She was glowing. It was not apparent that she was my mom, but she looked directly at me, and I hoped she was. She checked every box of my imagination. Same complexion as me. An athletic build. Her long, heavy locs were tied back with a red ribbon. The woman's face was perfect in every way, to the point where I could not stop staring at her. When our eyes locked, my heart fluttered, like the feeling of your first kiss.

I remember hoping and trying to be careful not to expect too much. I didn't want to feel the disappointment I felt with Scarlet again. I didn't move an inch.

Then Gail said, with so much ease, "Kita, there goes your mom."

Everybody in the family cheered when they saw her. Scarlet was screaming, "Debbie! Debbie!" LaVerne was crying and running toward her daughter. The adults hugged her tightly, rocking back and forth. Everybody wanted a turn. I was still frozen and didn't move a muscle. I wanted someone to say it out loud again: "Kita, there goes your mom." I wanted double confirmation.

After greeting everyone else, the pretty woman with my complexion locked eyes with me, and internally I stiffened. I was immediately conflicted and uncomfortable. The feeling wasn't like when I saw my dad. This time, I felt vulnerable and disconnected.

I didn't know what to do with my hands. I didn't like the way I felt. I didn't want to show people how overwhelmed I was. I didn't want to seem weak or ungrateful or anything. But I was so confused. *Is this real?* I thought. *Is this really finally happening?*

If my mom noticed my emotional turmoil, she didn't show it. She picked me up and spun me around while hugging and kissing my face. She was saying something in my ear, but I had no idea what it was. My trepidation was dissipating, but not all the way. I had to mash the rest of it down.

I remember nothing else about the visit. I don't remember saying goodbye. I don't even remember the ride home. But I remember that first moment with Debbie Africa.

Chapter 15

SAMBOR AND GOODE ATTACK

t was 1985. My parents didn't know it, but I was living like I was entirely out of MOVE. Scarlet and LaVerne weren't going to force the issue anymore. I ate like a regular kid. Cooked food, candy, junk, all of it. I began to lose my nurturing way with animals. I watched television. Darren got a cool, box-shaped haircut like Big Daddy Kane's; I wanted to look like him, so I cut my locs off with the same scissors that Scarlet had used on him. It looked awful. Darren laughed and called me Patchy. I also had neighborhood friends: Monty, Gordon, and Ray Ray, whose families had known my family forever. They saw Scarlet go from an ordinary person to a MOVE person and back to an ordinary person again.

Life was not at all ordinary for me. I felt like I was living a lie. I was like a fish out of water compared to my neighborhood friends. None of them knew what raw food was, none of them did push-ups or exercises, none of them had locs. I didn't always understand what they were talking about, especially early in our friendship.

"Ray Ray, what grade are you in?" I heard Monty ask one day.

"I'm in first going to second," Ray Ray replied. "What grade are you in, Kita?"

"What's that?" I asked. I'd been curious about school. Scarlet's kids went and made it sound like fun. But I hadn't heard much terminology yet.

"He's in MOVE. He doesn't go to school," Monty answered for me, like he knew my life.

I felt like an outsider. I didn't like it.

"Well can you play football or basketball?" Ray Ray asked.

"They don't play sports, either," Monty said, answering for me again. He stared at me.

Now I was annoyed. "I can play sports!"

MOVE carried with it a stigma that was hard to shake. It didn't matter that one of the core principles was being physically fit. Non-MOVE people didn't associate MOVE with anything fun. I was quite athletic, though. I played football and basketball, ran track, and boxed. Eventually, I was often picked first for teams. My new friends quickly got to know this about me. But I had to deal with their stereotypes in the beginning.

Once we got cool, though, I played outside with friends a lot. That was what I was preparing to do on the afternoon of May 13. I was going outside to play. That had become my new normal.

I walked out the front door of my house on Reno Street and saw my friend Monty, who was already outside. Monty was running up the street toward me. He was out of breath. "They dropped a bomb on MOVE!"

What is he talking about? I thought. "No, they didn't."

Monty gestured for me to turn and look up. I did. The sky was full of black, billowing smoke. I darted into the house and sprinted upstairs. Scarlet and a few other women were already crying hard, watching the event on the news.

I looked on, still in disbelief. "That lady on TV looks like Louise," I said.

Scarlet glanced at me. "It is, dummy."

Soon, LaVerne and Louise were both on the television in front of the Osage house, yelling and crying hysterically. I was so confused. I didn't know what to think or what to say. I couldn't process what I was seeing. All I remember is the fire, the smoke, and the police. "Mental chaos" is the only way to say it. The people I usually got answers from were just as confused as I was. Probably much more so.

"Another body pulled from the burned-down house on Osage Avenue," a news reporter said.

Each report described a devastating scene and posed terrifying questions:

"The body count is up to eleven, and five of them are children."

"Are there any survivors?"

"Neighbors are upset, screaming for Mayor Wilson Goode."

"At least 250 people, homeless."

I couldn't grasp all the information flooding the news. Every channel had the bombing on it. The adults pulled me and the other kids away from the television. The question everyone wanted to know was: How could this have happened?

After MOVE's original headquarters in Powelton Village was destroyed and the MOVE 9 were convicted, the organization had no intentions of backing down from law enforcement. Some of them might have been scared to fight the System but they weren't showing it. If anything, MOVE doubled down. Daily, they marched and protested for the release of the MOVE 9. Every inch of the community heard MOVE's voices booming through a loudspeaker, from Osage to the top of William Penn's hat at City Hall. Benny would typically organize the protests, and Louise and LaVerne would lead many demonstrations, while we kids, usually in tow, would sit outside of courtrooms or play at the closest park. Every now and then, the adults would have all the kids stand together and hold protest signs and banners. It was a powerful image. Benny kept these protests going, even when the people living on Reno Street stepped away from MOVE.

The constant protesting, combined with MOVE's belief system, general way of living, perceived connection to violence, and decade-plus-long history in the court system, made it a target of Philadelphia's senior leadership. They considered MOVE disruptive, unruly, and uncivilized. The city's accusations against MOVE were constant, including parole violations, illegal possession of firearms, making terroristic threats, disturbing the peace, and whatever else they could reach for and try to make stick.

The city's elite and powerful wanted MOVE gone. They thought MOVE was a stain that should be erased. In 1983 they elected a mild-mannered yes-man named Wilson Goode, the first Black mayor of Philadelphia, to do their bidding.

Goode was born into a humble family of tenant farmers in Seaboard, a tiny township in Northampton County, North Carolina. I once heard that Goode's family was so poor that he didn't own a pair of shoes until he was a teenager. In addition to the gross reality of poverty, Goode's dad was extremely abusive, used him as a punching bag, and eventually went to prison for slapping his mother in the face with a garden hoe.

Goode vowed to never be a callous bum like his father, and he would dedicate his life to constructing a positive personal narrative based on respectability, the power of education, and hard work. Seeds for this type of effort were planted in Seaboard during Goode's formative years, and the shoeless youngster packed that work ethic with him when he relocated to the Paschall neighborhood in Southwest Philly.

Goode was an honors student in high school, went to college at Morgan State University in Baltimore, joined the Reserve Officers Training Corps, and then entered the US Army as a first lieutenant in the military police.

After a brief stint in the armed forces, Goode returned to the Paschall neighborhood, where he married, bought a home with his wife, and served as a deacon at Paschall's First Baptist Church.

Goode began his public service career at the Philadelphia Council for Community Development (PCCD). He earned a master's in public administration from the University of Pennsylvania and ultimately became an executive of PCCD. All of these accomplishments made Goode the perfect prototype for the modern Black politician—educated, respectable, a veteran, and a skilled worker from humble beginnings that can connect with every demographic.

To his advantage, Goode was also very charismatic and easy to talk to. This guy never yelled, lost his cool, or expressed any emotion, really—the exact opposite of Frank Rizzo, the former police commissioner turned mayor whom he defeated in the general election. Rizzo wasn't afraid to hop in front of a camera and tell voters that Goode wasn't the guy for the job, would run the city into the ground, and do everything to protect controversial public figures like Louis Farrakhan, whom Goode knew. But Goode, wouldn't clap back. He just softly denied any serious connection to Farrakhan, as if that was the worst thing in the world, then continued to run his race.

Before Goode was mayor, he worked under his predecessor, Bill Green, as the managing director of Philadelphia. MOVE members like my grandmother and aunts would often meet with Goode about the police brutality and unfair treatment our family received from city officials. He would always listen to their concerns with a calm face before raising his arms and saying some variation of "I believe MOVE is innocent, and I really want to help you guys. I want to free your family members. As managing director, I don't quite have the power to do anything. But if I was mayor . . ." he'd say, trailing off.

Then Goode became mayor. He could influence the DA to do certain things, like drop all the trumped-up charges against MOVE, exonerate the MOVE 9, and authorize a hefty settlement as restorative justice for some of the damage that had been done. Somewhere along Goode's rise, though, he stopped caring about MOVE.

In one of his first major decisions after getting elected, Goode appointed and ordered Gregore Sambor, an underqualified leader who had served only six months as police commissioner, to develop a tactical plan for confronting and removing MOVE members from Osage Avenue. Sambor was so hotheaded that even Rizzo warned Goode not to use him. Goode also brought on Brigadier General Leo Brooks from the Pentagon as managing director of Philadelphia.

Osage had become MOVE's new headquarters. It was ground zero for Benny's confrontation with the city about the MOVE 9. Raymond and Moe had boarded up the house, strapped a bullhorn on the brick wall outside, and built two bunkers on the roof. One of them wasn't originally a bunker. It was a rooftop chill spot—and served as a way for the occupants to be on the roof without getting wet in the rain or covered in snow in the winter. But the other bunker was built in case MOVE ever had a confrontation with police. The corners were held together with industrial-strength angle iron. The exterior walls were plywood with constructed holes that Conrad said were for shooting.

From this house, demands for the MOVE 9's release happened around the clock. All the while Louise was demanding MOVE leave her house. The boards, bullhorns, and bunkers infuriated her to no end. The more MOVE constructed confrontational reinforcements around her house, the more she wanted them out. Louise wanted her house back.

Neighbors who had once been sympathetic to MOVE were becoming less so. Everything that happened on MOVE property affected them, too, because of everyone's close proximity, living in row houses.

Mayor Wilson Goode felt he had to handle the city's MOVE situation once and for all. He didn't want to fail at it, like Frank Rizzo had before him. So he authorized Sambor to do whatever it took to get the job done.

On the morning of May 13, Sambor called for the residents on Osage Avenue to evacuate their homes. He wanted to clear the block for the coming confrontation at MOVE headquarters. Then Sambor gave the okay for more than five hundred police officers to swarm the area surrounding Osage with weapons and tanks. He brought in the same police force that Rizzo said was trained and equipped to fight wars.

Benny, Frank, Conrad, Raymond, Rhonda, Teresa, Tree, Netta, Delisha, Tomaso, Little Phil, Ramona, and Birdie were inside the house. At first, they refused to come out. They refused to be intimated by the show of force outside their door. And *they* knew that the *police* knew children were inside.

A loud voice over a speaker made commands. "You must abide by the laws of the American government!"

"Man, fuck your laws!" Frank screamed back, using the MOVE bullhorn. "Fuck you, you unjust muthafucka. Let our people go!"

Cops were posted in various positions around the perimeter of the house. They were armed to the teeth with M-16s, M-1s, M-14s, 12-gauge shotguns, .50-caliber machine guns, tear gas, smoke grenades, armor-piercing antitank guns, and pounds and pounds of C-4, or Composition C-4, a plastic explosive commonly used by brutal governments during wartime.

"Your laws put our people in prison!" Frank continued, gripping the bullhorn handle tighter. "Your laws are the reason people suffer! Your laws are the reason that animals get killed! Your laws are the reason the air is polluted! Fuck your laws!"

To shatter open the windows, a tactical police unit lobbed small blocks of C-4 in front of the house, which blew the porch onto the sidewalk. Stakeout police barged into the evacuated houses on either side of Osage and drilled holes through the walls to pump tear gas into Osage from both sides.

The explosions of C-4 sounded like gunfire, according to police. In response, they opened fire. They claimed they believed MOVE was shooting at them.

A light show of firearms flickered in every direction, as police used handheld pistols and assault rifles to riddle the bunker with holes. An estimated ten thousand rounds hit every part of the house. Police then carefully entered Osage to survey the damage and see what they were facing. Their onslaught of bullets had hit four people. They could see right then that two were dead.

From surveillance, police knew that more people were in the house. When they couldn't find everybody, they assumed they'd fled to the protective bunker on the roof. But in actuality, MOVE members who were still alive all rushed to the basement. They felt it was the safest place to be. Their police standoff from 1978 was still vivid in their memories. And in that confrontation, they'd waited it out in the basement. This time they were expecting the same result.

Sambor was focused on the bunker, though. He gave orders to dislodge it; he felt it posed a significant threat because it was elevated and had shooting ports.

"The bunker gives MOVE a tactical advantage," Sambor said. "Take it down."

Soon after, four fire hoses, with the power to blast water ten stories straight up into the air, were aimed at the bunker and turned on. The bunker didn't budge.

Sambor and his police force waited a few hours to see if anyone from MOVE would surrender. But from the basement, MOVE was unaware of what was happening. Only that water was pouring down over them.

By 5:27 p.m., Sambor was tired of waiting for MOVE members to come out.

There were many things he could have done at this moment. He could've called the cops off and sent in a team of medics to piece back together the people he knew his cops had broken apart. He could have called in a negotiator to try to negotiate MOVE's withdrawal. Maybe he could have simply challenged MOVE to a waiting game to see if someone would crack. But he did none of these things. Goode wanted the house evacuated to make arrests, and Sambor wanted to kill.

"If we drop the bomb on 6221 Osage and ignite a fire," Sambor asked the fire chief, "could you put the fire out? How much damage would be done?"

I find it hard to believe that the fire chief, or anyone with any sense, thought this was a smart idea. However, Sambor decided that the bomb would do minimal damage and force the people inside Osage to come out.

With that decision, a Pennsylvania State Police helicopter flew over Osage and dropped two bombs of FBI-supplied water gel C-4 explosives on the house, to destroy the bunker. And then *BOOM*. The shock waves traveled through the air, penetrating the thickest walls of the tallest buildings. Windows in nearby cars and houses burst into millions of pieces. Miles away, you could feel an earthquake-like rumbling beneath your feet, rippling through the ground like waves on a lake. *Philadelphia Tribune* reporter Linn Washington said the bomb shook the ground he stood on. The roof on Osage smoldered and soon became engulfed in flames. The members of MOVE who were huddled in the basement were forced out by a mixture of smoke, heat, and actual fire.

They rushed through heavy dark clouds of smoke toward the back of the house, where the garage was the only exit. Conrad, carrying Tomaso, kicked the garage door open and was greeted by gunfire.

Tomaso was hit multiple times in the chest right away. Conrad retreated through the smoke to hand Tomaso's limp body to Rhonda, and then forced his way back out toward the firing officers, only to be shot in the head. His body fell into a stream of water on the pavement. The fire was so hot that it leapfrogged from Osage to the other side of the street. The temperature was about two thousand degrees—hot enough to melt steel.

The remaining MOVE members couldn't hold on much longer. Ramona kept trying to push the kids out the front door, yelling, "Run toward the park!" which was a block away from the house. The kids were paralyzed with fear after seeing what happened to Conrad and Tomaso.

Ramona had no way of telling who was still alive, and soon, she had to decide to save herself. The kids Tree, Netta, Delisha, and Little Phil ran out of the house, using the door Conrad had kicked open. All four children were shot by police when they came out of the house. Philadelphia police deny this detail, but Birdie, who was part of the fray to escape, always said he saw the children get shot. Rhonda pushed Birdie out of the house, too, and Ramona ran behind him. The heat caused Birdie to pass out. His small body fell to the ground, but the sizzling concrete snapped him out of it. Birdie had third-degree burns on 60 percent of his body, wrapped around his torso, arms, and legs. Ramona's skin was equally damaged. She had third-degree burns up and down her arms and legs.

Outside the house, Philadelphia firefighters and police officials were instructed to let the homes burn. There was no rescue attempt.

When the smoke cleared, nobody in the neighborhood knew exactly what had happened or how many people had been killed. Eventually folks pieced together that thirteen people were in the house. Nobody could have imagined that eleven of them were dead. Birdie and Ramona were the only two to survive. The block was torched, destroying more than sixty homes and leaving approximately 250 Philadelphians homeless.

Chapter 16

A NEW DAY

V isiting my parents sparked a new layer of complication in my life. They were still dedicated MOVE members, but the adults raising me on Reno Street—LaVerne, Scarlet, and Gail— had moved on and wanted no part of MOVE rules anymore. Trying to accommodate my parents' wishes for me, however occasionally, became a burden. Over time, it angered Scarlet because she was still young, and my ties to MOVE restricted her freedom. One of the biggest things was that while the other kids were in school, me and Whit were home all day. I didn't mind being at home, but I felt like I was missing out.

Darren and the other kids would come home from school raving about how much fun it was. Over and over, I asked LaVerne if I could go, too. The answer was always no. She knew my parents didn't want me to be in school. She wasn't a huge fan of the idea, either.

Through Benny's teachings as John Africa, LaVerne came to believe that school was the System's way of mentally indoctrinating people. "Why do you think it's illegal for you to keep your kids out of school?" I remember her saying. "School is about getting people on the System's program, so you can get the System's credentials, so you can make the System's money, working the System's jobs for people, for a System that is enslaving you with your own labor."

Whatever LaVerne's feelings about MOVE were at that time,

she continued to rock with some of the core beliefs. That didn't go away just because she'd left the organization.

LaVerne also believed in Benny's teachings about complete self-sufficiency, and how doing for self was the way to avoid being a slave to companies that exploit people.

"When Benny had the car wash," LaVerne explained another time, "we made all the money we needed without leaving the house, and we stayed strong. The opposite of sitting at a desk! We got strong scrubbing tires and carrying buckets of water. We worked together and built a family. Why should we trade our way of life for the System's lifestyle?"

These were things LaVerne believed and talked about often. She laid it out for everybody to hear, so I knew how she felt about me and school. I loved and respected her, but it didn't matter much. Attending school with the other kids was more important to me than fighting the System. I wanted to feel like a regular kid. I wanted to have fun and feel free without the threat of violence at every turn in my life. My need for salvation through normalcy overrode my need to be a revolutionary. I was relentless about asking to go to school.

Eventually one day, during the summer after the Osage bombing, when I asked again, LaVerne took a deep sigh and said, "Ask your father."

By this time, I was getting to know my dad. I visited him annually, and he called me every Sunday morning around ten o'clock. We talked about everything. It seemed like no topic was off-limits. He liked to reminisce and tell me stories about his life with my mom before prison.

I remember him getting comfortable on the phone. "One day in maybe 1970 or '71," he told me, "your uncle Benny and your uncle Fonnie, Benny's younger brother that could have passed for Benny's twin, went to visit your grandma LaVerne to give her a new car. Me and your uncle Joseph, who did not have a license, thought it was a good idea to take the car for a spin with your mom and your aunt Scarlet. Well, Joseph wrecked the car and Uncle Fonnie was pissed to the point of threatening Joseph's and my life. Uncle Benny intervened and helped keep your Uncle Fonnie off our backs."

Dad was using his limited time with me to teach me life lessons and decision-making skills that would breed self-determination and honor. Compared to the other men that I had seen with their kids, to me, he was raising the bar for parenting while introducing me to the realities of his life.

People I knew who had their fathers living with them would compare my dad to theirs and wish their fathers treated them with the respect and consideration my father gave me. I remember going on a couple of prison visits to see my dad with my cousin TT. TT was openly envious.

"I hate going to the prison with you," TT would say.

"Why?" I asked.

"Because I wish my dad was like your dad."

"At least your dad is home."

"I would trade places with you in a minute, Kita."

"I wouldn't trade my dad for anybody," I said possessively.

"If I were you, I wouldn't trade, either," TT would reply. "Not for anything."

TT's reaction was not unique among my family and friends. Tony and Kevin, my friends from across the street, also had a father in prison. They never received any mail from him. When their dad finally came home from prison, he didn't even recognize his kids.

My dad was always sending me pictures, whatever money he could, news about his accomplishments, baseball trophies, basketball trophies, boxing, tennis, high school diploma, and college diploma from Villanova University that he earned while incarcerated. He wrote me letters to stay in touch, clothes, and shoes to keep me well-dressed. It was important to him to stay connected to me.

In the eighties, my dad enrolled in a woodworking course, where the instructors taught him how to build furniture. My dad built bookcases, hope chests, and China cabinets. Every MOVE house had some of my dad's work. He made me a dresser and a night table, which I still use to this day, thirty years later. Dad was raising the bar, not just for parents in prison but for parents, period. And especially for fathers because where I'm from, having a father in prison was sometimes more common than having a father living with you. Hardly anybody I grew up with knew their fathers well.

My dad's involvement in my life, even from a distance, was why others cared about his opinion when it came to me. It was clear he wanted to guide me, and he had a deep compassion for my feelings and needs. That was precisely why, when the conversation of me going to school came up, LaVerne said, "Ask your father." And I was happy to ask him. I knew I could count on him to understand the freedom I craved.

In one of our Sunday morning conversations, I broached the subject. "Dad, all the other kids are going to school. Can I go to school, too?"

"What did your grandma say?" he asked.

"She told me to ask you."

I think my dad could hear the pleading in my voice. I was still a boy but I was old enough to have real opinions and wants. That mattered to him. To my shock, Dad did not hesitate. "Sure, you can go."

"Yes!" I pumped my fists and yelled "Woohoo!"

"Okay, okay," my dad said, chuckling. "Let me talk to your grandma."

I instantly created my own song and started dancing around the room to it. "Dad said I could go-o-o. I can go-o-o!"

I danced around the house, yelling and screaming with glee, and told all the other kids that I could go to school. They were happy that I was coming with them.

When the split from MOVE happened a year or so earlier, we kids would talk to each other about returning to MOVE someday, when we were old enough to do so on our own. None of that was on my mind as I danced around the room, excited about going to school for the first time. It was, by far, the boldest and most significant MOVE principle I was violating as a kid born into the organization.

Granted, almost everybody in MOVE had gotten more lax about the rules. Eating cooked food was taboo but was not met with nearly the same level of disapproval as in years prior. Every adult in MOVE was eating cooked food daily, except for Frank. Some MOVE members drank wine. Others smoked cigarettes and reefer. But still, they kept up their physical training, to remain MOVE-ready. I knew folks who could do a thousand push-ups in an hour, or sometimes up to five thousand in their daily exercise routines, in addition to doing five hundred pull-ups a day. MOVE law was still in place, even if not everybody followed it to the letter.

My mind was guilty about going to school, knowing how anti-MOVE it was. My dad helped me feel better about my desire to go. "Education is a tool," he told me. "Reading and writing are not necessarily natural. Animals don't read books. But we don't live in a natural environment. Your education will prepare you for the world you live in. Lions prepare their cubs for life on the plains of Africa. We have to prepare our cubs for the environment they live in. That's true education."

This was just what I needed to hear. My dad's words were like a life raft, and my guilt went away. That was a good thing for me because all the other Reno Street kids were enrolled months before Whit and me. Had I not started school, I'd have felt excluded and inferior to them. That's never good for a kid.

Before I went to school, there were multiple issues to contend with. The first thing was I was starting school two years late. Typically, kids go to kindergarten at age five. I was too old for kindergarten but too unlearned for second grade. So they put me in first grade. That wasn't too bad. The older kids like Whit had it a little tougher. The school staff put her in second grade, even though she should have been in fourth. But the worst situation was Darren. He was almost fourteen years old and in third grade, when he should have been headed to high school. I remember looking in his classroom and seeing him sitting at his desk. Everything seemed so small in front of him. He looked like a giant compared to his classmates. He tried to pretend to be comfortable, commenting on how nice his teacher Mrs. Wurts was, but it was clear that he was mortified.

"Why do you want to know how old I am?" he asked, as classmates treated him like some sort of overgrown oddity.

I'm sure there was some embarrassment for the other older kids from other MOVE houses who left MOVE and went to school. When my family left just a year or so earlier, so did others. All across Philly, schools were registering ex-MOVE kids who were starting school for the first time in their lives as teenagers. I'm sure Scarlet and other adults felt very embarrassed for us, too, but my mind was too happy to feel anything besides excitement.

Enrolling in school required a few documents for identification that proved tricky for me. I didn't have a birth certificate or any immunization records. The House of Correction jail where I was born didn't issue birth certificates. And when I was transported to a hospital shortly after my delivery, I wasn't issued one. I didn't have a Social Security card. We were running from the state all the time, and nobody obtained one for me. This was typical for MOVE kids.

Immunizations from a doctor were entirely out of the question. Other than dental visits that started when I was around seven or eight, the first time I ever went to a doctor's office for any type of medical treatment, I was twenty-eight years old. I was in Florida and drank strawberry soda. I didn't realize that I was allergic to red food coloring until I got a bad case of strep throat, aggravated by Cuban strawberry soda, which almost prohibited me from breathing. Needless to say, when I enrolled in school, I had no medical records.

LaVerne and Scarlet got on the phone with my mom to tell her the news of sending me to school and to try to help figure out how to maneuver around the identification obstacles.

"Debbie, what's Makita's real name? You named him Michael, right?" Scarlet asked.

"Yes," Mom answered with a quick and short response.

"What's Whit's real name?"

"Her real name is Anne," Mom replied.

"She looks like her father. Her name should be Michelle. Whit, do you want your name to be Michelle?" Scarlet asked her.

"Yeah, I like that name. 'Anne' sounds old."

Mom was answering the questions, but she wasn't thrilled. She had reluctantly told Scarlet she'd agree to let me start school after she learned my dad had already said yes and because I wanted to go so badly. My parents communicated through handwritten letters and through intermediaries on the outside. Hashing out big parenting decisions was sometimes thorny and slow. My mom realized what was happening but wasn't comfortable with it. Abruptly, she said, "Wait, wait, wait, wait. You really want to send my kids to school?" Mom was that concerned about it.

"Don't worry, Debbie, the kids will be okay. We talked to the school. We told them to put the kids that are around the same age in the same classes as each other. Makita will be in the same class with Rock and Mocky, and Whit will be in the same class as Diane."

Mom remained terrified. She had become okay with the cooked food we were eating but worried that school was too much of a violation of the MOVE principles. "I will teach my kids reading, writing, and arithmetic and give them an education myself," Mom told Scarlet.

But it was too late to stop what was already in motion. Dad had said yes, all the other kids were going, and I was dying to join them. Things were changing for me, and my mother couldn't be there to change it back. So she did what she could from where she was.

My mother started sending me kindergarten schoolwork to do, and I would have to complete the assignments and mail them back to her. She would grade them and send them back to me. She ordered me Worldwide Wildlife Fund magazines so I could learn about the importance of animals and the beauty of the environment. She tried to keep my education as close to MOVE principles as possible so I wouldn't lose them. I enjoyed what she sent me because it meant I got to correspond with her more. But her assignments to me through the mail never could have kept me from attending school with the other kids and wanting to live more like the regular, non-MOVE kids I saw around me.

Once LaVerne sat me down in a chair and pulled out the big scissors, it was really a wrap.

"Sit down, boy," LaVerne demanded. She sounded impatient and agitated. She was ready to get this part over with. I had never had a haircut. But LaVerne wanted me to be able to fit in with the other kids for my first day of school.

She draped a towel around me like a barber's cape, lifted up my sixteen inch-long locs and sliced through them like she was wielding a hedge clipper. Slice! Another loc down. Slice after slice, I watched the floor pile up with hair. I cried big, fat tears. It felt like I was losing a part of what made me, me. It also drove home that living by MOVE law was over for us.

A few days later, I was cleaned up, wearing new clothes and new shoes, and ready for my new life to begin. Before I left our house for my first day, LaVerne gave all the other kids and me a talk. It was my first time hearing it.

"When you enter the class, the teacher will try to make you stand for the American flag. Don't stand. She'll try to make you say the Pledge of Allegiance to the flag. Don't open your mouth. If she tries to sing that fucking 'My Country, 'Tis of Thee' song, walk out of the classroom and stay out until she finishes singing."

"Grandma, can we go now?" I eagerly insisted.

"Boy, shut up," she ordered. "If you have to go to the bathroom, raise your hand and ask. If she says no, get up, walk out the door, and go to the bathroom, and then go back to class. And make sure y'all kids stick together and don't fight each other the way y'all be fighting each other in this house. Okay, okay, all right. Give me a kiss. Bye.

"Wait, wait, wait, wait. One more thing." LaVerne touched each of our faces with a finger. "Don't you tell your classmates that you have anything to do with MOVE. They will be prejudiced, and they will fight you."

Finally, with my mental list of dos and don'ts, I was on my way with the other kids, at last. LaVerne walked us the two blocks to school. I was carrying my new lunchbox. It had the Smurfs on it. You couldn't tell me a thing!

LaVerne walked me to my teacher's classroom.

"Good morning, class! Say hello to your newest classmate, Michael Sims," Mrs. Lebowitz said with a sing-song tone. Scarlet and

LaVerne had registered me under my mom's maiden name, Sims, for school. Back in those days, a father's name couldn't be on the birth certificate if the parents weren't legally married or if the father wasn't present at the birth.

"Say hello to Michael, everyone," repeated.

"Gooooood moooooorning, Michael!" all the kids said in unison.

The classroom desks were set up in quadrants, where four kids sat together.

I quickly adapted and thrived. When I got to school, I was slated for the honor roll after the first semester. I made friends rapidly, using my athleticism to excel in sports.

I quickly started crushing on the prettiest girl in the classroom. Her name was Nakia Green. But Rock's mom had enrolled him in school a week before I got there. He had already impressed her with his bravery and willingness to fight anybody for her. One day he impressed her even further when he ran into traffic to save her punching balloon while we were on a school trip to the Philadelphia Zoo. MOVE children going to the zoo would be like Frank Rizzo's kids wearing "Free the MOVE 9" t-shirts. But there we were.

When Mom heard that Scarlet let me go to the zoo, she scolded LaVerne. "Mom, why did you take Makita to the zoo? You know better than that! What did those animals do to deserve people supporting their imprisonment?"

Scarlet intervened: "Debbie, you may still be in MOVE, but out here on the street, we are not MOVE members anymore. Stop trying to make us live MOVE life according to the way MOVE believes. We are not MOVE members anymore."

Mom was undeterred from the MOVE message, even in a prison cell. "Scarlet, John Africa has sparked a powerful movement for life. There's a new group called PETA. All they do is advocate for the ethical treatment of animals, and they are not MOVE members. This isn't only about MOVE. It's about taking a stand against injustice!" My mother was screaming all this through the phone receiver.

Scarlet tried to be patient with her sister. "Debbie, you are not out here with these kids. I hate to say it," she replied. "I don't want to hurt your feelings, but you are not here to see how things were for the kids when they were in MOVE. I was and am. I want these kids to have a normal life!"

This disagreement was the verbal personification of an unstoppable force colliding with an immovable object. LaVerne took the phone from Scarlet and said gently but firmly, "Scarlet, you cannot tell Debbie what she can and cannot do with her kids. They are *her* kids." LaVerne was trying to broker peace and keep my mom calm, even though LaVerne was the one who cut my hair. Scarlet saw the tightrope LaVerne was walking in the conversation and didn't care. She was insulted and wounded by the comment.

Scarlet fired back: "If Debbie doesn't like the way other people raise her kids, why don't she come home and raise her own kids?"

The words cut deep because Mom had a chance to be home with me and Whit. When she was arrested she could have renounced MOVE and come home. Instead, she pledged her loyalty to Benny and lost her one chance to raise us. Now, from prison, Mom wanted to dictate what happened with the kids that Scarlet was helping to raise. Scarlet was so angry and hurt about the situation that a week later she moved out and transferred her four kids to a different school. Reno Street went from having a house full of kids living in it to just three. I had never seen the place so empty, quiet, and cold.

When Scarlet moved out, there was no explanation and no heads-up. She just took her kids and moved on. I don't think Scarlet realized how attached I was to her and her kids. Before I knew who my mom was, Scarlet felt like my mom, and her children felt more like siblings to me than cousins.

My life was transforming in every way. School was hard and lonely. I fought a lot. When the kids in school learned I was a MOVE member, I had to fight what felt like almost every day.

It started with a simple round of the dozens in Ms. Marshall's class. People call it "roasting" each other today, but in Philly in the 1980s, we called it "bussin'." Terry, who lived on the other end of the block on Reno Street, was the champion busser in the class. At some point, I threw my hat in the ring.

I had the class laughing, talking about Terry's head being as long as a hoagie. Terry was talking about my lean body but was getting little laughs. A kid we called Pop, who was probably two years older than us, was laughing too hard at my jokes for Terry's liking. Midlaughter, Pop said, "Terry's whole family got hoagie heads. His dad is Mr. Hoagie Head. His mom is Mrs. Hoagie Head. He's Hoagie Jr., and his sister is Hoagie Head Juniorette."

The class laughed uncontrollably. When I think about it now, it doesn't sound funny at all, but in second grade, this was hysterical. Terry had had enough.

"At least I'm not a MOVE member," he said, staring directly into my face, as he jerked his head forward and poked out his chest, like he was ready to fight. The room went dead silent. One kid pointed at me and asked, "You a MOVE member?"

Terry pointed at me and said, "Yeah, he is."

The other kids did not say much, but the cognitive bias of each one in the classroom was in full effect. Most of them I had known from the grade before. They were my classmates in first grade. We had spent an entire year together and had become friends. Yet when Terry revealed that I was in MOVE, I was immediately stereotyped as a terrible person despite all of my classmates being my friends for over a year.

MOVE could have been better liked in the eighties. Kids made fun of our hair, and they made fun of our food. They made fun of our clothes and told us MOVE stood for Monkeys On Vines Everywhere.

Now my classmates were staring at me, as if I had betrayed them. They were mad that they had unwittingly liked and become friends with somebody like me—somebody in MOVE. That night, I realized how much of an embarrassment MOVE was to the people around me.

Depressed from this interaction in school, I went home and immediately threw myself on the couch and dozed off. I was afraid I would never be normal, no matter how hard I tried. I was getting haircuts. It didn't make me normal. I ate cooked food. It didn't make me normal. I broke every rule known to my young life in MOVE and went to school, and not only did it not make me normal, but the people there were insulted by my presence. It was a shallow point in my life. I felt like a fraud.

As if my day wasn't going badly enough, it was about to get much worse. While asleep on the couch, Darren shook me awake. "Makita, get up. They're outside," he said.

"Who's outside?"

"Everybody, and they wanna fight."

I wiped my eyes and shuddered at what I saw. Word about my family's secret had spread like wildfire. A representative from each class was at our front door, ready to fight. I scanned the crowd of what seemed to be about twenty kids and a few parents. Right up front was Terry. I wanted to kill him. Most adults would try to talk the crowd down and encourage a peaceful resolution, but not LaVerne.

Standing in the doorway facing the mob, with us crowded behind her, she let the mob know what was up. "Y'all motherfuckers want to fight? Do y'all want to fight? Well, you're going to get a fight today. You're going to get all the fight you can handle and more, motherfucker!" LaVerne yelled and then looked at us. "Y'all going to have to fight them because if you don't, they won't stop. If you run from them, you will be running for the rest of your life. Makita, Whit, Darren, y'all ready?"

We looked at each other, we looked at her. We pounded our fists in our palms with scrunched brows and nodded our heads yes.

She said, "Good, get 'em."

Without thinking, I darted out the front door and punched Terry in the face with all my might. I instantly drew blood. Darren fought Terry's older brother, and Whit hit his sister. Then it became a free-for-all. Everybody started fighting. People were falling to the ground. I was knocked to the ground in the commotion. While I was down there, I saw Terry trying to kick me, so I grabbed his leg and bit his shin as hard as I could. He reached in agony for his leg. I wouldn't let go.

I had learned in MOVE, "Don't mess with anybody, but if anybody messes with you, make them regret it." When Moe was constantly getting attacked by the police after he and Benny won the federal trial, Benny told him, "The next time the police attack you, give them something to remember you by."

So the next time Moe was attacked by the police, Moe hit one of the officers in the head with a tire iron, removing a section of the officer's ear. Every time the officer looked in the mirror, he had to remember Moe. I adopted the same mentality. I don't mess with anyone, but if you mess with me, I promise I will take it too far. I next saw Terry about fifteen years later. He was still limping. When I bit his leg, I was trying to crack his bone like I used to crack those Brazil nuts back in the day.

The fight felt like a victory because afterward, LaVerne's words came true. Those kids never messed with us again. In fact, whenever I saw them, they avoided me by walking to the other side of the street. But still, second grade didn't go great. I spent the rest of the school year fighting other haters and searching for personal solace. My wounds from that period have never fully healed.

Making matters worse, Ms. Marshall, my teacher, was in a custody dispute with her husband over their son. During class, her husband came into the classroom armed with a butcher's knife and violently attacked her. He stabbed her in the face five times. I wasn't in her classroom at the time of the attack, but I saw the paramedics wheeling her into the ambulance. I was afraid to look at her face. I kept my eyes on her arm as it dangled lifelessly when they rolled her across the grainy asphalt. I was shocked that she had even lived. After a few years of healing and recovery, she came back to teach again.

Whenever I graduated from a grade level, I visited my previous teachers. I never visited Ms. Marshall. I was too afraid to see her, too scared that my memory of her wouldn't match her current state. I imagined her wounds made her look like a victim of Jason Voorhees or Michael Myers, and I didn't want that to be how I remembered her. I was ashamed of myself for feeling this way. She probably needed all the hugs and love she could get. But my heart couldn't take it. I never went back to see her.

Chapter 17

HITTING ROCK BOTTOM

During this period, life seemed to be giving me five and taking back ten. I was born to wonderful parents, but they were in prison. I had a great group of childhood friends, and MOVE brothers and sisters, but they either shunned me, moved away, or got murdered. School was going great for a while, but then Terry ruined it for me.

A couple years later, in the fall of 1990, I started school fresh and new at Charles Drew Elementary School, which went up to the eighth grade. Aside from a new student body, I struggled with another big change. The teachers at Drew seemed to be a generation younger than the ones at Belmont. Up to this point, my teachers were LaVerne's age or older. They were very disciplined, wholesome, and organized. At my new school, many teachers weren't much older than Darren, which changed the classroom dynamics considerably. Instead of listening to jazz, Otis Redding, or the Temptations, they were listening to the same music that the students were listening to—Geto Boys, Kris Kross, and Public Enemy. The parental element felt missing or, at best, relaxed. To make matters worse, the fights that I thought were receding for me were rearing their ugly heads again. I was constantly in a scrap. So were the other ex-MOVE kids.

I couldn't seem to make any forward progress. This pattern continued when LaVerne's good friend Derek came home from prison to live with us.

Derek was six feet tall, with brown skin and a very muscular build. He reminded me of Jim Kelly from Bruce Lee's *Enter the Dragon*, in that he was a throwback to the 1970s. He thought everything from that time period was the best. So even in the 1980s, Derek was still rocking an afro, like he was Shaft or somebody.

He had a reputation for being a hustler. Ever since he was a young teenager, he had been in and out of prison. Now he was out again, and home on parole. The party was on.

Derek lived up to his reputation. The first thing he did when he got home was change the energy on the block. Neighborhood kids who always wanted to fight me suddenly wanted to become my friend because Derek was good at making money. It was never legitimate. Derek's version of a nine-to-five was selling crack and robbing the people who had normal jobs.

He'd rob any- and everybody, from the corner boys to preachers—liquor stores, toy stores, even local cheesesteak joints. Dude had no problem shaking down his enemies and sometimes even his friends.

The flip side was that often, after his escapades, Derek would return to the block and hand out the things he'd stolen, like Robin Hood. "Makita, you got any money?"

"No, I ain't got no money," I'd say.

Derek would reach into his pocket, peel off a couple of dollars from his wad, and hand them to me.

Sometimes he'd look at my friends, and then back at me. "Is that your buddy?"

"Yeah," I'd respond if it was my friend.

And he'd give them some cash, too. It doesn't sound like much, but a man handing me a few dollars in 1990 meant a lot for a few reasons. First, my parents were in prison. As much as my dad and I bonded when we could, it was still only when we could. We were highly restricted. We usually spent about twenty minutes a week on the phone and about six hours a year in prison visits. Second, even though a dollar is not much money today, it was plenty for me in 1990. Back then, with one dollar, I could buy a hundred pieces of candy. Or four bags of chips. Or four of America's favorite unidentifiable and colorful sugar drinks—what some cities called "quarter waters"—but we called "hugs." Or fifty cookies and five pretzel sticks, and still have enough money for five giant gumballs. With two dollars I could feast!

If I had one dollar extra, I could even buy a cheesesteak, which I often did.

Derek's generosity made my life on Reno Street more bearable. School was really not going well. I didn't feel good about myself. I think Derek could see that and looked for ways to lighten my mood. It helped that he was hilarious and didn't mind acting like a big clown sometimes. If the neighborhood kids were playing street games like ding dong ditch, hide-and-go-seek, or freeze tag, Derek joined us. He was always trying to find a way to keep the atmosphere happy and full of laughter. And, as my uncle, he was my biggest defender and cheerleader. Like with Darren.

Darren was seven years older than me and would impose his will on me when he could. If we were wrestling or actually fighting, I didn't stand a chance. He always beat me in football and basketball, which messed with my confidence. Derek noticed and would threaten Darren to take a bit easier on me and to show me a little mercy because I was so much younger and smaller than him. With Derek around, Darren knew he had to be cautious not to bully me, or else Derek would seek old-school, prison-style justice. That made me feel safe.

He had a serious side, too, which mainly showed in the way he told me what he felt was pertinent and made sure I was acting properly. Derek might've been doing the wrong things, but he wanted me doing the right ones.

I remember one day my friends and I caught frogs by the Fairmount Park pond. I had three or four hand-size frogs in a bucket. When Derek heard about it, he sent my friends to get me. I assumed he wanted to check out my excellent find because he was my fun uncle.

I joyfully showed him the frogs, and his face hardened. Derek was rarely like this with me. He took the bucket from me, walked it over to the bushes, and released the frogs into the tall grass.

I was perplexed. I just looked at him.

Before I could say anything, he sternly said, "Ain't your mother in jail?"

I said, "Yeah."

"Ain't your father in jail?"

"Yeah."

"Why do you want to put *them* in jail?!"

I lowered my head. The sound of MOVE talk was bouncing around in my mind.

"Think about what you're doing the next time you do it," Derek continued. He seemed disappointed in me, and I didn't want that.

The impact of that interaction was lasting. It made me respect Derek as a fair and decent human being. The respect level was high but something brought it down. I saw Derek punch his wife directly in the face. He beat up his wife really badly. Then I started seeing him as a walking contradiction. Kind of like Dr. Jekyll and Mr. Hyde.

He'd punch his wife in the face, stomach, and chest, and kick her in her ribs while she was on the floor pleading and vomiting. He beat her up in front of their children and put her in the hospital. Another time, after he beat her, I was surprised to see her cooking dinner for him and sharing a cigarette with him. Then they played cards together. I could never understand why a grown man would try to hurt his wife, or any woman. But I was seeing it a lot.

Everyone in the house on Reno Street knew this was happening. I was ashamed of my family because it was happening in our household. I was ashamed of LaVerne and Scarlet for not doing anything to stop Derek's behavior. I'd seen them talk to the police before and instill terror. I'd seen them beat neighbors to a pulp and not blink. I'd seen them fearlessly take on the most difficult MOVE members, including even Benny. But when it came to a woman being abused by Derek, LaVerne and Scarlet couldn't seem to stop it. Derek didn't always beat his wife in front of us. But when he did, he was vicious and uncontrollable. Hardheaded as hell, too. His physical strength wasn't something LaVerne or Scarlet could handle. They would holler at him, and he'd apologize to the household afterward. I even heard Derek sometimes apologize *while* he was doing the beatings. But it was a pattern that never let up. And it eroded my confidence in LaVerne and Scarlet over time. It seemed they didn't go as far with him as I'd seen them go with others in the public. It was the Frank situation all over again, except I was there to see this one. Even though I enjoyed the benefits of him living in the house with me, I expected LaVerne to kick him out of the house. But she didn't. His wife begged her not to.

This went on for about two years—Derek being my protector, making everyone on the block happy, beating his woman. Meanwhile, his hustling and violent behavior were catching up to him. He robbed a couple of guys on the corner who were shooting dice. When he turned to run after the robbery, one of the gamblers pulled out a gun and shot at Derek. Luckily he got away, catching only two bullets in the foot.

Before long, Derek's drug dealing turned into drug use. His addiction led him to violate his parole, and police took him into custody. The parole violation meant that he had to serve the remaining three years of his original five-year sentence. Then he would have been eligible for re-release. But some of the robberies he committed and was convicted for were added to his time. The judge threw the entire book at him.

Derek's prison sentencing came at the time that President Bill Clinton was promoting the three strikes rule. The rule stated that if an individual committed three violent or drug-related felonies, they would receive a life sentence in prison without parole. Twenty-eight of the fifty states had adopted this rule in some form since the 1950s. With the president of the United States supporting it, prosecutors were beginning to use it more regularly.

Repeat offenders needed to tread lightly. In 1995, a California man named Jerry DeWayne Williams faced twenty-five years to life for allegedly stealing a slice of pizza.

Pennsylvania didn't have the three strikes rule, but New York did. When a gas station robbery was pinned on Derek in New York City, that was the third strike. So once he served three years in Pennsylvania, he was shipped to New York, where a judge pulled out that old rule book.

Derek tried to fight the case, claiming his first offense came when he was a minor, which would mean he only had two strikes. But the judge didn't care about this argument. Derek was sentenced to fifty years to life in prison. He becomes eligible for parole in 2042.

Derek's arrest had a ripple effect on me. From then on, it was one bad thing after another, like dominoes. The bullies in my neighborhood returned because Derek was gone. And all the fun in the house was gone with him. It got rolled away in the back of a paddy wagon.

LaVerne descended into a deep depression. She had lost so much. When Derek was home, his presence revealed a side of La-Verne that I had forgotten about. LaVerne was an entertainer. She was a singer in her church choir and loved dancing and listening to music. I remember how excited she got when Lionel Richie's "You Are" played on the radio. She would sit me on her lap, bopping to the rhythm and singing that song. She loved other songs like "Happy Birthday" by Stevie Wonder, "The Girl Is Mine" by Michael Jackson and Paul McCartney, and anything Luther Vandross ever sang she thought was heavenly.

This song came a little later, but when Luther Vandross and Gregory Hines released, "There's Nothing Better Than Love," La-Verne forgot that any other music had ever existed. It played in our house on a loop until the record player needle grounded down to nothing. After the bombing and the deaths, all the fun-loving singing and dancing seemed to disappear. But when Derek returned from prison, he brought her back to life. When he returned to jail, she sank into a deeper depression than I had ever seen. She grieved because of the bombing, the kids who were murdered, her brother Benny, and all the other adults. They were always on her mind. She framed and hung pictures of everybody on the walls. Adding to her grief, three of her five children were imprisoned with life sentences.

She'd lie on the couch for weeks at a time, getting up only to go to the bathroom, and sometimes she didn't even do that. Asking her questions could sometimes lead to short answers laced with frustration while she smoked her twentieth Salem 100's cigarette of the day. She couldn't be bothered, she'd say. Sometimes I'd go to someone else's house—usually Louise's or Scarlet's—and spend weeks with them.

Eventually LaVerne and Louise had decided to sue the city of Philadelphia for dropping the bomb, and she would ensure she got it right. While working on the lawsuit, LaVerne sat at the desk that Benny built for her. Once she got that in her mind, it consumed her every minute. *Click, click, click, click, clack, clack, clack, clack, click, click, click, click, clack, clack, clack, click, click, clack, clack, clack,* screamed from her typewriter. Nonstop. I mean, nonstop.

When I got up for school, I could hear it. When I came home from school, I could hear it. I could hear it when I came in at night, after roaming the streets all day. I could still hear it when I woke up at 2:00 in the morning to use the bathroom. It never stopped. And the suit did grant a victory—an insult but still a victory. For the bombing of her house on Osage Avenue and the killing of her son Frank, the city of Philadelphia gave Louise a settlement of $500,000. Public sentiment about the figure drew ire. Many people in the community believed that if MOVE was a white organization, the number would have been a lot higher.

With little guidance and supervision, I started getting into a lot of trouble. My grades in school were dropping. I was still going, but I was skipping certain classes to cut up and chase girls. That was when a friend from the neighborhood, Malik, said to me, "You should start hustling and make some money."

Derek had introduced him to the drug game, and he was making a lot of money. Considering I was always hungry and fending for myself, I considered it. Malik said in this slow, methodical voice, "This is how you do it. Take this razor right, cut off a little piece, and fill up the little tubes with the shavings, and that's it. These are caps. There are four sizes. Treys, nickels, dimes, and dubs. If you sell them to pipers, you can make some money."

I hung out with Malik and learned the ropes. He took me to the cookhouses, the storehouses, and the selling corners. He had only one rule for the game for me to follow: Don't get high on your own supply. I never officially agreed to sell with him. After the introduction to the drug world, it didn't really appeal to me.

The cookhouse had a few locks on the door, which also had two two-by-fours to reinforce it in case of a raid by police or rival dealers. The storehouses and cook houses were filthy and grimy, and they smelled like death. The people running them looked like zombies. It all looked like something out of a horror movie. In my mind, I told myself that this wasn't for me. I didn't want this kind of life, always looking over my shoulders or wondering if the cops or some other dealers were coming to take what I got.

I wasn't feeling it. Until one day, Malik was off at school, LaVerne was at the typewriter, the refrigerator was empty, and I was starving. I went into Malik's room, grabbed a couple of caps, and went to the selling corner. I was really nervous, but I was hungry, and my hunger pushed me to overcome my nerves. After a few minutes of waiting, a man came walking up. As he got close, he looked at me and stepped back skeptically. "What you doing here? Where's Malik? "

"Malik's my friend. He's not here today. I am. What do you want?"

He hesitated, like he was skeptical because I was so young. But it didn't deter him. "Give me a trey." That was three dollars' worth of crack.

He looked at it. He examined it closely. I was shaking in my Pro Wings discount sneakers, terrified, but I didn't want him to know it. I had to be strong because the look on his face was like he'd take advantage of me if he could. I had to play it off.

In a commanding tone, as he examined the cap, I said, "It's real."

He gave me a look of contempt and slowly walked away. I assumed the first one was the hardest to sell, so now that I'd broken the ice, I figured I could do this even though I was still nervous. If I had to quit right then, I already had enough money to buy myself a cheesesteak and some fries. But if I sold a little more, I would have enough to buy Whit some, too.

My second customer came up just a few minutes later. He was tall and slim, and was wearing a bomber jacket that looked like it used to be really nice. He wasn't in good shape. He looked greasy, like he worked on cars all day. He came stumbling over to me. The transaction was all right. He taught me something and was a smooth talker when he did it. "Let me show you something, young blood. When you make the exchange, you got to do it smooth, like you're shaking my hand. That way, people can't see you doing what you're doing, even though they see you doing what you're doing. You got that? You got to be smooth."

He even practiced with me a couple of times. Dude bought a nickel cap, and then he rolled out. I felt a little more comfortable. It was strange that adults were helping me become a criminal, but at least this guy wasn't trying to kill me.

Near the selling corner was a tiny block called Sloan Street. It was so narrow that a car was too wide to ride down it. It used to be filled with row houses like the other streets, but they were mostly torn down. One place was left in the middle of the block, and it was dilapidated.

The vacant lots around it were overgrown with tall weeds that had trash, old tires, and burned-up cars tangled in them. The house was too scary to feel safe anywhere near it; the only people who went there were pipers, rapists, and killers. As I waited for customers, a man came falling out of the first-floor window of that old house. He wore a dirty brown peacoat and jeans that looked like he'd been wearing them for months. His eyes were lifeless. His teeth were brown, and he smelled like rotten ketchup.

"What you doing? What you got?" he asked.

I frowned up my face, pretending to be tough. "What you need?"

"I need a dime."

"I got it. Show me the money."

"Money's down here. Follow me, and I'll give it to you." I walked with him until I came to the other corner of Sloan. He tried to get me to follow him toward the old house, but I stayed at the intersection where neighbors could see me. "Come on," he insisted.

I stayed put. "Bring it up here," I said.

He went back into that house window and came out with $10. I made the exchange smoothly like the second customer taught me, while never taking my eyes off the man. He took the cap and said in an angry parental-type voice, "Go home."

My face pretended to ignore him, but inside I was trembling.

I wanted to get home as soon as he said it, but I couldn't show fear. I could hear LaVerne's voice telling me about how the System people were dangerous and couldn't be trusted. *They will kill you, rape you, beat you*, she'd said. She always urged me to stay away from them. I watched the man stumble back down Sloan Street and waited until he climbed back through the window. Then I ran home as fast as I could. My heart was pounding through my chest. I was so out of breath I thought I would have an asthma attack, and I don't even have asthma. I did have eighteen bucks in my pocket, though. That was enough money to eat for the next few days and feed Whit, too.

The bottom of West Philly was no joke. People were hooked on drugs, prisons were popping up all over the state as fast as construction workers could lay bricks, and people were dying at alarming rates. The drugs were making people crazier than they already were.

Five or six years passed. I was thirteen years old. I knew many people who had been killed either by police or by thugs. I also learned about a lot of people who were in prison. I was clear that I wanted no part of either life. I wasn't clear on how to avoid it, but my desire to escape it gave me a drive. I know far too many people to name everybody who was shot, stabbed, killed, or in prison. D Rock, Malik, Derek, Man, Boomie, Neil, Unji, Rel, Coke Bottle Glasses George, Aisha, Bruce, Tyrone, Kareem, Pop, Mike Mike, Mark, Na Na, Kyann, JR, Man Man, and the list goes on and on and on. To tell their stories would take writing another book.

The straw that broke the camel's back for me was a fight that Whit got into at school. She has always been a pretty up-front person. She'd fight if she had to, but she wasn't looking for it. What Whit had was a mouth and a lot of opinions. If she didn't like something or someone, she'd show it. No ifs, ands, or buts about it. When one of her classmates named Donna, who was way too big and strong to be a teenager, said some negative things about Whit, they got into a face-to-face confrontation on the way home from school. Whit tried to walk away after telling Donna, "If you don't want me talking about you, then stop talking about me."

But Donna wouldn't let it drop. She took off her coat, gave it to her instigator friends, and started throwing a barrage of punches at Whit's head, landing all of them. I saw blood jump out of Whit's lip while her head was repeatedly hammered. I jumped in between the girls, but the crowd of teens, cheering Donna on, pulled me away. I yanked my arm, swung wildly, and freed myself just as the cops showed up to disburse the crowd. Whit got beat up pretty bad. Later, when the bruises and swelling began showing on her, it was worse than I thought. I was feeling more aches and soreness than I did at first, too. We had been in a serious fight.

Whit was afraid to go back to school, for fear that Donna would seek a Round Two. So the next day, we told our teachers everything that happened. LaVerne took the matter all the way to the school board to make a formal complaint. The school board and the PPD said there was nothing they could do about a squabble between teenagers at school. They said they had more important issues to deal with.

Whit decided that she wasn't going back to school until something changed. She didn't feel safe or heard. I decided I'd stand by her side and wouldn't go back, either, until she was ready to go back. She never went back, so neither did I. By March 1992, I was a thirteen-year-old sixth-grade dropout headed in the wrong direction.

Chapter 18

BACK ON A MOVE

MOVE was on the move, and I was about to be on the move with it.

I was young, but I realized I would forever be judged by someone else's idea of me, based on their feelings about my family. People who were my friends probably would have remained friends if only I weren't stained with the stigma of MOVE member. No matter how often it happened, the reaction from my classmates and my peers always hurt. Some kids I spent time with every day. I went to the movies with them. I went to sporting events with them. I dated a couple of great girls. But being connected to MOVE ended almost every relationship I had—romantic or otherwise.

I was in physical fights all the time, and I was on a path of getting into the kind of serious trouble that it's hard to come back from. I wasn't in school, I wasn't in MOVE, I was just . . . out there.

I sought out the MOVE organization in a real way, a sincere way. I wanted to learn my heritage before I lost the rest of my memory about it. It was just in time to escape the downward spiral I was on and just in time to witness the next stage of the MOVE organization's evolution.

A couple of months into my protest against school officials, shortly before I quit school for good, I was watching television when a familiar face popped up. It was Ramona Africa.

Ramona was the only adult survivor in the 1985 bombing on MOVE's Osage Avenue headquarters. She was indicted on riot charges related to the bombing. Then she was convicted and sentenced to seven years. There was rampant controversy around Ramona's sentencing, after the serious injuries she sustained in the attack and the nation's astonishment that the attack ever happened in the first place. This brought newfound attention to Ramona specifically. There couldn't have been a better person in the spotlight to talk about MOVE. Ramona had superior intellect and was a master orator. She knew how to communicate well with the public, even from prison. During her time behind bars, she became a major figure in activist circles. And there she was on TV.

"Ramona Africa is scheduled to be released from prison in just a couple of days," the news reporter said.

My eyes lit up. I hadn't seen Ramona in person in years. Seeing her face brought back so many memories. I told LaVerne I wanted to go see her.

"That's fine with me," LaVerne said. "You need some MOVE law in your life."

Ramona and I were always very close. When I was a little kid, she took us down to Ninth Street to the Italian Market and allowed me to eat my grapes without putting garlic on them. She was always kind and fair to all the kids. I missed her terribly.

Mom was scheduled to call me that day. I knew she and Ramona were cool, not only because they were MOVE members in the same prison but also because they were sisters-in-law. Ramona was married to my mother's brother Chuck since the early eighties.

When my mom called, I asked about Ramona right away. "Mom, are you going to see Ramona anytime soon?"

"Yeah, I'll see her soon. Why?"

"Can you ask her to pick me up when she comes home?"

Mom took a deep intake of breath. "I'll ask her, Kita."

I was too eager to leave it at that. "You think she'll do it?"

"Yeah, she'll do it if I ask her to."

My heart fluttered. I was on pins and needles, waiting for the day to come, and finally, it did. Ramona was released from prison on May 13, 1992. She pulled up in front of my house the next morning.

The doorbell rang at about 10:00. LaVerne answered the door and there Ramona was. LaVerne greeted her warmly with hugs and smiles. When I saw Ramona, I was stunned that she had kept her promise. I didn't expect that she would have lied to me when she said she'd come and pick me up, but it was obvious that she had made me an early priority. She was scheduled to be on nation-wide radio and television programs and had speaking engagements lined up. She came home from prison in a limousine.

Ramona looked directly at me with a smile on her face. She said only two words: "You ready?"

"Give me one minute," I said. I ran upstairs to my dresser and started pulling out clothes and tossing them in the air, looking for something to wear. I quickly changed and jumped down the thirteen steps from the second floor, practically right into Ramona's arms.

I hugged her so tightly, and she hugged me tighter. We hopped in the car with a MOVE supporter named Beverly, and off we went. Ramona accepted me as if I were leaving LaVerne's home for admission into an institution of higher learning called MOVE University. And indeed, my experience with Ramona was like a college education. I was about to get a PhD in MOVE history, MOVE theology, and MOVE physiology, and LaVerne knew it. I could tell she was proud of me. Some of the other kids were bigger, stronger, and faster than me. But LaVerne knew it wouldn't be that way for long. I could tell that she wanted me to be better than I was. She didn't care how I got there.

Beverly had a couple of kids in the car who had locs. I assumed they were with MOVE kids. However, as soon as I heard one of them call Beverly Mom, I knew they weren't official MOVE members. Even to this day, the original second-generation members who have never left MOVE still don't call their parents Mom or Dad.

Ramona took me around to the half dozen or so MOVE houses in the Philadelphia area and reintroduced me to everyone. She was staying at a MOVE house on Kingsessing Avenue in southwest Philly. She took me to another MOVE house on Fifty-Sixth Street, where Moe and his family lived. When we got there, Moe greeted me with a smile and a handshake. Pam ensured I was safe with the dogs when they tried to intimidate me. Every house had the nostalgic smell of raw food floating around in the air.

When Osage was bombed seven years prior, I knew people had died, but I didn't know who exactly, and I was afraid to ask anyone. I saw how upset everyone was when it happened, and I didn't want them to have to relive bad memories. As Ramona took me around to meet people, I sought out those I remembered, especially the kids. Allen and Taylor, who I hadn't seen since we were little kids at Osage and had only vague memories of, worked for Moe and his new home-improvement business.

To my thirteen-year-old self, they felt imposing from our first reintroduction. They were seventeen and eighteen, doing most of the work in Moe's business. They were hanging drywall, running electrical wire, installing plumbing pipes, and painting. Occasionally, they would counsel me like big brothers and tell me what had been happening in the organization in the years I was gone. They explained to me something new for the kids called D-Day, or distortion day. The name came from Benny, who used to call junk food "distorted." Because MOVE kids' diets were so strictly regimented, we considered any food that wasn't raw as distorted. Over time, all nonraw food we gave the general moniker of "distortion." Basically, distortion was the good-tasting stuff.

If you have had some distortion—Now and Laters, Lemon-

heads, Chick-O-Sticks, cookies, donuts, even a can of tuna fish—
you were very popular. We were allowed distortion all weekend
long, unlimited. On weekdays, we could eat one cooked meal per
day and then everything else had to be raw.

Everybody still had to exercise daily, and the main exercises were
push-ups, pull-ups, bricks (which were our versions of dumbbells),
and running. We took care of the animals. A lot of this I remembered from when I was younger.

Things sounded a little less restrictive overall, but it still seemed
constrained. Every refrigerator had locks, as did the cabinets and
closets. This was to monitor what you ate. When it was D-Day,
the kids could borrow the keys and get whatever specific food they
were approved to have. Then the keys had to be returned. There
was definitely more freedom than before, but still not that much
freedom.

Some young people in MOVE wanted to learn but still had
not gone to school. This was true even for folks in their late teens.
Bert forbade Allen and Taylor from ever going, and the rest of the
nearly dozen kids who never left MOVE were illiterate. I wouldn't
be surprised if some of them didn't know their ABCs. Darren had
always been the leader among the kids while I was growing up.
Watching him struggle to read was uncomfortable. Allen and
Taylor couldn't spell the word "the," and they were teenagers. But I
didn't care about any of that. I was just happy. I had spent the previous seven or eight years being rejected by people who I thought
were my friends. Once they knew my connection to MOVE, no
matter how loose it was at the time, they saw me as an outcast.
Being with Allen, Taylor, and the others in MOVE, I felt reunited
with something. Like I was finally home.

I wanted to do everything the MOVE kids were doing, no matter what they were doing. One day I heard that Beverly and Pam
were gathering the kids and taking them down to Cobbs Creek

Park to swim. I didn't have any swimming gear and I couldn't even swim, but I was still going. I waded into the stream with all my clothes and my shoes on. The kids taught me how to doggy-paddle, and the adults laid blankets on the grass and pulled out raw food for everyone to snack on.

I went home that night, and even though it was a simple day, I told LaVerne all about it. She was happy to get a break from me, and I was glad to get a break, too. That night, I couldn't sleep. I couldn't stop thinking about my new experiences and what else I needed to learn. The following day I asked LaVerne if I could visit the MOVE house at Fifty-Sixth Street again, and she said, "Of course." Ramona had reunited me with the people there, including Moe and his family. I didn't know it at the time, but Moe was going to make a MOVE man out of me. He was the daily example for manhood in MOVE.

The next time I visited his house, I stayed for a whole weekend. I got to see Pam and Ramona in action as MOVE spokespeople. They had become the faces of the organization. Ramona handled MOVE activities and MOVE 9 legal updates, and told MOVE's side of the story about the bombing to the media. Pam took on all the major advocacy for Mumia Abu-Jamal's case. Mumia was now on death row for killing a cop, despite nationwide skepticism about his guilt and protests for a fair trial. His first trial was wildly controversial. The judge was heard by the stenographer saying, "I'm going to help the police fry the nigger." Pam was working hard to make sure Rizzo didn't pull the switch.

Both Ramona and Pam were well-versed in MOVE's mission and always represented the organization well together. They were a combustible but dynamic duo, like fire and ice or thunder and lightning. They spoke all over the world—from community centers, churches, mosques, and private organizations to venues like Madison Square Garden. On the college campus circuit, they were particularly popular. Invitations from Harvard, Yale, Princeton, Vassar, and other elite institutions were normal. Ramona took note, however, that she'd never been invited to speak at a historically Black college or university.

In their presentations, Pam would deliver a speech with passion and fury, while Ramona was excellent with conveying complex and methodical information. On my visit, they were scheduled to speak at a community event. Ramona kicked things off. I was in the audience while she talked to a few hundred people in the crowd. She pointed me out, telling the audience I was born in a jail cell. That my parents had been in prison my entire life. She asked the crowd what I had done to deserve that.

Pam pointed me out, too. She told the crowd that I was a boy born in the belly of the beast and that I had been gone for a while, but now I was back On a Move.

When they were done speaking, a line of people approached me with sympathy, hugs, kisses, and consoling words. I was horrified. Ramona noticed.

"Does it bother you that I say that you were born in prison?" she asked me after the event was over.

"Yeah, it does," I answered. I was ashamed of it. It didn't seem like a thing to be telling people. I'd spent the previous years ignoring it myself. Ramona blurting it from the stage and having people feel sorry for me was not what I wanted.

Ramona looked right at me. "Kita, you should be proud of that. Your mother had to be strong to give birth to you in a prison cell."

I had never thought of it that way. Ramona's words were spinning in my head. "Any example of strength is a powerful example, and you should be proud to be connected to it."

"It's just all these people knowing my secret," I said, "I feel embarrassed. I don't even know my own history."

That was all Ramona needed to hear. She gave me lots of things to read, to help with my personal understanding of MOVE. I read "The Guidelines" for the first time. I read Benny's writings daily. The information was so authentic and inspiring to me. How can Black people not fight for animals to be free? At one time, white people saw us as animals. How can we not want clean air to breathe? MOVE's beliefs just made sense to me. I didn't want to do anything else except learn more about the organization. For myself, I could begin to see the value of what MOVE offered its members and the community, the missteps it had made in service of its mission, and also the deliberately grave injustices committed against it. I could see it all, based on my own judgments.

Ramona had also planted the seed with me that I needed to work on getting my parents out of prison. Among the MOVE children at the time, Whit and I were the only ones alive whose parents were in prison. For Ramona, that meant that we were in positions of power. Ramona went to Whit first. Hers was the face that people saw when they saw my mother. Whit was the baby my mother held on the platform at MOVE headquarters in 1977. Whit's in all those pictures that everybody knew. So naturally, Ramona and other MOVE people tried to get Whit to be involved in MOVE's efforts with the public. Whit refused, though. She didn't want the responsibility or the public attention. I was the next option. Ramona knew I was enthused with MOVE's beliefs and Benny's teachings. And I didn't mind the public-facing parts of MOVE's work, even though I didn't feel adequate for the job.

Still, it was settled. I was just thirteen years old when Ramona put me front and center. She never let me miss anything regarding my parents' legal cases. "I could never convince people to free your parents the way that you can," she told me.

I became a constant presence at court hearings, lawyer meetings, and community action meetings to get support for the MOVE 9's release. I never resisted any of this because I wanted to be involved. But I would not have participated without Ramona's push.

I learned that my uncle Chuck would memorize the MOVE "Guidelines" and recite them at demonstrations back in the 1970s. I started doing the same thing at demonstrations in the 1990s. I attended protests calling for the release of the MOVE 9, Mumia Abu-Jamal, and many other political prisoners. I also protested with groups and organizations for the protection of animals and the environment. I would choose a section of Benny's writings that would fit the demonstration's theme and then recite it onstage. I wanted others to hear about MOVE's work and beliefs based on what was true and not on what they'd seen on the news.

The reception from crowds was usually polite and inspiring. Sometimes I could see in the faces of the audience that they agreed with what I was saying. Preserving life, protecting all animals, taking care of your body, eating real food, fighting for justice in a city still recovering from Rizzo's racism. "The Guidelines" didn't sound outlandish. I got more confident onstage over time and started to bring my personality to my recitations. Before long, I started writing raps about MOVE and performed them onstage. I became a staple at MOVE events. The adults would speak first, and then I would come on. My youth and renewed interest in MOVE, after having been away from it, made older MOVE members see me as a future ambassador in the organization. I was certainly becoming the face of the second generation of MOVE. I was honored that the organization trusted me to represent it.

I still had a long way to go, though, to being MOVE-ready.

Nineteen ninety-two continued to be a big year. A few imprisoned MOVE people started to come home. First, Ramona was released from prison, followed by Sue, Carlos, and Consuewella. Each had a unique personality.

Sue was the only white member, and she was a drill sergeant–type character. Carlos was a Puerto Rican member and had a laid-back personality. Consuewella was just mean. Sue came home and hit the ground running, getting back into the groove with MOVE. The first thing I remember about her was trying to get everybody to exercise. She was trying to run the organization like an army barracks. With her, I had a daily routine that lasted all day with few breaks in between. I had to get up early and walk the dogs, change the water, feed all the animals at the house, and then go run five miles. Over the course of the day, I had to do a thousand push-ups and a thousand combined reps of bicep curls, overhead presses, tricep extensions, and other weight-lifting moves, using a set of bricks. While I was doing that, she'd be telling me about why I needed to work even harder.

She'd been that way as long as I'd known her. I remember visiting my mom in prison while Sue was still there and feeling Sue's fiery spirit. "Come on, boy, you got to get back what the System stole from you. How many push-ups can you do?"

"I don't know," I answered.

"I bet I can do more than you," she said. "You should be able to do at least twenty."

I laughed. "Are you challenging me to a push-up contest?"

"I'm challenging you," she replied without cracking a smile.

Sue made such a big deal about it. Now, we had an audience of about thirty people, all watching me. Darren used to try to make me exercise, but I was so weak that I struggled to do ten push-ups. Hanging around Allen and Taylor for a few months got me up to doing a few more. But with all those eyes staring at me, I could muster only thirteen in this contest against Sue.

"Thirteen?! Thirteen?! All you can do is thirteen? That's pathetic. I'm an old white woman, and I can do more than you," Sue said, just getting started. "The other kids around here are laughing at you, ya know. Thirteen!"

Then Sue got down and did twenty-five push-ups. "The system stole so much from you, Kita. You have to get as much as you can get back."

I don't think she was being mean to me. I think she was really shocked because the other kids could do so many compared to me.

My mom, who was watching, said nothing.

Sue turned to her. "Debbie, your mother did a job on your son. Allen and Taylor did fifty push-ups each, and they weren't even tired afterward. Your boy struggled to do just thirteen. You should never forgive the System for what they did to your son."

My mom just nodded silently in agreement.

I was humiliated.

From then on, I vowed to work my body as hard as I could for as long as I could. By the time Sue came home and brought her drill sergeant mentality with her, I could handle it a little better. Like others, Sue made it clear that if I was representing MOVE, I would not be allowed to be weak. I admit, I liked the way that felt. I felt purposeful and important—like I had something to live up to. That's critical for any teenage boy. I was no exception.

Over the next four years, the formal education I had abandoned was completely replaced with my learning and living in MOVE. I was traveling all around the world with Ramona and Pam. I was working with Moe at his home-improvement business. I had developed a physique like Bruce Lee, and my locs were back and dangling past my shoulders.

I had been studying Benny's teachings so avidly that I could recite fourteen pages of "The Guidelines" word for word. I had gotten sharp enough to defend MOVE's position in any argument and turn your crowd into my crowd. I even had a run-in with Jesse

Jackson on the voting issue when he came to Philly, and I stood my ground.

This was a different vibe from when Ramona first started speaking about MOVE publicly in 1992. She faced occasional hecklers and people who blamed MOVE for the bombing. MOVE was enjoying a complete energy shift. People were giving me gifts like money and jewelry and fancy clothes. I was meeting revolutionary heroes like Geronimo Pratt. I met Tupac Shakur's mother, Afeni Shakur, Reggie Schell, and Sonia Sanchez. I was connected to celebrities like Kenny Gamble, the founder of Philadelphia International Records, I picked up donations from Joe Frazier, and I even sat next to Danny Glover on a panel discussion about American policies.

Aside from my parents' freedom, there was only one thing missing: someone to share my life with. Although I was young, I was clear about what I wanted. I wanted what my dad had. My mom was all my dad needed to be happy, and I wanted to be MOVE-married like him, to a MOVE woman. But unfortunately for me, all the MOVE girls on my age level were either taken or related to me.

The MOVE adults, especially Bert and Sue, could see that MOVE's teenagers had started to become interested in one another. More than curious, actually. Relationships were already happening—sometimes with non-MOVE members. Our hormones were raging.

Bert was very concerned about what our raging hormones might lead us to. She knew some of the teenagers were having sex with one another, and she felt that if we were making adult decisions with our bodies, then we should be making adult decisions with our minds. She didn't want any Maury Povich situations around paternity.

So Bert gathered all the MOVE teenagers around to talk about commitment and MOVE marriage. She believed that the time for it had come for some of us. She felt that if a person was good enough for us to give our bodies to, then why wouldn't they be good enough to commit to?

"Y'all don't wanna be hoes, do y'all?" she asked us, waving her hands broadly at the group. "Messing around with all these different people! Gettin' all crabbed up!"

I knew this applied to me, too, but I was too young for it to matter. I wasn't like Allen and Taylor. I wasn't there yet with girls.

It did matter to Whit, though. And she was having none of it. She said, "I'm not marrying anybody." She was sixteen years old, and she wasn't ready for anything like that. Whit wanted to date around like a regular teenager. She'd already had a couple boyfriends. Nothing serious. Just innocent, typical teenage relationships.

Bert hated this. She felt committed partnerships protected us and helped us prioritize what was important. "I know the System teaches that you're supposed to get married when you're older, put your career first, and *then* have a baby and whatever. They want you to wait until you are older and don't have as much energy."

Whit was unmoved.

Bert continued, "Doesn't it make sense to have a baby when you are a little younger so that you can grow up with the baby and run around together as they grow up? The System sure got it backward, but we ain't System people. We're MOVE people."

Whit shook her head. She wanted to feel in control of the major decisions in her life, and she felt like Bert was trying to steer her toward a choice that wasn't hers. This was absurd to her. She didn't want to do it.

Allen and Violet were excited by the idea, though, especially because they were always sneaking off together. Jay and Melissa, who were a couple, didn't argue, either. Made sense to them. Taylor wanted to marry Whit but knew better than to say that now.

Bert meant what she said and didn't care about Whit's opinion on the matter. Bert was influential in MOVE. She was Benny's widow and was managing $2.5 million in settlements from the city of Philadelphia after the bombing on Osage Avenue.

The sum included settlements to the parents of each of the five children killed. An actuary came in and did one of the most gruesome things you can do with a child's life. They estimated how much the children's' worth to society would've been if they lived up to their expected potential. That expectation was determined by the jobs and social standing of their families. That meant that Tree and Netta, whose grandfather was a cop, were rated higher in expected earnings and potential benefits. They came from a household that was secure and wasn't broken, so the likelihood that Tree and Netta would've been successful was deemed higher. That was in contrast to Little Phil, also killed in the bombing, whose mother, Janine, was a high school dropout and whose father, Phil, was a street thug. The actuary didn't think Little Phil would've done as well because his parents didn't have as much going for them. Then there was Tomaso, who had a white mother and a Black father. Tomaso's maternal grandfather was an engineer. Sue said he invented the ejection catapult seat in airplanes. Tomaso was rated as potentially very high-earning.

Settlements for the five children made up the bulk of the $2.5 million settlement. These settlements initially went to the kids' parents. But all the MOVE adults were in prison. Bert was the person closest to getting out. So everybody signed their money over to Bert. Bert used the money to support all of MOVE. She bought properties around Philadelphia for MOVE families to live in rent-free. From the interest earnings on the settlement, she paid for everyone's monthly expenses and bought all the food that everybody ate. She didn't have to touch the principal.

People listened to Bert. And Bert felt that Whit would be better protected if she had a MOVE man around her in a stable living situation, especially with our parents still in prison. Bert even took it a step further and got my parents involved. My father told Whit the same thing I told Whit: "If you don't want to do it, you don't have it do it." He was irate with Bert's attempts to persuade Whit. "Who are you," he told Bert, "to say to somebody that they have to do something like this? Who are you to say to somebody's parents that they have to do something like this? You don't run people's lives."

My mother reacted a little differently. She knew the consequences awaiting Whit if she agreed with my father. Among other things, she knew Whit would've been banished to Reno Street, and Reno Street couldn't have been the only consequence on my mother's mind. She knew why we had left, and she felt much safer with us in MOVE, even if it meant getting MOVE-married young. So she tried to look on the bright side of the situation.

Whit didn't see it that way, and I agreed with her that it should be her own decision. "If you don't want to do it," I said, "you shouldn't do it."

My relationship with Whit was always a little fraught. I was her annoying little brother. She waved me off. "Shut up, Kita."

The conversation ended with no resolution.

Bert wouldn't let the issue go, though. Later, in a conversation with other MOVE members, Bert was clear about Whit's need to marry. "With all this foot traffic coming around the organization, some people are supporters, but some people we don't know. Whit is young, pretty, and shapely. Without her parents out here to protect her, she's vulnerable. I don't want to be responsible for anything bad happening to her. If she doesn't want to get married, that's fine, but she'll have to return to Reno Street with her grandmother."

When this got back to Whit, who'd been staying at Fifty-Sixth Street, she was furious. "How you going to make somebody get married, Bert? It's my life. You can't make me get married."

"No, I can't make you get married," Bert pushed back. "But I can decide to protect this organization. And as I said, if you don't want to get married, you don't have to. But you do have to go back to Reno Street with your grandmother LaVerne."

Whit packed her belongings and left. She did okay for a few weeks, trying to live the MOVE lifestyle outside of MOVE. But there were more reasons other than bad school experiences and neighborhood bullies that had driven Whit and me back to MOVE after our years away from it. We'd felt vulnerable and unprotected from what was happening around us.

We had a close friend of the family who was a Philadelphia police officer. He was never part of the police squads that attacked MOVE, even though he was from our district. We found out he was a sexual abuser. Whit saw him inappropriately touching a young girl. Later we heard of him sexually assaulting several neighborhood girls. The reaction from certain family members drove a wedge between people that, decades later, still has not mended. It also highlighted the collective and very visible defense that MOVE provided, despite whatever criticism or misgivings Whit had about it. Bert knew how protective that defense could be. MOVE marriage was part of that.

As for me and my dating life, I was still a long way from figuring it all out. And it wouldn't have mattered much anyway. Whenever the teenagers would sit around and talk about the best pair-ups for marriage, nobody ever picked me.

One day I came into the house sweating from a hard ten-mile run and walked in on a conversation that quickly turned into a heated discussion about me.

It started with the usual pair-ups. "I know she don't wanna do it, but Whit should marry Taylor. Allen should marry Violet, and I'll marry Jay," Melissa said.

"Yeah, and Robin should marry Kita," Violet said, laughing and pointing at me as I walked into the kitchen. Robin was a beloved child of MOVE and considered a gem. Everybody adored her.

Melissa didn't crack a smile. Instead, she rolled her eyes and sucked her teeth. No one opposed the idea for the couples until my name came up. The eruption of disapproval was eye-opening.

Melissa was not usually a person who would speak up, but when she did, she was steady and unwavering. If she had a strong opinion, people paid attention. Turned out, she had a strong opinion when my name came up in the marriage conversation.

"I hate him. He's so sarcastic and mean. He picks on the little kids, punching them all the time. He teases them when they play Nintendo. Plus, he never shares his distortion. The other day, he took my bike and messed it up. Kita would be a horrible husband for anybody acting like that."

I didn't realize the bad feelings my peers were harboring against me. Hearing them talk about me so derisively, it stung. They talked about me the same way I talked about kids in the System. I was a great ambassador for MOVE publicly, but internally I was also a jerk. The idea of no one in MOVE considering me a good match immediately fueled me to get better. I believed Bert when she said marriage was a cornerstone in MOVE life. I wanted what my dad had.

Robin was Taylor and Allen's annoying little sister. She liked me about as much as a vegan likes pork bacon. Hearing my name practically caused steam to blow out of Robin's ears and nose. She always had an opinion about everything I was doing, and she hated my boasting.

I couldn't help bragging all the time. Growing up athletic in Philly, I became a prolific trash-talker. I'm talking Gary Payton–level. I was reckless about it. Anybody could get it. That was fine on the basketball court or football field, where trash talk is part of the game and part of the fun. But I didn't know how to turn it off. I carried trash-talking over to everything I did. If I was washing dishes and Rock was drying them, then I'd be like, "Ha, I bet I could wash the dishes before you put them away, you scrub."

If I was frying chicken and Rock was making potato salad: "Ah, I bet you I could make my chicken taste better than your potato salad, you bum."

And if we were headed to school: "I bet I beat you to class, slowpoke."

My competitiveness and my trash-talking wasn't something the MOVE kids had ever experienced. To them, I was a brute.

In the early days of my reentry to MOVE, Allen and some of the kids were still figuring out how to play Nintendo. I was having fun crushing him and the whole family and busting out laughing the entire time. The house rules were: you lose, you move. There were two seats in Allen's bedroom–game room: the winner's seat and the challenger's seat. The winner could play as long as they wanted and as many games as they wanted until they lost. If the winner went to the store, came back three hours later, and found someone sitting in the winner's seat, the winner could make them move.

When Taylor, Allen, and the other kids played with one another, they swapped the winner's seat all the time. It was very collegial. Nobody ever sat in the winner's seat long. Everybody got a turn. When I started playing, I would go back home to Reno Street and come back three months later, demanding my seat. "I pissed on you. You ain't no match for me, mop top. I just busted your ass, bum-ass garlic ninja. Give me my seat. Go take a walk."

Robin had seen this firsthand. Allen and Taylor were her heroes. To see her big brothers get treated this way, as I laughed and bragged about it, infuriated her. Her eyes would lock in on me with her lips curled up, as she sat on the edge of her seat, watching every game, anxious for me to lose, begging her brothers to beat my ass. Eventually it happened.

When Taylor finally beat me, the whole house cheered like their team had just won the heavyweight boxing championship of the world. And no one cheered louder than Robin. She got all up in my face, "Loser boy! Woo hoo! You suck!" But she was not laughing, and she was not happy. She wanted an end to the name-calling and bussin' on each other.

Meanwhile, Whit was starting to have second thoughts about walking away from MOVE. Life at Reno Street reminded her of why she left.

Whit sat down for a make-nice conversation with Bert. Bert's opinion about Whit needing to marry had not changed one bit. If anything, from the conversation, Bert felt even more strongly that Whit would benefit from marriage. Bert believed it would give Whit a firm anchor to build a life from. Bert could see Whit was reconsidering the idea of marriage even though she wasn't fully warming to it. As an added incentive, Bert assured Whit that Taylor would take care of her, love her, and protect her. And that if he didn't, he'd have all of MOVE to deal with. Finally, the tipping point was when Bert said, "If you get married, you can have a baby. And you'll get to love your baby the way you always wanted your mother to love you."

Whit asked to think about it. A couple days later, a bunch of us from MOVE were on our way to see the film *Menace II Society*. It was a big hit in the theater that year. It's the story of two teenagers struggling with identity, loss, and purpose in the midst of Los Angeles's hyperviolent and dangerous crack era. MOVE members of all ages wanted to see the movie. It spoke to us. Me, Jay, Melissa, Allen, Taylor, Bert, and a few others all gathered to head to the movie theater.

Whit caught sight of Taylor coming out the front gate of the house as we left, wearing his favorite green-striped T-shirt. She stopped Bert on our way out and solemnly said, "All right, I'll do it."

"You'll do what?" Bert asked.

"I'll get married."

"What? To who?" Bert replied, confused but with a smile spreading across her face.

Whit was dropping Bert into a conversation that Whit had been having in her head for days. Bert hadn't caught up yet.

"To Taylor. I'll marry Taylor."

Bert was thrilled. And relieved. It was like a problem had been solved.

Melissa, who had been standing next to Whit, piped up. "I'll do it too, Bert, and then we all can get married." Melissa was pretty happy about it.

"Really?! Okay," Bert said, smiling. "Melissa, who do you want to marry?"

"I want to marry Jay," Melissa answered.

Jay was eating an orange nearby, completely unaware of what was happening. Bert called out to him, "Jay, do you want to get married?"

He took some time to swallow the orange slice, then answered hesitantly, "Uh, yeah. Yeah, uh. Yeah, I guess I'll get married."

Bert said, "Okay, you're married."

"That's it?" Whit said.

"Yeah, that's it. What did you expect?" Bert answered, "This is MOVE. We don't do all of that romantic, committing-to-the-System's-laws-only-to-end-up-divorced five years later. We put priority on devotion, not that Cinderella, fairy-tale bullshit. Enjoy your life together. Now let's go to the movies."

A few months later, Allen and Violet followed suit and made their secret relationship official, too. Bert said they were married and that was it. MOVE marriages were so unconventional that they didn't even jump a broom.

The newlywed couples all gathered for the backyard party with MOVE members and supporters congratulating them on entering adulthood. I had never been to a wedding before, in MOVE or otherwise. I didn't know what was supposed to happen, but what I saw didn't seem like it was supposed to happen. No tuxedos, no fancy dresses, no ceremony, no rings. Taylor got married in the same green-striped T-shirt he wore to see *Menace II Society*. In my life, I've seen eight marriages among MOVE's second generation. Of the eight, only one ended in divorce. The other seven have a combined twenty-nine children, four grandchildren, and nearly two hundred years of marital history together. The emphasis on being united was much stronger than the romantic idea of a wedding dress and a honeymoon. That unity is the bedrock for family, for community, for growth, for health, and for wealth, however you measure it.

Chapter 19

STEPPING UP

Watching my peers step into man- or womanhood encouraged my desire to improve myself. If I was going to live up to the standard of a MOVE-material husband, I had a lot of work to do. I had to be strong. I had to be clean. And I had to learn to be excellent.

The first thing I decided to do was focus on my physical appearance. In my mind, I thought nobody wanted a raggedy husband who didn't look like he could do anything. So I started working out hard. At Reno Street, besides sports, I spent most of my time playing Nintendo and watching television in the house. I didn't exercise much between football and basketball games. That had to change.

I remembered the workouts Scarlet and Marie did. I designed my own workout routine based on the physique I was looking for. This was the most rigorous physical work I had ever done in my life. It was composed of three parts—floor, bricks, and cardio training.

My floor training started at 50 push-ups, 50 sit-ups, 50 leg raisers, and 50 squats. My bricks were 50 curls, 50 lateral raises, 50 punches, and 50 butterflies. My cardio workout was a one-mile run and three minutes of boxing or hitting the heavy bag.

Getting through my first day felt like torture. Remembering my defeat by Sue in her push-up contest, I wanted to make sure I could do at least twenty push-ups on call. But when I first started,

I quickly realized that when you start out exercising, your muscles have to adjust to the movement—not just as you make the motion, but also internally. So even though I was able to do twenty push-ups on call, once I started a routine, I dropped down to just five per set. I had to push myself to stay with it.

I was so embarrassed by my own weakness I would hide behind walls and go into other rooms to exercise alone. This was where Taylor and Allen got their revenge on me. They had grown up exercising like this all their lives. Unlike when we played Nintendo, they were in the winner's seat, and I was in the challenger's. They led the pack in the running when we went to the track. When we did push-ups, they could do in one set what took me ten sets to do. They were so strong. I once witnessed them taking turns lifting the rear end of a car off the ground.

"You weak motherfucker," Taylor would say. "You play all of those video games, but you can't lift your own body weight. If you were as strong as you are good at Nintendo, you'd be a bad motherfucker."

I was so embarrassed. I felt like I needed to be reborn with the genes of Hercules to compete with them. Sue saw me flailing and intervened, reminding me of something Benny had said to her years earlier: "You may never get as strong as some people, but a strong effort can give you a level of strength you can be satisfied with."

I took that statement seriously and applied it to my life, exercising and otherwise.

For my next workout, the first set of push-ups I did hurt like hell. The second set was worse. I did my fifty and felt like my arms could not recover. Next was sit-ups. They were just as challenging. Every lift made me question how it was possible that people actually did this all the time. When I finished, I lay on the floor for a long time. I was already starting to feel the pain. The next day, I could barely walk. Everything hurt. I was so sore my legs could not bend at the knees. I could not move my arms to put on a T-shirt. Trying to walk down the steps at the MOVE house on Fifty-Sixth Street hurt. I was tearing up and I didn't even know it.

Ramona saw me limping. "Why are you walking like that?" she asked.

"I'm sore from exercising."

"Uh-huh. You overdid it, huh?" Ramona smiled. "Well, I know you won't want to hear this, but the only way to get unsore is to do the same exercises that got you sore in the first place."

That evening, I massaged my own body as best as I could and got back to work. Ramona was right. Although the pain didn't totally disappear, by day three I could at least walk down the steps again. I was setting new rules and boundaries for myself. This required a new kind of discipline for me. It was hard to keep going, but I kept going.

Within six months, my 50 push-ups total turned into 50 per set. My one-mile run turned into five miles. Eventually I could do 1,000 push-ups in a day, 500 sit-ups, and 500 leg raises. I did brick reps by the thousands, and my running distance increased to more than ten miles.

It took me a long time to work up to this routine, but I did it every day once I did. I matched my workout regimen with way more raw foods. I stopped looking at it as a punishment and more like something that gave me an advantage.

The physical work I did unlocked an understanding about myself that propelled me mentally. It gave me a foundation for enduring pressure. The mindset I had during the burn from my intense workouts transferred to challenging situations in the real world. I was learning that no pain is forever. I would use that message and think to myself, *If I can make it this far, I can go a little further, and step by step, I inched my way to the next level.* Classic no pain, no gain attitude.

I was seventeen years old and feeling strong in my body and mind. I was feeling proud of myself. I was feeling secure and maturing every day. Others could sense it.

After years of training my mind, body, and soul, I got a call from Sue, summoning me to the house for a meeting.

I walked up to the third floor into a dark room where she sat with Bert. "Kita, it's time. You're getting married," Bert said.

"What?" This was one of those *What are you talking about, Willis* moments. I wanted to be married, but I wasn't about to marry just anybody. And yet I definitely wanted to see where this conversation was going. "What do you mean I'm getting married? To who?!"

"To Robin," Sue said, as if this was somehow obvious.

"To Robin?!" I shook my head over and over again. "No, no, no, no, no, no, no, no, no. Are you kidding me?"

I saw Robin all the time and had never once thought about her romantically. She was one of the younger teenagers, around fourteen at the time. I wasn't thinking about Robin at all. I had dated a few other girls outside MOVE who were older than me. College-aged and college graduates. Robin wasn't on my radar. I continued my protests.

"Robin hates my guts! Why in the world would you pair me with Robin?!"

But what I also knew was that a few weeks earlier, a group of younger folks in MOVE were in the kitchen, discussing unmarried MOVE members and who might still pair up. They were comparing the different personalities of people and how various pairings might gel or clash. When my name came up, the tone was way better than it had been years before. Nobody described me as a jerk. They had watched me mature. Then the unthinkable.

Violet commented that Robin seemed to like me.

"What?!" Allen said. He and I were cool, but he was protective of his little sister. "Kita is too old for Robin."

Melissa, who never defended me, quickly replied, "He ain't no older to Robin than you are to Violet."

Allen was stunned. He had nothing to say to that. I was also amazed. As far as I knew, this was the first time I had ever heard anyone pair me with someone in MOVE *and* defend my pairing when faced with opposition. I recalled that exchange as I sat in front of Bert and Sue. I couldn't help but think that this was the culmination of that previous conversation.

Bert and Sue loved to play matchmaker and push people to get together. I didn't have a problem with it as long as the person they tried to match me with was someone I liked and liked me back. In this case, as far as I was concerned, Robin was not a match for me.

Sue wasn't playing around. "You're getting married."

"No, I'm not. That girl hates me like Jordan hates Isaiah."

"Well, let's see about that," Bert said. "I'm calling Moe."

She dialed the phone, as I sat silently, wondering what the hell was going on.

"Moe, does Robin like Kita?" Bert asked fast and in a hurry. "We tryin' to see something."

I could hear Moe in the background. "Hey, Robin! Bert's on the phone. She wanna know how do you feel about Kita."

"What did Moe say?" Sue hastily asked. She put her ear up against the phone receiver Bert was holding, then started talking right into it. "What did she say, Moe?"

"Shhh, Sue, I'm trying to find out," Bert whispered.

It was quiet for a moment, as they waited for Moe to relay Robin's answer.

Then it came.

"She said yeah. She over here smiling," Moe said with a laugh.

Bert and Sue erupted with cheers, singing about how they would have another MOVE wedding.

"Wait, wait, wait. Hold up, hold up, hold up," I said. "This is way too soon. I need some time to figure some things out first. Come on, man. This is too much."

"What do you need to figure out?" Bert impatiently asked.

"First, I'm glad she seem like she likes me, but she's still too young. I mean, she's fourteen."

"Well, how old does she need to be?" Bert asked. "How old do you think she needs to be for you to approve of y'all being together?"

"I don't know. She got to be at least fifteen. We're both still teenagers, but three years is a big difference at this age."

"That's not a big difference," Bert explained. "My grandmother was thirteen when she married my grandfather, and he was twenty-one. You are just too modern and civilized. Robin is at a good age to get married, and she's still clean, and she ain't been messed over by all of them no-good motherfuckers in the System."

I couldn't believe what I was hearing. Except I could.

This was the MOVE way. Adulthood was not determined by what the government said. Driving age, drinking age—on those matters, MOVE wasn't guided by legalities. They said it was guided by nature. But that was not what was happening here. This was Bert wanting me to pair up. She said it was time, and she considered Robin my best match.

I was not entirely convinced. I had to see for myself. I heard what Bert said, and I understood it, but I still had to speak to Moe and get his approval. I had to talk to Robin's mother, and I didn't need to do this by proxy. I had to speak with Robin, too, of course.

The next day, I went to Fifty-Sixth Street, where Robin lived.

"Are you here for Robin?" her mother asked, grinning at me.

"Yeah, I am here for Robin. I just want to talk to her, if that's all right."

"Yeah, she's in her room. You know where it is."

I made my way to Robin's room, and I was shocked when she greeted me at the entrance with a smile and wrapped her arms all the way around my neck. I didn't know what to do. This felt wrong. She just didn't seem old enough for me yet. And the last time I'd spent any real time with her, she was begging her brothers to destroy me. I couldn't get comfortable with her. It was an awkward visit, and I stayed only twenty minutes.

Word spread that Bert and Sue wanted me and Robin to marry. Robin and her parents were on board. And Robin was being nice to me. It felt so odd. I couldn't get past the fear that her niceness was an act and that I might end up being the butt of a cruel joke. That was how sour my encounters with Robin had been before this. I knew I was maturing into a different person—into as good a man as I could will myself to be—but I was astounded that Robin was checking for me.

She was cute enough, I guess in a young lady sort of way. I could admit that. Muscular, athletic, strong. She was developing her body and mind in the MOVE lifestyle the same way I was. I liked that a lot. It was a sign that we might be able to build together and that we could be great support for each other. All good things.

For the following several months, I kept thinking about it.

Pam took some of the kids on a camping trip in Vermont that spring, and Robin went with her. While she was away, Robin found a pay phone in the rural town and called me. "Hey."

"Hey," I said back. "Who are you looking for?"

"You, stupid."

"Oh, okay. What's up?" I didn't know what to say to her. I was a confident person, but everything about Robin suddenly unnerved me. Everything felt weird and new.

I could hear Robin smiling through the phone. "Nothing. I just wanted to tell you about Vermont. It's not like Philly. It's green! Everywhere is green! There's a park up here with a giant crater that a million people can fit inside of, just like the one at Clark Park, but it's way bigger. And there are so many stars in the sky at night. They look like they're all connected to each other."

I remembered that was how the sky looked when I visited my dad for the first time. I felt a twinge of connection to Robin, hearing her recognize the sky's beauty.

"Anyway," she continued, "what's going on back home?"

"The usual. Whit wants a divorce from Taylor again."

"Oh. What else is new?" she said dryly.

We both laughed.

"Well, I got to go. I'll see you when I get back home, okay?"

"Okay," I said. And then we hung up.

I couldn't stop thinking about Robin after the call. I couldn't wait for her to get back to Philly. I knew what I wanted then. No more doubts.

When Robin returned, Bert planned our wedding. Well, our wedding party. It was a bit of an upgrade from the previous three couples' but still pretty primitive. No dress for Robin, no suit for me, no rings, no minister. Just a commitment to each other that has lasted since 1997.

Chapter 20

STEPPING IN

A year later, in 1998, Merle Africa, one of the MOVE 9, died of cancer in her prison cell. MOVE had been protesting for the MOVE 9's release for nearly twenty years, without any progress. I had been visiting my parents in prison twice a year. But the fragileness of their mortality had not occurred to me. Merle's death changed that. It dawned on me that my parents could die in prison, too. I always thought that just like Ramona came home, they would eventually come home. Just like Sue came home, they would come home. Just like Consuewella and everybody else had come home, something would happen, something would work out, and they would come home. But Merle dying in prison gave me another reality.

Merle's death was eye-opening in other ways, as well. It gave me a new perspective that compelled me to clash with verbiage I often heard among MOVE's most confident leaders.

MOVE members like Sue had the mentality that if you did your work to be a good MOVE member and acknowledged John Africa as God, then that mentality would propel you beyond any sicknesses and any ailments. You would be invincible, even indestructible. It didn't start out that way, but soon Sue had the kind of personality where once she believed in something and locked in to it, she became blindly determined about it.

For instance, you might ask her, "How did Frank do at the track today?" A bunch of us would go there every day to exercise.

Sue might reply with something descriptive but innocuous like "He was as fast as a cheetah." Except Sue wouldn't mean that only metaphorically. With all of her heart, she seemed to believe that Frank had run as fast as an actual cheetah because he was the most loyal and disciplined MOVE member and ate only raw foods. Cheetahs can run seventy miles per hour. To give context, Usain Bolt's top recorded speed is twenty-eight miles per hour. But everyone knew better than to question Sue or disagree with her, or else they'd have a serious fight on their hands.

Sue's literal interpretation of Benny's teachings about the benefits of a raw food diet was wrong. In MOVE, life is not just the duration our physical bodies are tied to our nonphysical bodies. Life is the sun, the moon, the stars, the earth, the water, the sea, the air—life is everything that is natural. And it's precious. The core MOVE principle that all life deserves our efforts to preserve and honor it was always taught alongside the belief that the essence of life is going to be here forever. Over the years, Sue began to conflate this belief with her own misinterpretation that human beings can live forever, too. In Sue's mind, so as long as you did your work and believed in the power of Mama and MOVE law, you would not die. She became completely devoted to these beliefs. Other MOVE members did, too, but Sue was by far the most extreme.

So when Merle died in prison, Sue was dismissive and said, "Merle must have been violating the teaching of John Africa." She believed that Benny had cured Merle of cancer, and the cancer couldn't return unless Merle had been violating MOVE law. See, back in the day when MOVE headquarters was in Powelton Village, Merle was always sick. MOVE members, especially Sue, credited Benny with helping Merle get better, with a regimen that included a special diet, extra love, and attention. Eventually, while in the bathroom one day, Merle screamed in pain and horror. LaVerne and others ran to see what was happening. Floating in the toilet bowl was a clump of fatty meat and blood covered with tentacles. Every day after that, Merle got better and then she wasn't sick anymore. Marie and Consuewella did some research on the foreign item that Merle had passed. They believed it was a tumor. For Sue, this meant Merle was cured of her cancer. And she saw Benny's teachings as the only determinative factor. So when Merle died, Sue blamed Merle. Not how the prison treated her or fed her or didn't give her the opportunity for exercise as Merle had before she was imprisoned. In Sue's world, everything came down to what was in your mind and how close or far from MOVE law your beliefs were.

I was always curious how Sue reconciled all this with the 1985 bombing and the eleven MOVE members who were killed, including her son Tomaso. When I asked her, her face immediately darkened, and a wall the size of the Hoover Dam seemed to form between us. She was insulted and perplexed by my question. When she finally found the words, she screamed at me, "They're not dead!" She said she thought they were somewhere else and that if we did our work, our reward would be to see them again. Like they were in some utopian MOVE world, where they were as strong as wild animals. Bert shared this viewpoint.

I think the agony of her losing her son and seeing so many people she cared about treated heinously warped her thinking, beyond anything in reality or MOVE law. Really, she was no different from the zealots who are found in all the world's most popular organized religions. When faced with a trauma too difficult for the mind to process, it can create inexplicable thoughts. It's just when those thoughts are held by billions of people over hundreds of generations, it seems normal.

I rarely ever saw anybody challenge Sue. As children, we didn't really argue with any of the adults. Now that I was twenty years old and MOVE-married, I still wouldn't dare challenge Sue. I just came to understand that I couldn't believe everything she said.

I knew that Merle didn't die just from thinking the wrong thoughts. She had cancerous tumors in her body. But Sue believed that Merle died because she'd strayed away from MOVE's beliefs, so she vilified Merle in death. Sue told people that Merle was a violator of John Africa's teachings and that Merle set a horrible example and made Benny look bad because she died in prison.

Sue's behavior after Merle died became a huge problem for the second generation of MOVE members, me included.

This was the first test of the second generation's faith in MOVE.

The question became, for me, if everything comes from the mind, and one's physical state has nothing to do with anything— like Sue says—then why did Benny prescribe a particular diet for us? Why did we exercise? I agreed with Sue that the mind and body are tied to one another. But to believe that everything is mental made me wonder: What are we doing with our bodies?

Eventually I gathered the nerve to ask Sue about this. She didn't take my question well. She saw it as a challenge and an offense. It widened a rift between us that had opened with my question to her about the bombing. To this day, my relationship with Sue has never mended. It's a sad truth. But I don't dwell on it now and I didn't dwell on it then.

For me, the much bigger issue became MOVE's plan for getting the remaining MOVE 9, including my parents, out of prison. The idea that people were beginning to die in there was chilling to me. I had important questions.

What is our plan?

What is our goal for the MOVE 9's release?

What is our program for the children that MOVE-married couples are having?

What is our plan for the future of the organization?

I posed these questions to Sue, and she went and dug up a letter Benny had written to her twenty-five or thirty years earlier. The opening line read: "Forget all that future planning."

Sue recited that line whenever she wanted to neutralize anyone's question, argument, or comment about what MOVE should do next. She would say, "John Africa said forget all that future planning." If we wanted to plan to purchase land, "forget all that future planning." If we wanted to make provisions to secure housing for the MOVE 9 upon their release, "forget all that future planning." She'd sometimes add, "You're so confused and crazy because you always worry about the future."

What I learned later was that Benny wrote that letter to Sue because she had issues with anxiety. After all, she was in prison and thinking about whether she was going to come home and ever see her child again. Benny was telling her, "If the future makes you feel bad, forget about it. Stop thinking about it because it makes you feel bad and focus on what's happening now."

Some people take comfort in looking ahead and in thinking and dreaming about what they will do later on. If that makes you feel good, if that helps you pass your time in prison, if that motivates you to be a better person, then you should do that. But Sue had these problems to such an extreme and found Benny's words to her to be a comfort, so she indiscriminately applied his words to everything and tried to apply them to everyone except Bert's son, Zack. To me, she was stifling the future of MOVE in her refusal to have a conversation about it. It bothered me that we didn't have a plan for getting the MOVE 9 out of prison, or for MOVE more generally. I voiced my concerns to Sue and to Bert, who both had a lot of power and support within MOVE. Everyone in MOVE felt indebted to them and grateful to them, in one way or another. Sue and Bert knew this. So, whenever an argument or a disagreement came up, they would quickly pull out something like *After all I've done for you, you're going to betray me by taking his/her side or believing what he/she said. I would never steer you wrong.*

That became a problem for me. Using MOVE law, it didn't even make sense. Again, I made my case to Sue and, this time, to Bert, too.

If it's wrong and against Mama to plan, why do squirrels bury nuts for the winter? Why do bears fatten their bodies up before they hibernate? Why is it that the birds fly south? Life plans always, and to say it is unnatural to plan is ridiculous.

My logic was too sound to refute. I won the argument over whether or not MOVE should make plans. This sullied my already rickety relationship with Sue. And I could tell Bert wasn't too happy with me, either.

I was still very young and had more questions than answers from the duo. I had plenty of MOVE work to keep me busy, especially my traveling around with Ramona and Pam. Robin and I were newly married, so I couldn't push my bigger thoughts and questions about MOVE very far. I didn't like being away from Robin for long. So I decided to let things sit for a moment. No need to keep rocking the boat when I didn't have paddles. I started reading a lot. My formal education ended really early, but my mind was alive. I liked reading.

Maya Angelou's *I Know Why the Caged Bird Sings* made me I think of Merle Africa a lot. Merle was a tormented soul with only her beautiful singing voice to connect her to the freedom she mourned for. What made her so special to me was that she helped bring me safely and lovingly into the world. During my birth, it was Merle who sang to drown out the noise from my fussing as the MOVE women welcomed me into the world. She helped ensure my safekeeping during a time of uncertainty. Whenever I went to visit my mother, I would always see all four women from the MOVE 9, including Merle. And now she was gone.

Who among the MOVE 9 might be next?

I became haunted by this question.

I never wanted to take for granted that everyone I knew would always be alive or be how I remembered them, so I started visiting everyone much more frequently. I started calling everybody I knew that was ever in MOVE. Not just the prisoners, even though I made jail visits regularly. I visited the kids who had since grown into adults and had kids of their own. I called the supporters I remembered so I could see their faces and hug them. I visited MOVE members who had left the organization, because I wanted to see people who understood something few others could comprehend. Because of my blood relation to a third of the MOVE members, and because of how the prison visiting policies were set up, I got to see all of the people often. It was important for me, but of course it was extraordinary for them. Some prisoners were separated from their families for years, sometimes decades. Making the connection with them fulfilled something vital in all of us.

I especially liked feeling more connected to the network of prison visit opportunities. I was older by then, so I was sometimes organizing the visits myself, seeing three women at the female prison instead of four. I never did get used to that.

My dedication to MOVE and to Benny's teachings as John Africa was so profound that I was only able to see the good in MOVE. I felt privileged to be part of it. However, Merle's death made me question that a lot, too.

Merle died in March 1998. Later that year, Robin gave birth to our first son, born on the birthday shared by three people significant to me: my hometown hero, Will Smith; my close friend's mom, Brenda; and my sister, Whit. All were born on September 25.

Robin and I delivered the baby ourselves in our bedroom. We didn't see a need for doctors, midwives, epidurals, medicine, or anything else. We credit Benny for that idea and both of our mothers who gave birth to us without hospitals or doctors. MOVE life insulating us from the thinking that childbirth must be handled by a medical professional in a hospital. Most of MOVE's teachings, fundamentally, were about shielding people from the System's training. Robin will tell you it worked well in this instance. Thirty minutes from start to finish was all it took for her to push our little Alex right out.

My introduction to fatherhood was like my introduction to love—terrifying. The fear of messing up was always on my mind. I never really saw a father hold a baby or be with a baby. I was so scared that I wouldn't know what to do. I had always been envious of other people who felt as comfortable holding babies as I was not. This didn't change just because Alex was mine. I was afraid to hold my son, fearing I might drop him. I was scared to get too close. I didn't want to breathe on him wrong. I don't know if part of that was because I didn't have parents growing up in the house and didn't know what to do, or if it was just how all fathers feel. Or maybe my mind was playing tricks on me, confusing me with this idea that I wouldn't be a good parent myself. Whatever it was, it was terrifying.

Would I have the answers to the questions Alex asked? Could I give him the confidence that he would need while growing into a young man? Would I be strong enough to make him strong so that he could navigate the world? For a moment I even thought, *How the hell do I do this?* Because I knew the trouble that I experienced. I didn't want my son to go through what I had gone through as a child.

I had a conversation with my friend Kakuya Shakur, the daughter of Black revolutionaries Assata Shakur and Kamau Sadiki. She told me, "I decided to bring a child into this world, knowing what this world is." And that was precisely how I felt.

But I also felt that if there's any challenge I'm faced with, any life that I'm responsible for, I'm going to do whatever I can to provide the best opportunities. I would ensure that Alex's life would be better than mine was. MOVE teachings helped.

Benny instituted certain rituals in MOVE for what we do when a baby is born. First, we fill the room with raw food, all kinds of foods. Peanuts, sweet potatoes, mangoes, grapes, oranges, pineapples, just all sorts of raw fruits and vegetables. That smell from all that raw food in the house is what always gives away that a new baby has arrived or is coming shortly. A baby is a big deal in MOVE.

The purpose of that is not only to give the mother and the baby fresh, wholesome, good, solid, healthy food. It's also so that the baby can have good air to breathe because those foods are nurturing. You don't get nurtured only by consuming these foods. They provide a wonderful aroma, and that's nurturing, too.

Another ritual is once the baby is born, there's a month of acclimation so the mother can bond with the baby. There are no interferences. None. Babies will lay on their moms, bare-chested, both of them, bonding skin to skin. It keeps the nervous system calm, the heart strong, and the confidence level high. Bonding is so essential for the mother and the baby. That strengthens and gives those babies and the mothers much-needed security that they carry with them for the rest of their lives.

To avoid illness to the new mom and baby, no one is allowed to come visit the baby until thirty days after the birth, unless you are a very, very close family member—like the baby's grandparents. It's up to the mother's discretion, but normally if you're a cousin, an aunt, a sister, a brother, or anyone like that, you'll have to wait thirty days. Once the baby gets more acclimated to the world outside the womb, more visitors are allowed.

Although I was afraid of Alex at first, my love for him has always been off the charts. It was overwhelming. I was excited to get to know him. And once I did, the connection was clear as day. I swear he could hear my thoughts. If I was upset about something, I could see in his facial expression that he knew what I was thinking. I'd never experienced anything like that before. I can only describe it as a deep feeling of connectedness.

I got that feeling again exactly three years later when our second son, Koby, was born, on Alex's birthday, in that same bedroom that Alex was born in.

Koby loved to touch and feel his mother's skin. From the moment he was born, he loved to put his arms around Robin. He liked to touch her face, her arms, and her hands. Even when he got older, he would reach for her face if he was lying down.

Having two sons made me want to go harder at doing things MOVE's way, because I wanted them to be strong. I didn't want them to go through what I had gone through—living with uncertainties, drugs, violence, bullying, all that. My sons made me take MOVE's work more seriously. MOVE had saved me. That was how I was feeling. I still feel that way now. I wanted to repay my saviors by raising strong soldiers for MOVE.

As the firstborn, Alex was raised on an entirely raw-food diet for the first fifteen months of his life. With Koby, we were a little less strict. I guess I resolved to myself that a little cooked food every now and then wouldn't kill any of us. Growing up, MOVE had me scared that if I didn't eat raw food only, I would die or something. Bert used to say if you brought a man that was from a thousand years ago into today's time, he wouldn't be able to live in our polluted environment. He'd die quickly because his system was so clean that today's air would kill him. That was always in the back of my mind. But in time I got to see that I didn't die. And Alex didn't die. And Koby would be asking for stuff because his big brother had tasted it before and told him how good it was. I was still a MOVE man, and yet fatherhood had softened me in some ways and toughened me in others.

I had two sons and a good MOVE woman, and I was continuing MOVE's larger work with Ramona and Pam. They had me on the road regularly with them at events. Whatever money came in from those activities went straight to the organization, which supported my young and growing family. Robin, the boys, and I had a two-bedroom apartment at the big MOVE house on Kingsessing Avenue in Southwest Philly. We lived in the same building as Ramona. Things were good, and I was happy. Fatherhood was growing on me, and Robin was a phenomenal mother.

My relationships with Sue and Bert weren't improving but weren't getting worse, either. I knew what would set them off. I was mostly staying out of their crosshairs, even as I continued my personal crusade to keep meeting, visiting, and staying in fellowship with other MOVE members, past and present.

This was a very confusing time in my life. The big questions I had about the future of MOVE I had let rest for a while. But I was a dad. I looked at my boys and could think only of the future.

Every day I was having moments with my sons that my parents never got to have with me. First steps, first words, all the milestones. The mundane moments were my favorites and I didn't take them for granted. The ordinary intimacy—like playing in the park, seeing their reactions to tasting ice cream for the first time, teaching them to swim, and finally going to Disney World—made me feel wonderful but guilty. Because no matter how much time passed, I always kept the other kids on my mind. Tree, Netta, Delisha, Little Phil, and Tomaso would probably have had kids.

And they didn't live long enough to get the chance. I was living a good life that they should've been living, too.

Getting to know my sons and maturing into fatherhood got me thinking more and more about my parents. They'd been in prison for twenty-three years already, with no plan for their release.

I went to see my parents twice a year. And from the time each of my kids were a year old, Robin and I took them for visits.

I remember the first time we took Alex to meet my dad. By this point, he'd been transferred to Graterford, a prison that was only about an hour away from Philly. With my dad so close, I started visiting him all the time. Sometimes as much as four times in a month. My mom was seven hours away still, near Erie, Pennsylvania, at a prison called Cambridge Springs. The distance made it difficult to see her as much. So Dad met Alex first. That was a good day. I remember my dad holding Alex and just staring at him with a smile on his face. Every now and then Dad would lift his head up and look at me, the whole time smiling, and then look back at my son Alex. He just kept smiling and looking back and forth. I felt like I was making my father proud, and I felt proud of myself. Mostly I felt like I was on the right track and so far from the road that I could've been on—the road that I had been on just a few years earlier. To see that my father was approving of the decisions that I was making and the way my life's trajectory was headed—it meant a lot.

But I was scared, too. My dad is amazing. I'd had a lot of accomplishments over the years, but I knew there would have been ten times more of them and they would have been ten times greater if my dad had raised me himself. I felt wistful about it sometimes, yet there was a sense of *If my father's proud, it must be good.* And Dad was proud. He was adoring and proud to be a grandfather.

I felt like I had a real village. My family unit was tight. Robin and I moved as one, and our boys were growing and thriving. In MOVE, though, by the end of 2001 things weren't going so smoothly. A dramatic custody battle was underway, and I had to pick a side.

After Benny was killed in the bombing, his MOVE wife, Bert, married again. Her husband, John Gilbride, was a MOVE supporter and not a member like Bert. Members carried the surname Africa and were made members by Benny. Or they were the children of original MOVE members. Usually, members had a deeper commitment to Benny. MOVE always had more supporters than actual members.

So MOVE member Bert married MOVE supporter John. They were married about eight years and had a son named Zackary. At the time of their split, Zack was five years old. John wanted joint custody. Bert wanted full custody. It led to a very public feud—one of those nasty, disgusting fights over a child. And a mystifying one. During the custody battle, Bert and John spent a lot of time together outside of court. She would cook him breakfast in the morning before they stood in front of the judge and squared off and hurled hateful statements at each other. It was the strangest thing I've ever seen.

John was a good dude, from what I observed. He was a person whom I considered a friend beyond MOVE. Probably the only person like that for me at that point. MOVE people didn't have outside friends. We had supporters, and we had other members. We also had blood relatives outside of MOVE, but interaction with them was seldom. Nearly all our lives were spent with MOVE people.

I think John and I got along well and really enjoyed each other's company because we had interests in common that had nothing to do with MOVE. I didn't have many people in my life who shared those interests. My peers in MOVE—meaning those in the second generation—didn't grow up doing what I was accustomed to doing. They didn't watch basketball, and they didn't watch football. They weren't involved in competitions. They didn't go to the playground and play organized sports. John did.

So we got kind of close discussing those things together. With or without MOVE, John could've been a friend of mine. He took me to my first and second Philadelphia 76ers games. It was so much fun because it was uncharacteristic of MOVE to be there. We ate hot dogs I wasn't supposed to be eating. We drank soda I wasn't supposed to be drinking. We were playing hooky from life. It was such a breath of fresh air. When Bert and John split up, I was surprised.

None of it was my business. I was happy for it to be none of my business. Then Bert asked me to testify on her behalf and make it my business. Bert was one of the most "important" people in MOVE, especially after Benny was killed. My first instinct was to protect her. Protecting Bert felt like protecting MOVE itself. So I agreed to testify against John. I showed up to court and told the judge that I believed John was not a great father. I had seen John with Zack. John didn't know how to hold Zack and wouldn't listen to Bert about how to do it. He worked one hundred hours a week, every week, and wasn't home much. I had experience with fatherhood at that point and had set a high bar for it. I knew I didn't clear the bar myself some of the times, but I wasn't going to lower it to make it easier to clear—for myself or for John. That was how I thought of it at the time. The judge asked me particular questions. I gave him very precise answers.

I knew my testimony surprised John. I'd like to think that he understood, but I never asked and he never said. What I do remember is that during a questioning session in court, the judge asked John if he missed any MOVE people. John said he did. The judge asked who. And John said he missed me. I missed him, too.

After some deliberation, the courts sided with John. He and Bert would share custody of their son. I didn't think that was bad. After all, Bert and John basically behaved as if they had shared custody of Zack anyway. John was frequently at Bert's house when he wasn't working. To me, it almost seemed like Bert was low-key trying to get back with him.

But the court's decision outraged Bert. She felt like a grave injustice had been carried out. I think she remembered how Benny acted in court and won, and thought she'd have similar good fortune.

The night before the first scheduled child-custody exchange was filled with anticipation. We weren't sure how Bert was going to react to handing over her son, but we MOVE members had made up our minds that if she decided she didn't want to give Zack to John, we were not going to let John have Zack.

Just months earlier, Whit had come to the Kingsessing house to support Bert on this issue. She brought with her her clothes, a sleeping bag, food, and her four kids. Whit told her husband she'd come back home when Bert's custody matter was resolved. Three or four other MOVE mothers did the same. We slatted up the Kingsessing house, just like in the confrontations at Powelton in the seventies and at Osage in the eighties. My father and Chuck were outraged at Bert's decision to involve MOVE members in her custody drama, especially since John had a right to see his own son. Dad tried to convince Whit and me to leave Kingsessing, but we refused. We all went to bed ready for a confrontation. But that never happened.

I woke up early the next morning to Pam Africa yelling, "John is dead! John is dead!"

She was listening to 1340 AM when Philadelphia radio icon Mary Mason announced the news. We were all stunned.

John had been shot through his car window as he sat in the parking lot of his apartment building. MOVE was among the top suspects. Police brought every MOVE man in for questioning. I remember being brought in. They questioned me for several hours. Nothing ever came of my questioning or from the questioning of anyone else in MOVE. Bert later told me that John had gambling debts in the hundreds of thousands of dollars. But the police never had enough evidence to charge anyone, and all the leads were apparently dead ends. The case went cold. No arrests were ever made. No murder weapon was ever found.

After a while, I was too disturbed by the developments to hear any more about it. I have deliberately not followed the story of John Gilbride's killing, even all these years later. I've not read the articles or watched the stories, and I would tune out when Bert talked about John in a negative way. His murder fucked me up. I regret getting involved in the custody battle between him and Bert, even as I look back and know why I did. Any time the battle lines felt like MOVE versus another person or entity, I had been taught from birth always to pick MOVE.

Chapter 21

THE EXIT STRATEGY

Two thousand eight marked ten years since the passing of Merle Africa. It also marked the thirty-years of my parents being in prison. By then, they had each come up for parole one time and each been denied. My parents refused to admit any responsibility in Officer Ramp's death during the 1978 standoff at MOVE's Powelton headquarters. By then, Robin and I had our third son. We were on target for birthday landings. Our baby boy, Tommy, was born on Bert's birthday. For a person who grew up being taught that birthdays were just another day, the universe sure had a way of pointing me back to specific dates.

The birth of a new baby had me thinking about the newness of fatherhood yet again. Not that I could ever really get away from it. Robin and I already had Alex and Koby. But something about a new baby and all the new possibilities it represents makes a person think about the future. With three sons, I wanted to be the present, everyday type of father for them that my dad wasn't able to be. I knew I was getting to experience what my dad wished he could get. I was always trying to appreciate it, even as it sometimes daunted me.

I could feel time passing. Like, really passing. Alex was already ten years old. Would he ever see his grandparents free?

I remember lying in bed as a child and imagining when my parents were coming home. I'd sometimes look out the window and watch the moon. I used to wonder if my parents might be looking at the moon at the same time.

I would look at that moon and say to myself, *I know by the year 1995*—or 1998 or some other random year—*my parents are going to be home by then.* I didn't have anything to base my expectation on other than hope.

Or I remember when I asked my mother, "Debbie, how old are you?"

"I'm thirty," she told me.

I was just a kid then. But suddenly I was the one who was thirty and taking my three sons to see my mom, who was still in prison. Never in my dream on the moon did I expect to be this way.

I remember the first time Robin and I took Alex to meet Mom. We packed up the car and drove four hundred miles north and west toward Erie. Alex was little. Gurgling, trying to talk, full of energy. We wanted to make sure he was comfortable for the long drive. We did our best. I felt excited for Mom to meet my first child. I had butterflies in my stomach. Honestly, I wasn't sure what to expect.

MOVE women raised me. My grandmother LaVerne, and my aunts Scarlet and Gail, specifically. Then when I got older, Ramona became an important figure for me. When you're a kid growing up in MOVE and your parents are in prison or dead, several adult women sort of replace your mother. That was why it hurt so badly when Scarlet told me she wasn't my mom.

Janet and Janine Africa, who I knew were my mother's MOVE 9 codefendants, felt almost as much my mother as my mother. Merle, before she died, did, too. I loved my mom. I was happy she was my mom. But I didn't know her much more than I knew the other women. When it comes to motherhood in MOVE, there's a village-raising-the-child mindset that is encouraged and welcome. Other children born and raised in MOVE will tell you the same.

The MOVE 9 men served their time in facilities that were

different from one another. I couldn't visit my dad and see Delbert, too, for instance, because they were at different prisons. But the MOVE 9 women were always in the same prison together. I rarely visited my mother without also visiting the other women. That bred a special kind of relationship. The same way I would write my mother letters, I wrote the other women letters. So when Alex was born, he used to say he had three grandmothers. He would call my mother Grandmom Deedee. He would call Janet Grandmom Janet, and he would call Janine Grandmom Janine. It broke my heart that Merle never got to meet him.

I remember getting to the visitor's room at the prison and seeing Janet and Janine with my mother. Robin handed Alex to her. Mom held him for a couple of minutes. She was thrilled and so loving. She cooed at him and kissed him all over his little chocolate brown face. She rocked him back and forth and whispered in his ear. And then Janet said, "All right, Debbie, my turn."

Mom kissed Alex again and handed him over.

Janet held him and was doing the same thing Mom had just done. Then she walked Alex around the visitor's room a bit and one of her friends noticed. "Hey, Janet," her friend asked, "is that your grandbaby?"

"Yep!" Janet said with a huge smile on her face. She looked content and peaceful.

Janine, who'd been looking on the whole time, had been patient enough. "Hey. All right now."

And then Janet handed Alex to Janine, and she held him and did her thing. It was really beautiful. And it felt totally normal.

I think my mother wanted that experience for Janet and Janine. They both had kids who were killed in the 1985 bombing. Neither of them would have a chance at grandchildren in MOVE. Mom wanted them to feel the grandmotherly love that she was feeling. Of course, it wouldn't be the same. But it was something.

I was proud that me having children could provide a sense of connection to a baby for Janet and Janine, and of course for my mom.

When Koby and Tommy were born, it was the same thing. All three grandmothers kissed and cooed and shared in the cuddles during my and Robin's prison visits. The boys were getting older. They understood where their grandparents were. It was all they had ever known.

My children have been learning about MOVE all their lives. At some point each of them has realized what that means. As they grew from babies to small boys and got more curious about why our lives looked different from others', Robin and I kept it real with them. They've been hearing about MOVE since they could understand language. About legacy, about who I am, about who their mother is, and about the sad tragedy to which they'll always have a link. They don't remember when they started learning these things. And I don't remember when I started telling them.

By the time Alex was ten years old, Koby was seven, and Tommy was four, I was really starting to question how MOVE was being managed. I was very satisfied and confident that Benny's teachings as John Africa work. But the people making decisions about MOVE—Bert and Sue—weren't doing their work. Everybody was saying the right thing about getting the MOVE 9 out of prison. But I hardly ever saw movement on it. There was no plan. My children were getting older. I was getting older. My parents were getting older. Merle had been dead for a decade. And still, no plan.

Shit hit the fan for me for real when Philadelphia's Major League Baseball team, the Phillies, went on an epic run and then won the World Series.

For years, I'd heard that Benny said no Philadelphia sports team would win a championship because of what city officials did to MOVE.

It seemed like he was right. Philly's football team, the Eagles, had a Hall of Fame–caliber starting quarterback in Donovan Mc-Nabb and made several deep-season appearances but couldn't bring home a Super Bowl win. Philly's hockey team, the Flyers, were pretty competitive but hadn't won a Stanley Cup since the 1970s. The 76ers you could forget about. Allen Iverson got the team to the NBA finals in 2001, but they only won the first game in a best-of-seven series. They had to watch Kobe Bryant and Shaquille O'Neal lift up the championship trophy and victoriously spray champagne around the locker room.

But then the Phillies, in their 2008 season, were playing their hearts out and winning. It started to look like they could go the distance. I mentioned Benny's talk of a curse to my mom.

"That's not what he said," my mom told me with a laugh, before she clarified it. "What Benny said was, if a Philadelphia sports team won a championship, it would be a good opportunity to use the attention from the fans and eyes that would be on Philly to let people know what's happening with MOVE. Benny always said that using that momentum would be smart. He said we should never let a big opportunity like that go by without making sure we took advantage."

Well, the baseball season began in late March. The Phillies won the World Series in late October. That was seven months. And in the course of that seven months, the city of Philadelphia went from being happy the team was winning, to curious about how long they'd keep winning, to hopeful about winning each play-off series, and then to ecstatic at the final win. The city was in a great mood. It was exactly the circumstance that Benny had said MOVE should exploit, in a good way. We should've been using that energy to get in front of people who had influence and who could help us make headway with the MOVE 9's release. Yet nothing from the organization was happening.

I sent Bert and Sue the parole denial letters that came in the mail, and neither of them had anything to say. They didn't have a plan. There was no event, no protest, no march, and no statement or action from MOVE's leaders at all. There was not one thing in place to use the momentum of the Phillies' win for MOVE, with all of America's eyes on the city. There was no urgency to getting the MOVE 9 home. This wasn't how MOVE was supposed to behave. MOVE protested other things all the time. Their silence during the Phillies' World Series run made me livid.

I was sitting at a MOVE brother's house and listening to the radio while playing the board game *Monopoly* when I heard the news. I am a *Monopoly* pro. I put my skills up against anybody. I know the strategy. I know the rules. But I was losing. And I was getting beat because, in my mind, I couldn't understand how I just heard on the radio that the Phillies won, and there was nothing MOVE was doing about it. It took me back to Merle and how things were when she died. I could feel myself getting angrier and angrier. Why in the world wasn't there a plan?

I knew better than to take this to my parents, especially my dad. If I told him I was really worried about him being in prison or worried that he and my mom weren't going to make it, my father would say, *Mike, don't worry. We got this. You just raise your family. You make sure you're doing what you gotta do so you don't end up in here. Take care of your sister, take care of your wife. Make sure you send your mom some money.* That outlook gave me long stretches of peace in the midst of all the nonsense and confusion in how MOVE was being managed. Dad wanted me to focus on my life. He and my mom and others who were imprisoned were handling their business. They wanted me to handle mine. So I did, even though my feelings about MOVE's management never went away. I held my tongue and followed the lead of Bert and Sue, and whatever the MOVE 9 needed, I would try to make their time in prison easier.

And then, in 2010, two big things happened. My grandmother

LaVerne passed away. I hadn't seen her in years. I had foolishly let Bert and Sue drive a wedge between us and manipulate me into thinking that LaVerne was a bad person. LaVerne didn't help with that because she was a shoot-first-and-ask-questions-later type. I wasn't a person who could handle verbal confrontations with people that I cared about or that I thought should care about me. La-Verne being so impatient didn't help our relationship. But when she died, I had actually tried to convince myself that I probably didn't care. I hadn't seen her in a long time, I told myself. She was mean the last few times I had seen her. I almost convinced myself I didn't care. And then one of her favorite songs—"There's Nothing Better Than Love" by Luther Vandross and Gregory Hines—came on the radio randomly. I realized I cared a lot. I downloaded the song and couldn't stop listening to it. I couldn't stop. I wept. The tears were just pouring down my face like a faucet. That was the first thing.

The second thing was my uncle Chuck. He was the youngest of the MOVE 9 men. Chuck turned fifty years old in 2010. He was aware of his age, and he told me so.

He started pushing me. "Mike, we gotta get outta here. You gotta do something. Man, I just turned fifty in here! We gotta get outta here. And I'm the youngest! That means your mother is older."

This was the first time I saw any of the MOVE 9 ever express a whiff of anguish about wanting to get out of prison. When I would question them about the time they were doing, *to a person*, they were even-tempered about it. Never panicky. I think it was because of what they considered MOVE's work to be. A protest against the Philadelphia Zoo on a Saturday morning when most patrons were going to show up—that was a MOVE activity. And then the next week, when they'd go to a reservoir, where the city was pumping chemicals into the water—that was an activity. And then the following week, when they'd go to the circus to protest against Ringling Brothers Barnum and Bailey—just an activity. In

MOVE, these were all activities. It was what the group did. The MOVE 9 going to prison was also just another activity. That was how they seemed to think of it. They didn't want to be there, obviously. They had always talked about missing people and wanting to be home. But they never talked or behaved like they wanted saving. What they wanted was justice. And they wanted the courts to give it to them. They weren't going to strike a deal. They weren't going to admit any guilt. Their time in prison was part of MOVE's larger work.

My earliest memories of the MOVE 9 was when they were in their twenties. I repeatedly heard from them, "We gon' fight the System. We don't care. We'll die in prison." And "We'd rather die in prison than live under the System's stranglehold." That was still how they felt in their forties and fifties. Their fight against the System never changed. They were just doing it from prison cells instead of the zoo or City Hall.

But that changed when Chuck turned fifty. It was the first time I saw real panic and dread from anybody in the MOVE 9. Chuck told me straight-up, "We gotta get outta here."

"And Bert and them are wrong, Mike," Chuck continued.

He was clear with me about how Bert and Sue had warped Benny's teachings in a way that paralyzed MOVE.

"What do you mean, they're wrong?"

"Man, the Coordinator didn't want us to be in here for all these fucking years, Mike! We have been in here all this time. Merle died here."

"Chuck, but you know this is your activity. This is what y'all been saying. It's up to y'all how to do it."

"I know it's up to us. And I'm one of the ones saying, 'Let's get the fuck up outta here!' How the fuck we gon' get outta here? Hey Mike, you better stop listening to Bert and Sue, man. They fucking up. Just go tell 'em what I said."

This changed everything. Chuck's words sparked new urgency in me. I got in touch with Paul Hetznecker, who had been MOVE's counsel since the mid-1990s. Paul was a good lawyer and fought hard on MOVE's behalf. But his methods weren't effective. None of the MOVE 9 was getting any closer to coming home.

By 2010, Paul and my father had had disagreements they couldn't come back from. Paul filed a brief that excluded witnesses whom my father felt strongly should have been included. Meanwhile, Paul had begun advocating for another path altogether: try to get paroled.

"Judges don't want to hear your case," Paul explained to my father. "I think you should focus your attention on getting your parole and forget about getting back into court. You all have exemplary prison records. If we start the process of getting you parole, I think you have a great shot at getting it granted."

Dad refused to consider it. "You won't get another cent from us if you don't file what I want you to file," he said.

I understood where Dad was coming from, with wanting to be exonerated. But it seemed like an uphill battle. Nothing Paul had ever tried ever worked. But taking Paul's approach would also be an uphill battle. I slept on it and decided parole was the shorter route home. My big question was then, how would I convince my father to do something he strongly disagreed with? How would I convince the rest of the MOVE 9 to agree to this new plan? They made decisions regarding their case as a unit. They would all have to agree and that was not even close to happening. Phil was writing my father five-page letters about his reasons for abandoning the appeals process all together and instead going for parole. Phil's wife, Janine, plus Janet, Delbert, and Eddie, agreed with Phil. They had no confidence in the legal system getting them home and weren't going to admit any culpability in the death of the policeman. Chuck agreed with Dad 100 percent. Take no parole.

And then there was Mom. "Listen to your dad and Chuck," she said.

It was settled. The MOVE 9 were not feeling Paul's parole idea. The disagreement severed Paul's relationship with the MOVE 9 but not between Paul and me. I had been there when MOVE chose Paul as counsel over legendary civil rights attorney William Kunstler. I knew Paul had great ideas. And I thought his best idea was the one he was fired for suggesting.

Knowing the MOVE 9 like I did, I was clear about one thing. They might resist something at first glance but if they saw it working, they would give it a chance. So I decided to get the ball rolling on the parole idea, but I didn't tell anybody about it except Robin. I understood the seriousness of what I was initiating. Had they found out, the MOVE 9 would've been angry that I was defying their explicit wishes. Bert and Sue would've said I was violating MOVE law, which would have been a guaranteed ostracization and shunning from the rest of the organization. I had to move stealthily and steadily.

My grandmother LaVerne was gone; MOVE's biggest opportunity in years, with the Phillies win, was squandered; and my faith in MOVE's leadership was at an all-time low. It was into this environment that Robin and I had our fourth child, a girl. We named her Alia, like the singer, just a different spelling.

All my kids had been born on a significant birthday. Alia was perfectly set up to be born on my dad's. But she decided she didn't want to share her day with anybody we knew. So she let Dad's birthday come and go and arrived three days later, on October 9, 2011.

Robin and I already had three boys, so everyone was hoping for a girl for us. When word got out, a lot of people broke the newborn-baby rules and came to see her. Everybody was excited.

By the time Alia was born, a lot of my early fatherhood insecurities had subsided. I held her the day she was born. In fact, Robin had a hard time taking her from me. Alia slept right between us every night. Before she would fall asleep she'd always turn to face me while sucking her thumb and twirling my hair with her tiny hands. I couldn't wait for a year to pass so I could take her to see my parents. The MOVE women followed their same pattern with Alia as they did with my boys, kissing and cooing.

New babies were often sidetracks from how much time was passing. Before long, taking my kids on prison visits consisted of conversations of how tall the boys were growing to be.

"Oh Janet, Alex is as tall as you now," my mom commented.

Janet, who was four feet, eleven inches tall, playfully denied that and wanted to see for herself. "Come here Alex, let me see whose shoulder is the highest," she called out. Alex stood up out of his seat, and before he took one step toward her, she recognized his height and said, "Never mind. Sit down, you giant." He laughed and approached her anyway, and gave her a big hug while lifting her off the ground.

Visiting the MOVE 9, especially visiting the MOVE women, was always a joyous occasion. But in those next few years, things permanently changed.

Internally, I was transforming and maturing. I was an adult in years but not in confidence or wisdom. The next few years were a huge transitional period for me, where I was adjusting to the reality that many of the things I'd been taught to believe were lies. It started to register that leadership in MOVE wasn't trying to get the MOVE 9 home. And that was hard to accept. But it was true.

Something within the organization would have to change. But most people were comfortable with the way things were. And when I tried to get support to start bringing the MOVE 9 home, I was usually met with shrugs. Anybody who could've helped was living in a MOVE house that Bert owned and driving cars she bought them. I needed to become brave enough and courageous enough to stand up to my family. That took me many more years to do because I felt indebted, the same way everyone else did.

One of the most outrageous incidents from this period for me was Birdie's death in 2013. Birdie was the only surviving child of the 1985 bombing. Afterward, his father raised him outside of MOVE. I last saw Birdie when I was a little boy. When I heard that he drowned and had been found dead, I was grief-stricken. But when Bert heard about it, she ridiculed him. She said, "That's what his ass gets. He should've brought his ass back to MOVE." I couldn't believe it. These were the people I had let be in charge of my parents' fates, as well as the fates of the other MOVE 9 prisoners who were still alive.

Two years later, in 2015, Phil Africa, Janine's husband, was the second member of the MOVE 9 to die in prison. Any hesitancy I'd felt about not going full tilt to getting the MOVE 9 home was over. Phil's death was the final straw. I was ready to fight.

Of all the second-generation MOVE members, and some of the first-, no one was closer to Phil than I was. Phil and I were so close that he told prisoners and guards I was his son, the same way Janet described Alex to her fellow inmates as her grandson.

Phil's actual son Uju was in the house on August 8 during the first confrontation between MOVE and the city. He was just a one- or two-year old baby at the time. When Phil and Janine were arrested, Uju went to live with his grandmother, who was not a MOVE member and did not raise him according to MOVE teachings.

Phil hadn't seen Uju since he was a little kid. Uju was so young on the last visit that he didn't remember it. Uju and I connected when one day out of the blue he showed up at the MOVE house on Kingsessing Avenue. He and I immediately started hanging out together and catching up on what we missed about each other's lives. Uju asked me if I would go with him to see his father. I said to him the same thing my father said to me when I asked him if I could go to school: "Sure!" Phil hadn't seen Uju in more than thirty years. I was happy to help them reunite.

Phil's death hurt me and enraged me.

Bert and Sue responded to Phil's death the same way they responded to Merle's. They blamed him for not following Benny's teachings closely enough. There was no outcry from them against the System that kept him in prison for all those years. As they did with Merle, they believed Phil set a bad example for MOVE by dying in prison.

It was a cold-hearted response to the death of someone who spent thirty-seven years in prison. He knew his son Little Phil got killed in the bombing. He had a grandchild whom he never got to know. His incarceration permanently separated him from his wife.

And then, to top it all off, Phil died because he refused medical treatment from the hospital. They said he had cancer. Phil was reluctant to believe the doctors and refused medical intervention in part because Sue and Bert convinced him that MOVE members don't get cancer. They told him that if he really had cancer, then he wasn't really in MOVE. They told him if he continued to study and believe in Benny's teachings, then his mind would be strong enough to overcome whatever was happening to his body.

So Phil didn't get medical treatment, and he died in prison. He was cheated out of thirty-seven years of his life, thirty-seven years without his family, and he lived through his children's violent deaths. I could never forgive Bert and Sue for that.

Of course, it heightened my worries about my parents potentially dying in prison, too. At that time, my father had some ailments. He was prediabetic and had high blood pressure. One day in the shower, he nearly passed out and felt he needed to see a doctor.

He and I started talking about what needed to be done. I was trying to avoid my dad going to hospitals because he was in prison, where the care for inmates is suspect. We were trying to figure out what he was eating and if there was a way to strengthen his immune system. Whatever was going on, we wanted to try to fix it.

Sue got on the phone and told me I was a violator of Benny's teachings if I encouraged my father to go to the hospital. And she said my father was a violator of Benny's, too.

By then, after the death of Merle and now Phil, there was no way I was taking Sue's or Bert's advice, direction, or suggestions. While I did agree to be careful, I tried to help my dad through whatever he felt made the most sense for his health.

My father felt he should go to the hospital, and, fortunately for him, he did because he discovered he was severely anemic. His iron levels and hemoglobin dropped so low that he needed to change his diet. My dad, who was a strict vegan and had been for more than twenty years, was malnourished because of the poor-quality food prison had to offer. He actually needed to start eating meat. With this new information, my dad was able to care for himself with relative ease. I stocked his books with money so he could buy all the meat he needed, and he ate like a champ. I'm happy about that. But left to Sue and Bert, he'd still be suffering and probably much sicker and maybe dead. It made me really want to get him home. And it cut, once and for all, whatever thin thread might've still connected me to Sue and Bert.

I stopped trusting Bert and Sue for anything. And I mean *anything*. They saw me as a rebel, once a loyal subject but now the irritant that was upending their plan to keep the MOVE 9 in prison. They tried to ostracize me with the second generation of MOVE. They told people I was trying to replace Benny and become the new Coordinator of MOVE. It was all nonsense.

The things that I cared about—the future of MOVE, getting the MOVE 9 released—were never on their agendas. In terms of what MOVE did and how MOVE functioned, it was like they were stuck, psychologically, at the bombing from 1985. It was like Sue and Bert were replaying MOVE's greatest hits, protest-wise, and they didn't want to change the record.

But I did.

I kept up my efforts with the parole board. And in 2016, thanks to Chuck, we were finally able to get a lawyer on board. I had tried every attorney in Philly for years. I'd go to movement lawyers and ask for their representation, they'd say they'd help and then not return my calls. I'd call money-hungry lawyers and they never answered the phone. Years earlier, on one of my trips with Pam to California I met with Johnnie Cochran through an introduction from boxer Rubin "Hurricane" Carter, who was wrongfully convicted and then exonerated after nineteen years in prison. Johnnie heard who I needed him to represent and said to me, "Son, I already dodged a bullet—are you trying to get me killed?"

Everywhere I turned, a door was slammed in my face. Chuck was growing further frustrated. Delbert was breaking down crying at the mention of Phil's name. People were suffering from so much lost time.

All of the surviving MOVE 9 members got a letter from a law student named Brad Thompson that had a plan to represent victims of systematic injustice. Chuck was the only person to respond to the inquiry. I first met Brad at the MOVE conference, where we briefly talked about how he could help if he were to pass the bar exam. I stayed connected to him by phone, cheering him on. Once he passed the bar, we began to develop a strategy. It was simple, and it was the same thing Paul Hetznecker had advised years before: try for parole. Dad reluctantly agreed with this tactic, though he never let me forget he didn't like it. He wanted a court to overturn his conviction so that he could be completely free. But we strong-armed him, and Dad caved to me. Brad and I, with Chuck and my dad's guidance, constructed what I called the three-legged stool plan. I remembered reading John Africa's writings. He would say "the System is controlled by pressure." Whenever he wrote about pressuring the System, he mentioned the courts, the prisons, and the streets. So I tried to think of ways to apply pressure in those places. It's not hard to apply pressure. But you do have to know where the pressure points are. The people most directly in a position to free my family were at the Pennsylvania Department of Probation and Parole.

"We're going to put together intentional support packets that will show how great your family is," Brad said. "But I need help to do it. We need to make sure it gets into the correct hands. We have to bypass the MOVE haters and see to it that it doesn't end up in the trash. We also need help to do this."

Once Brad became a lawyer, he began work with the People's Law Office out of Chicago. Brad felt we needed a Pennsylvania lawyer's support. So he called for help from Bret Grote, who was chief counsel for political prisoner Russell Maroon Shoats. At this point, the MOVE 9, except for my dad and Chuck, were largely indifferent to the path home from prison. Some of them didn't feel they had much to come home to. So I didn't have resistance from them about *how* to get them released. Only my dad and Chuck were telling me they wanted to come home. With the rest, I had to play my moves like a chess game. I knew getting my dad and Chuck would make it easier to get my mom. And if I had my mom, I knew I could nudge Janet and Janine to get on board. Bert and Sue couldn't find out anything until the MOVE 9 were in full agreement. That way they couldn't derail the whole thing. It felt like I was trying to swim and not get wet.

The organization's internal disagreement on legal issues created fragments throughout the group. Sue was a vocal opponent in every way. At a MOVE study session I attended where we were discussing MOVE 9 business, she busted in the front door, interrupted the meeting, and said the unthinkable: "You can do all you want to do with them lawyers and it ain't gonna mean shit. The MOVE 9 ain't supposed to come home. You're just wasting your time." I was surprised she said this in front of everyone at the meeting, but I was glad that she finally said it without beating around the bush.

I did have a few people cheering me on, though. I could always talk to Moe. We were always close, even before he was my father-in-law. He supported what I was doing and said he saw no wrong in it. Pam was encouraging even though she was conflicted, too. DeeDee, one of the women in an adjacent jail cell when I was born, provided great support for me. When I'd reach out to Moe for guidance, in typical MOVE fashion he'd say, "Don't listen to that bullshit, Mike. You just keep on doing what you're doing. Sometimes you have to be an army of one. Don't let them stop you."

That was all I needed to hear. I went into overdrive. I set up meetings with officials and street organizers so frequently and with so little notice that others didn't have time in their schedules to attend. But I never made any decision without consulting with each of the MOVE 9. I needed cover in case Bert or Sue tried to interfere. I needed to be able to say, "The MOVE 9 already approved this."

The talks with Brad Thompson and Bret Grote became more common. I also kept looking for help from others. Whenever I came across an activist, organizer, or official who could assist in any capacity, I brought them into the mix.

I took many of the lawyers, supporters, and even an ex-cop investigator turned supporter to meet the MOVE 9. We crisscrossed all over the state of Pennsylvania visiting and getting acquainted. I also took the investigator to meet Delbert, Eddie, and my dad. The MOVE 9 women said they didn't need a visit from any type of cop, retired or not. They felt that if the MOVE 9 men thought the cop was okay, then the cop was okay.

The calls, the meetings, and the traveling absorbed nearly every waking hour of my days. Things seemed to be moving. Until Delbert and Eddie changed their minds.

Bert and Sue found out what I was up to and talked them into backing out. I had to talk Bert and Sue into backing off by telling them my parents and Chuck would be coming home without the others. That seemed to fend them off. The last thing they wanted was to deal with angry MOVE men who were not restricted by prison walls anymore. The grace of quick thinking saved me in that moment, but I knew Bert and Sue would continue looking for ways to interfere.

To get ahead of their next step, I called Bert and Sue to set up a family meeting about MOVE 9 business. I thought including them in the decision-making process might keep them at bay. They both sounded awful when I called, and they told me they weren't feeling well enough to meet. Then I called Ramona, to see how she felt about meeting. Ramona sounded worse than Bert and Sue. She said she hadn't been feeling right for quite some time and even a conference call was more than she felt able to participate in. But she did have enough energy to give me a quick pep talk.

"Listen, Kita," she told me, "you've been in this organization all of your life. You have plenty of MOVE law and you know how to talk to people. You are going to have to handle this situation. If you need help, I'll be here. But right now, you must do this on your own."

Music to my ears.

The ball was now in my court, and I wasn't giving it back. Not until I had secured the release of every living MOVE 9 member. Adding to the good news, something amazing happened. I got a huge sign of encouragement. The Philadelphia Eagles were headed to the Super Bowl. This was the universe conspiring with me. This was the moment.

Chapter 22

SECURING THE PACKAGE

I didn't know how I was going to do it. But I knew Benny had represented himself in court and had freed himself. If there was a way to free the MOVE 9, I figured it had to be in his writings.

I scoured every page like a man possessed, searching for some sort of knowledge that would apply to the situation the MOVE 9 was in. I had all the old cassette tapes Bert had given me when we used to be cool. The tapes contained mostly jazz music from the 1930s, but in certain spots Benny's voice would echo through the tape player. I played cassette after cassette from beginning to end, usually listening to thirty minutes of Dinah Washington or Nat King Cole and eventually thirty seconds of the needle in the haystack. On one tape I heard a deep deliberate voice say, "They don't know how to fight MOVE." I listened intensely. On this tape, Benny talked about how to apply pressure. He said, "What are you going to do when MOVE people begin demonstrating at your houses, at your churches, at your synagogues? . . . The System is controlled by pressure and we're going to keep the pressure on you, in the courts, on the streets, and in the prisons." I went back to those old letters my mom was writing to me with the captions, and the answer was there all along. Apply pressure in the courts, on the streets, and in the prisons.

I had read Benny's writings about the importance of applying pressure, but hearing him talk about it was so very stirring for me. Any fears I had about Bert and Sue were completely gone. I was in the zone. So much so that I stopped being as guarded about my plans. There was no pushback they could give me that I didn't have an answer for.

Benny had a phrase about how to apply pressure "on the streets, in the courts, and in the prisons," which meant that we had to maneuver and work as often as possible in those three areas: street pressure, prison pressure, and legal pressure.

On the legal side of things, I felt the MOVE 9 should apply for commutations and pardons through the Pennsylvania Board of Pardons. It required extensive paperwork. I used my own money to pay for the forms because Bert refused to use money from the MOVE settlement to cover the costs. Bert and Sue convinced the MOVE 9 women that accepting commutation would imply they were admitting guilt.

In a fit of rage, I went to Bert's house and demanded, "Show me where it says that. Find for me on the printed form I sent you where it says anything about admitting guilt." She couldn't find it after looking for twenty minutes.

"Well, it's implied," Sue said. We've heard of people who have done it and it's an unwritten rule that you have to say you are guilty."

I was pissed off but mostly at myself. I should have never gotten so comfortable showing my hand to people who had made it clear they were working against me. I guess my past memories of what a family I thought we were blinded me to the reality that they were my biggest hurdles. They were finding every excuse they could think of to stop the freedom process. But no matter, I proceeded with my hard push.

I put MOVE's new legal team—Bret Grote and Brad Thompson—in touch with the previous lawyer, Paul Hetznecker. Paul had absolutely no interest in getting involved again. He told me the MOVE 9 case was a "bottomless rabbit hole" while we sat in his office downtown. "MOVE members are not trained attorneys yet they think they know everything about the law. They are unreceptive to new findings or issues of clarification. They seldom all agree on anything. Their personalities are defiant and arrogant. It's so frustrating when I attempt to move the case along and get held up by one of them because of something they heard from an ignorant jailhouse lawyer." Paul was out for good.

Ironically, the reasons for Paul's reluctance were the exact problems that were being spit in my face like from a llama. But Brad and Bret assured me that they could handle the case with or without Paul's help. I trusted that.

With the legal part in play, I spent more time on creating the "streets" part. We already had a lot of support from years of demonstrations, forums, rallies, and speaking engagements, and I had worldwide contacts. I wanted to make the MOVE 9 known on a more mainstream level. A few years earlier Ramona had introduced me to a Hollywood producer named Tommy Oliver. He was very interested in making a documentary about MOVE history. He and I took many trips to the prisons to meet the MOVE 9 and Mumia, too. Watching him work on his film projects gave me insight on marketing and promoting with narratives. Using this knowledge, I crafted a social media and publicity campaign to raise awareness for the eyes of key members of the parole board and other officials. All those years of traveling with Ramona and Pam were paying off. Unfortunately, Ramona was now on the sidelines. It was too bad that an illness put her there.

I continued working with Bret and Brad. I intensely read the parole denial letters. We had to challenge the reasons for denial. The denial letters said things like, "Lack of motivation for success," "Failure to accept responsibility for the crime," "Minimization of the crime, "Lack of support from the prosecuting attorney." None of the reasons cited seemed consistent with the information I knew about the MOVE 9. But it wasn't me who was judging them. My approach was to whittle the list of reasons for denial down to none.

I started with the easiest one: "Lack of recommendation from the prosecuting attorney." I told Brad, "We need to get that removed. How can the original prosecuting attorney have a say in parole? He hasn't seen the MOVE members in over thirty years. He doesn't know them. The prison officials at every prison holding a MOVE member recommends them for parole. That should be good enough."

Brad agreed. The parole packet we compiled included that information.

Everything on the list of denials we had a good response for except for one: "Failure to accept responsibility for the crime." The surviving MOVE 9 members were never going to admit to killing anyone. We needed a workaround and gave this issue deep thought. We had to find out what the parole board wanted to see.

I got Mom to ask one of the longtime guards what the parole board was looking for. Mom found out that the parole board doesn't come out and ask direct questions. They have a conversation with an inmate and surmise by the responses what the inmate's true intentions are.

I shared this tidbit with the MOVE 9 members and the lawyers. It would prove valuable.

We also found out that the parole board recommended MOVE members attend anger management classes, and reentry-into-society classes.

Mom signed up immediately to take the classes. She signed up for everything that was available, got on the waiting list for what wasn't available, and took classes that weren't even required. Dad was angered by the idea of taking classes. He said to me, "Mike, I have taken every class this prison offers." He didn't see how taking more would make a difference. The rest of the MOVE 9 outright refused, including Chuck. They were all insulted.

Janet let her feelings be known, screeching, "Anger management?! Them motherfuckers would be angry, too, if we did to them what the fuck they did to us."

I couldn't really care less about what hoops the board was trying to make the MOVE 9 jump through. I just didn't want to leave any stone unturned. And I didn't want anyone left behind for my lack of effort. Mom was giving full effort. Dad felt he had already done all the stuff I was asking. Delbert, Eddie, Janet, and Janine remained unmovable. They were okay with me trying my parole plan, but they wouldn't take the classes. Chuck felt it was destiny that I'd get him out and there was nothing more he needed to do. "No classes are necessary," he said.

I pursued Dad's and Mom's cases. The others wouldn't listen, but I left the door open in case they changed their minds. As for my father, I admit, a huge motivation for me was how much my dad loved me. As he put it, "I would spend the rest of my life and die in this prison before I ever see you spend one day hurt." I knew that if I didn't try everything, I'd never be able to sleep at night. I'd never forgive myself if he died in prison. Same thing with my mom.

Mom's next parole board hearing was in May 2018, a few months after the Eagles beat the greatest NFL quarterback of all time to win the Super Bowl. We got another crack at it. It was her ninth appearance in front of them. She anxiously called me and told me she felt good about how the hearing went. A few days later I got a call from an unfamiliar Harrisburg, Pennsylvania, number. I was at home by myself.

"Hello?" I answered.

"Hi," a young man said. "Is this the son of Debbie Sims, prison number 006307?"

I was on guard immediately. "Who dis?"

"This is Agent Johnson from the Pennsylvania Board of Probation and Parole. Is this Michael?"

"Yes, this is Michael."

"I understand that you'll be the home provider for Miss Sims if she is to be paroled?"

The space around me fell still, and my heart jumped through my T-shirt. "Yeah," I replied, trying to sound like I wasn't filled with a sudden nervous energy.

"Okay, great. When can I come look at your house to make sure it's suitable for her as a stable and safe living environment?"

"You can come right now!" I couldn't believe what I was hearing.

"How about this evening around six?"

"Perfect!"

"Okay, I have some questions first. Do you have any drugs, alcohol, firearms, other dangerous weapons, vicious dogs, or animals in the house?"

"No, unless you count a kitchen knife."

"Kitchen knives are not a problem. Okay then, sir, I'll see you tonight."

"Wait, Agent Johnson, does this mean that my mom is coming home?" I was dying to know.

"No sir, it only means that the results of the parole hearing are positive. I can't say for sure what will happen. But I can tell you that the guys upstairs don't call me unless they are scheduling a release."

"Okay. Thank you, Agent Johnson, I'll see you tonight."

I hung up the phone and jumped as high as I could. I called Robin right away. The house was tidy. Robin always kept a clean house, so we didn't have to do much.

When I got home, I gathered my kids Alex, Koby, Tommy, and Alia to explain the situation.

"Y'all, it's a good chance that Grandmom Deedee could come home." I didn't want to get their hopes up, but I had to tell them because they needed to know. I was scared but so excited. My emotions were all over the place.

"Really?!" they all answered, beaming. I could see their eyes light up. I could see them hoping as much as I was hoping.

"Yes, really." I smiled big. "My question to you guys is, since there's six of us living here and we have five bedrooms, would either of you be willing to give up your bedroom for your grand-mother?"

With no hesitation, all the kids hollered, "Yeah!" Then they start running around the house discussing with each other whose room was the biggest so Mom could have a nice-size space. Then I remembered that we needed to relocate a few things. Around the house, we had swords, a bow-and-arrow set, and throwing stars, and the kids had BB guns. No firearms.

The next day, Robin talked to my mom and sneakily found out her favorite colors, which were a mix of pastels. By the time I got home at the end of the day, the walls in Mom's new bedroom were painted. Robin and the kids were not playing around. They also decorated the room with paintings that Mom had sent home from some prison art classes that she took. Things were feeling really good.

Still, I tried not to get my hopes up too high. I didn't want to be disappointed.

Then two weeks later, the news came. I was driving home from work. My phone rang. It was Mom. In a voice barely above a whisper, she told me her parole papers arrived. She was whispering because she didn't want Janet and Janine to hear her.

"Kita, are you driving?" she asked.

"Yeah, Mom," I said impatiently. "What's the word?"

"The Pennsylvania Parole Board has approved me to come home."

Best words I ever heard: "approved to come home."

I was overcome with so much adrenaline and emotion that I almost drove off the road. We chatted for a moment, then I told Mom to call again in a few hours when I'd be with Robin and some of the other family members that I trusted to keep our secret.

Then I called Robin straightaway. She had been my rock through the whole process. I was talking so fast when I called her to share the news, she couldn't understand a word I said.

"Honey, calm down. Now what are you saying?"

I repeated myself. "My mom got approved for parole. She's coming home."

That's when Robin started screaming with excitement so much I couldn't understand a word *she* was saying. I wanted to share the news with the world, but I knew better. Bert and Sue did not need to know Mom was coming home until Mom was in my car with me. I could not trust that that would not try to sabotage her release in some way. I'd heard of cases where news of "cop killers" were released from prison and their release was held up because of backlash from police and cop-loving citizens. That was the last thing I needed to happen for my mom.

The next week was painstaking. It was nothing but waiting. I couldn't sleep. I could barely eat. It was unbearable. We didn't know exactly when she would be released or when we could go get her. But then on June 15, 2018, at 7 a.m., my phone rang. There was an unfamiliar Erie, Pennsylvania, number on the caller ID.

"Hello?" I answered.

"Hi, is this Michael Africa, the caretaker for Debbie Sims Africa?"

"Yes!" It could only be one thing.

"Good morning, Michael. I am Mr. Stuart. I have your mother right here with me and we're trying to figure out when you can come and pick her up."

I knew the prison was seven hours away, but I told Mr. Stuart, "I'll be there in twenty minutes."

"How soon can you safely get here?" Mr. Stuart replied.

I laughed. "I can get there tomorrow morning."

"Great. We open at eight. Can you get here at seven? We'd like to avoid any media attention."

"I'll be there at seven a.m. Thank you, Mr. Stuart. Have a nice day."

It was the most exciting news of my life. My mom was coming home. Forty years of waiting was finally coming to an end. I couldn't stop smiling. My cheeks were hurting. The best part about it was I got to share the news with my mom's number one, from day one. Minutes later my phone rang.

"You have a collect call from a Pennsylvania Correctional Facility SCI Phoenix."

It was Dad. From the moment we found out Mom had gotten parole and would be coming home soon, Dad called me several times a day for updates.

"Hey Dad, I got a call from Mom."

"Yeah?"

"I'm picking her up tomorrow."

Dad was dead silent for a full five minutes. The only way I knew he didn't hang up the phone is because I could hear background noise. I couldn't tell if he was crying or smiling. But I knew this was a real dream come true and a huge relief. He had loved my mom since he first met her in West Philly on Reno Street in 1969. I think at times he wanted her to have her freedom more than he wanted his own. Finally, he answered with one somber, satisfied word, "Great!"

I explained to him that although I was happy to get this far, I wouldn't believe Mom was coming home until she was in the car with me. Dad agreed. I told Mom not to tell Janine and Janet because I knew they would've been uncooperative. If they knew Mom was going home, they would most definitely tell Bert and Sue immediately.

At this point I had three things to do. Number one was "securing the package," the code phrase I used that meant Mom was in my car and on her way home. Number two was securing myself. For that I needed Robin and Alia along for moral support, and Moe. My boys stayed back to finish getting the house ready for the Welcome Home party they were throwing with a few family members. I asked my sister Whit if she wanted to go with me for the ride, and she said no. I guessed Whit would see Mom when she was ready. Brad Thompson came for the ride, though, in case we needed his legal expertise at the very end. Bret Grote would've come but he was in court. Third, I wanted the event documented. So I called Tommy Oliver. He was more excited than I expected him to be. He came immediately from a shoot for his television show *Black Love*.

We drove from 11 p.m. until 6 a.m. to the prison. We drove through the night in dense, foggy Pennsylvania mountains and in and out of rainy weather patterns. As we walked to the entrance, a guard opened the door. I could see Mom standing and waiting. I finally realized this was real. I walked up to her and gave her a giant hug. Then Robin hugged her, and we all hugged in a huddle, taking in the moment. The two guards at the desk had gotten to know Mom over the years. They were crying. They were so happy to see Mom finally going home.

Robin and I bought new clothes for Mom to change into. She had been wearing a brown prison uniform since she was in her early twenties. Mom went into a restroom to change. When she came out, she looked like new money. I'd never seen her in person in any clothes other than prison browns. We grabbed her bags and her storage trunk, and we walked to my car with me pumping my fist in the air. Mom held my hand as I led her to the car. We piled in.

The pick-up time for Mom was 7:00. Dad was calling my phone at 7:01. "This is a call from the State Correctional Institution at Phoenix." Before he had to ask, I said "Dad, I got the package. The package is in my car about to go home." Dad said one word: "great."

Before we took off, I had to make calls to our family. I called Whit first. She was so shocked she didn't know what to say. I took a picture of Mom and I sitting side by side in the car and sent it to some friends with the message, "Share this."

We had a list of people to call on the car ride home.

"Mom, who do you want to call first?" I asked her. She wanted to call her sisters Scarlet and Gail, then her aunt Louise. The call to Louise was amazing. "Debbie! Debbie! I'm jumping ten feet off the ground. I may not get that high but I'm definitely trying!" she said as she gasped for breath.

I called Violet and told her and Allen. Violet was one of the kids in Virginia in the Seed of Wisdom. Violet said she had some news, too.

"Let me share mine first," I jumped in. "Check this picture out. I'm texting it to you." The picture could say it better than I could.

"That's nice, Kita. I'm happy for you." She sounded too sad to be happy for me.

"What's wrong?" I couldn't understand that sadness in Violet's voice.

"Ramona is in the hospital. She was diagnosed with stage IV cancer. And while she was there being checked out, she had a stroke. It's bad, Kita."

My heart sank. I kept the news to myself to allow everyone else to enjoy the moment of my mom coming home. There were relatives and friends she had never met in person or hadn't seen in decades. Everybody we could think of reached out. But there was no sign of Bert or Sue. Not a visit, not even a phone call to welcome Mom home.

It didn't stop anything.

By June 2018, I had incredible momentum. Now that Mom was home, I knew there was no way we couldn't get the same result for my dad, Uncle Chuck, and the remaining MOVE 9 prisoners.

On the ride home, I was looking forward to watching Mom eat the food she hadn't eaten in years. I didn't realize how much she was trapped in a time warp. The last time she was home was in 1978. A lot had changed by 2018. When she went to wash her hands, she was looking for knobs on the sink, but the sink had sensors. Mom was thinking about how different things were, and the analogy she came up with was she went to prison during *The Flintstones* and came home during *The Jetsons*. Cars moved at what seemed like lightning speed. This was not something we all experienced, but Mom was so used to the rate of people that cars seemed to move faster for her.

We rode back home, and as we did, Mom looked out the window at all the animals on the farms and modern civilization. She was shocked to see buildings that were much taller than the Philadelphia City Hall. In the 1970s, it was uncommon for construction to be built higher than William Penn's hat. A giant statue of Penn wearing his signature Quaker hat is at the top of City Hall, as a symbol that nothing was bigger than the laws of the city's government. By 2018, Philadelphia had skyscrapers that dwarfed William Penn.

Mom received hugs and kisses from her sisters and family and friends, nieces and nephews, people who she watched grow up through pictures and whose voices she heard change over the years through phone calls. She got a chance to watch old videos of the kids in home movie collections. She got a chance to see herself in her own bedroom. Mom ate one food plate after the other. At first, she didn't realize she could get seconds because no guard was standing to give her permission. Being home was a lot to adjust to. But it was glorious nonetheless.

Chapter 23

THE MAN WITH THE FREEDOM PAPERS

I couldn't pay Bert and Sue any mind. I had to make sure I secured the release of the greatest man alive, my dad. I knew I needed reinforcements.

At that time, Wilson Goode, the former mayor, was honored with his very own street sign, Wilson Goode Way, in a section of West Philly called Wynnefield. This honor came with a large group of protestors at his house and in the neighborhood calling for the privilege to be revoked. With pressure on his back, Wilson Goode gave an interview on WURD, a local Black talk radio station, and said he wanted to support MOVE for the rest of his life.

Hearing the FOP leader's comments, I knew reinforcements could help, so I called Wilson Goode. Dad and I spoke at length about the comments the mayor made. Dad wasn't shocked by what Goode said. One of Dad's issues with Bert dated back to 1988 when Goode made similar comments in support of MOVE that Bert was unwilling to follow up on. Of course, one could understand why a MOVE member would have a hard time meeting with the man who dropped a bomb and killed eleven MOVE members. But if they can meet to collect a check for $2.5 million, why not meet to free our people?

Now, more than thirty years after the bombing, we had to see if Wilson Goode's claims of support were true. Someone would have to meet with him in person.

"It has to be you, Mike." Dad explained. "Anybody else would fuck it up. You can't leave our freedom in the hands of anyone that doesn't have the kind of care for us as you do."

This was not something I wanted to hear. I was certainly not going to meet with the "Boogie Man" without full approval from the entire organization. I needed to get approval from the parents of the children who had been murdered in the May 13 bombing. I went back to my box of tapes for guidance and strength, looking for anything to help clear my blurred vision. After hours of listening, I heard Benny's voice say:

"Anybody that wants to help MOVE do what we're doing, we welcome them."

He said, "Anybody." I knew if I shared that quote from the Coordinator with the group, they would be forced to step aside and allow the meeting to happen. Armed with Benny's own words in case I needed it, I called a MOVE meeting.

It was a very emotional and occasionally heated discussion. Everybody showed up—about forty MOVE members. Not supporters, but actual members. It was by far the most attended MOVE meeting we'd had in years. People were pissed at me for even suggesting such an idea. I was prepared to abandon the idea myself, because to be honest, I had no interest in meeting the man who was responsible for murdering my family. If everyone was not on board, unanimously, I was not going to do it. Because everyone listened to Bert, I knew that to win over the rest of the organization I had to get her to sanction the move. After hours of debate and argument, I brought into use my quote from Benny's writings as John Africa. I emphasized the word "anybody." The room was silent. I dressed up my statement with a simple question. To Taylor, who had been one of the most vocally opposed, I asked him, "If it was your father in prison, would you take every opportunity to free him or allow your emotions to overlook an opportunity?"

Taylor hung his head and said nothing.

I asked the same question to Allen and Violet.

Finally, I asked the question to Bert about her son, Zack, who we all went through the custody drama for. After a long silence Bert said, "If it will help the MOVE 9 get out, I don't see why we shouldn't do it. But since it is your father, Kita, you're gonna have to be the one to do it. Plus, you understand the case, and you have the right temperament."

I was so over Bert, but I needed this moment with her in front of everybody. With Bert's approval, all the other MOVE members would fall in line and stay off my back. My plan was working. Checkmate.

I was happy with the feeling of progress, but the idea of actually meeting Goode in person nearly stopped my heart. I left the MOVE meeting shaking.

The following morning, on September 22, 2018, I made the hardest phone call I ever had to make. My hands shook so much I dialed the wrong number five or six times before getting it right. While contemplating what to say, on the third ring a raspy man's voice said, "This is Wilson Goode."

It was chilling! I struggled to speak but then found the words. Mayor Goode was expecting my call, so I dove right in. "Mayor, all my life, you've been the boogeyman. And I really don't know what to say to you. You . . . you said that you were willing to help."

Feeling my discomfort, Goode cut in. "My father spent time in jail, too, so I know you want your father home," he said. Just as he had on the radio, Goode again pledged to me that he would do whatever he could to get my family home. We set up an in-person meeting. We only spoke for about three minutes, but I knew it was the start of many conversations.

Ahead of our first face-to-face meeting, again, I called Tommy

Oliver and asked him to film it. I wanted everything documented for posterity.

As the date approached, it was hard for me to think about it. I felt like I was betraying the memory of my young MOVE brothers and sisters that this man's police force murdered. But I had to put all that aside and focus on the task at hand. My dad would do anything for me. I had to give him the same effort he gave to me no matter how hard or uncomfortable it was. I also felt a tremendous respect for the other MOVE 9 members, too. As much as they were a pain in the ass, they still deserved to be free. Wilson Goode wrote support letters for the MOVE 9, which I took to lawyer Brad Thomson so he could add them to the parole packets. I felt it was a good rebuttal to the FOP. I endured months of mind-numbing and emotional torment, but at least I had something valuable to show for it. Those letters were a building block that I also had sent to newly crowned district attorney Larry Krasner, a prosecutor whose political campaign trumpeted the slogan "Progressive DA."

In September 2018, Dad saw the parole board. It was his ninth appearance in front of them, just like it had been with my mom. He called me on the phone and told me he felt good about the interview. "The agent only asked just a few simple questions. It was very different from all the last interviews. He asked me, what did I plan to do if I were to be paroled. I told him, 'I plan to live with my wife at my son's house with my son's family.'"

A couple of days later, I got another call from Agent Johnson. This time I knew it was him because I had saved his number in my phone under "The Man with the Freedom Papers." We did the same question-answer process as when Mom was about to come home.

After a few weeks, I got the call from Dad informing me of his release date, which was two weeks away—October 23, 2018. Dad had spent more than two thousand weeks in prison and now had only two more to go.

His pickup day finally arrived. Unlike driving to get Mom, SCI Phoenix is only an hour away from home. When we got to the prison the guards had the doors locked. They were having a meeting that felt like it was taking forever but was actually five minutes. They finally opened the doors and let us inside. After we'd waited about thirty minutes, Dad came walking into the room escorted by a prison guard. The first time I met my dad in 1982, I'd asked him if he should come home with me. Finally he was coming home with me. Gray-bearded, with less hair on his head, the old man was finally free. We hugged each other a long, long time. Robin and Alia hugged him while the boys, my mom, and the rest of our crew were back home planning another Welcome Home party. We went into the bathroom, and he snatched off the prison browns and changed into the clothes we bought him. Then I put my arm around his neck and said, "Alright Dad, let's go home."

What was about to happen is hard for me to describe today. "A long time coming" doesn't quite capture it. I'm not a religious dude, but knowing my parents were about to see each other for the first time in forty years was an out-of-body experience for me. They knew they still loved each other. For decades, they wrote each other letters and declared their undying devotion. I don't know that either of them ever expected they'd see each other again. They held on to the hope of it. And now it was about to happen. I was driving my dad—my hero—back to Philly not just to be with family but to be with the love of his life.

I was forty years old, and I had never seen my parents together. I had never heard them speak to each other. I had never seen them touch. I had never seen the two people who created me in the same room. I'd never seen them argue or seen my mom cut her eyes at my dad, or seen my dad lose his patience with my mom. I had never seen a man and a woman who loved each other disagree about something and work it out.

They defied every odd and were making their ways back to each other.

Mom was at home anxiously waiting for my call. I dialed the number. She answered before the first ring finished.

"Kita?" Her voice was full of expectation.

"Mom, I got the package."

After a long pause over a trembling voice, Mom said one word. It was the same word Dad said when I picked Mom up and talked to him. "Great!"

Dad and I had more calls to make. We called Whit. She was at work and tried not to scream too loudly. My other older sisters, Dee and Reecy, whom my dad had before he committed to my mom, kept repeating, "Oh my God! Oh my God!"

My father was the youngest of eight siblings. Only four of them were still living. We called them next.

"Hey Big Sis," he said to my aunt Neat. "I'm on my way home." She burst into tears of joy. He called my Uncle Pete, whose reaction was the best. Hearing Dad say "I'm on my way home," Uncle Pete let out a long Woody Woodpecker giggle. When we called Uncle Jimmy, Aunt Olivia answered the phone. Uncle Jimmy was in the middle of a surgical procedure.

Meanwhile, Mom was interrupting the calls to Dad's loved ones because every fifteen minutes she wanted an ETA from us. Dad couldn't believe how fast everything was moving on the road. He asked me to slow down. So the one-hour drive took thirty minutes longer. We finally got to the house.

Mom and Dad saw each other and collided into each other's arms. The house full of people erupted with cheers. I was happy I could help reunite two people who desperately wanted to be back together and who deserved to be back together. To see them connect to each other was worth every bit of anguish. It was worth every moment with Wilson Goode. It was worth every argument with Bert to see those people finally get a chance to have the only thing they really wanted. I cried like a child. There was not a dry eye among us. People had risked their lives and their kids' lives fighting to free the MOVE 9. After two had died in prison, two were finally home.

Over the following two years, Wilson Goode kept his word. I continued meeting with him about bringing Janet, Janine, Eddie, Delbert, and Chuck home. And we did. In that order.

Delbert was home for about six months before he died of prostate and bone cancer.

Chuck was home for about a year before he died from colorectal cancer. He died eight years to the day after Birdie.

EPILOGUE

Grief is winding and still I smile.

I think about the children in the MOVE bombing every day. Netta, Tree, Delisha, Little Phil, Tomaso, and Birdie. The bombing itself, I don't think about every day. But the kids, I do. It's always been this way for me.

I remember asking my grandmother LaVerne a couple months after the bombing, "When can we go see them?" I told her I missed everybody. I wanted to see them with my own eyes.

LaVerne paused. I didn't know what she was thinking. But now I know she was weighing what to say to me. It was 1985. I was only six or seven years old. I had been surrounded by so much death and violence, but I was still learning how to be with it. LaVerne had to gauge how much I could take.

She didn't say, "The kids are dead," which was the truth. Instead, she said, "You want to see Tomaso?" It was the first step in her offering me a new way to think about what happened to my family.

My answer was quick. "Yes!" I said, "I haven't seen him in a long time. I want to go visit Tomaso and them."

LaVerne looked at me, pausing from washing dishes in the kitchen sink. "Look outside. Look out the window."

Just as I did, a bright red cardinal landed on a tree branch.

"Whenever you miss your brothers and sisters, if you want to see them, look outside. See life, and you'll see them."

I never asked to see the kids again.

I could've easily been in the Osage Avenue house and died in the bombing. The kids killed in the bombing could've easily been at the Reno Street house and still be alive. It feels so random. I see adults today that I imagine the kids would look like if they had lived to be grown. I remember seeing a woman at a farmer's market about Tree's age—so around fifty years old at the time—and I couldn't stop staring. Robin had to yank me away. I didn't see the kids get killed. As many times as I've heard the story and seen the news clippings, there's still a small tinge of hope in the back of my mind, like, *maybe they're not really gone*. I know the truth. But like I said, grief is winding.

There's a town not far from Philly called Lancaster, Pennsylvania. And on the way out there, there used to be a big sign for directions to a farm that read "Tomaso's Tomatoes." I've never heard of another person named Tomaso before. I've gone to that farm to try to see the owner. To see if he had pale skin and resembled the kid I used to play with in the snow. To see if it's the Tomaso I knew. The closeness among the members in MOVE has kept memories of those killed alive—in heart, in mind, and in spirit.

What's odd for me sometimes is that theirs was a very public death that made major international news, but it's so little remembered and even more poorly understood.

I think most people don't know what MOVE is and never knew what it is about. That includes some of the people who were in it. Some people think MOVE is a bunch of bad motherfuckers that you best not mess with. Some people think MOVE is the people who helped their son when he was getting bullied at school. Some people think MOVE is a group of people who helped them pass their time in prison a little more easily and helped keep the guards off their backs. I think, overall, society thought MOVE was a crazy cult of people who wanted to fight the police. But you'll get different answers from different people.

Most people don't know MOVE members were animal rights activists. Most people don't know MOVE members were environmentalists. Most people don't know that MOVE members were prison rights advocates and civil rights activists. Most people simply don't know.

Part of the reason for the misunderstanding is the cult stigma that the public associated with MOVE almost from the very beginning. Honestly, I think MOVE, in some ways, was cultish. But so is Christianity, so is Buddhism, so is Judaism, and so are all the rest of the organized religions. But those groups aren't called cults. It reminds me of how some people use phrases like "Black on Black crime," but you never hear them say "white on white crime." So I don't like when people categorize MOVE as a cult, though I understand why they do. My position is, if you are ignorant about MOVE, I would like for you to become educated.

Boiling everything MOVE is and ever was down to the word "cult" makes it easy to keep people away from the positive aspects of the organization. If people are not having their babies in hospitals because they're having them at home, I wonder how doctors would feel about that. I wonder how pharmaceutical companies would feel about that. If zoos were no longer allowed to hold animals captive and on display, I wonder how zoo owners would feel about that. There's a lot of money wrapped up in the industries of which MOVE has strong opinions. MOVE's beliefs, if acted upon, would disrupt larger systems. It behooves the directors of these systems to classify MOVE with a negative connotation because MOVE is interfering with their money. You don't need to like MOVE to see how deep-pocketed businesses benefit from writing the organization off as cult members.

One thing that MOVE didn't do well was to deliver a clear message. It's been interesting to watch animal rights groups become more accepted within mainstream American society. Same with environmentalists. And women having children at home and at birthing centers is not considered countercultural or weird. People for the Ethical Treatment of Animals (PETA) has really clear messaging. It's right there in the name. When you see them, they're at furriers and farms protesting against animal abuse, and so on. It's really clear. MOVE didn't do a good job of being clear in that way. MOVE did the protesting, but cursed the cops and made such a ruckus that the news headlines were usually more about the ruckus than the reason for the protests. So I'm not surprised at the misunderstanding the public has about the organization.

MOVE's mission is simple. It's to protect all life: people, animals, and the environment. That's it.

At its peak, MOVE had about fifty members and another forty to fifty people who were considered close supporters. The number of people who rooted for MOVE or who sympathized with MOVE is much, much larger. I look at activist organizations today and see so many similarities. It's heartening and disheartening at the same time. Heartening because a new generation of folks have taken up the same fights MOVE fought, disheartening because those fights are still necessary.

In March 2023, legal ownership of MOVE was transferred to me. My family—meaning the blood family of my great-uncle Benny, who is known in his teachings as John Africa and who founded MOVE—has entrusted me to take our legacy into the next chapter, with our eyes open and in a positive direction. I am the Legacy Director. Bert and Sue, who led MOVE for many years after Benny was killed, still consider themselves MOVE members. But I don't follow them anymore because they have moved so far from my understanding of John Africa's teachings. They're on their own path and I'm on mine. I don't know if it was the sheer magnitude of the trauma from the bombing and everything that came after, if it was the millions of dollars they had at their fingertips, or if it was their position of influence after Benny was killed—but something in Bert and Sue would not allow them to propel MOVE forward. And they resisted steps that anybody could have taken to propel MOVE forward. Benny, when he started MOVE, said it best: "When things don't move, they die." Bert and Sue forgot that along the way.

To wear the MOVE label is to be attached to a fraught history that invites uncomfortable questions and constant scrutiny. I don't blame anybody for supporting the work but not wanting the burden of the label. This goes even for my immediate family.

But being a member of MOVE means something to me. It means working to make a change and doing the activities that the organization has always done to make people aware of the System's imposition on life. You are a MOVE member only if you do those things. The others don't do those things, so they're not members. MOVE members are active.

I would like to see the future of MOVE be what it was intended to be. It's such a big task, a daunting task. It makes me feel vulnerable a lot of the time but confident, too. At times, I have felt that nothing I've done to recast MOVE in the public's eyes was working. But I'm confident that it can because history is remembered by how it gets recorded. This book is my recording. I know it matters. Freeing my parents is a recording. All of my work to inspire people to keep moving despite the challenges they face is a recording. I'm On a Move, and I have no intention of slowing down. The more goals I reach, the more momentum I gain.

As a birthday present to myself, on September 15, 2023, I enrolled in a GED program. I'm working on getting a MOVE curriculum in Philadelphia public schools. After watching the positive results of the HBO documentary *40 Years a Prisoner*, about my quest to free my parents, I plan to get more films about MOVE history made. As soon as I earn my GED, I'm headed to college to become an investigative journalist. Not the kind that searches for missing people, like Jimmy Hoffa, but rather the kind that explores the ingredients in food products that rob us of our health. I want to uncover more stories that are shaping the fabric of this country but are ignored. Every journalist—no matter their professional objectivity—brings their lived experience to their work. I know my experience will be valuable in that respect. I think MOVE's mission of valuing all life will be an important addition to any newsroom. I want to keep contributing to history's record. I want to keep blending the two paths I'm on.

I've thought a lot about why all this still matters to me. Why haven't I totally abandoned the principles? The answer is certainly not nobility or any heightened sense of myself. My foibles are many. It's not personal strength. People in MOVE were strong people. I think what it comes down to is this: I know what MOVE has done for my life. Living on Reno Street and almost getting seriously caught up, MOVE was a safe haven for me. I owe my family for making the effort they made to raise me into the man that I am. My gut feelings about what MOVE is, at its best, haven't changed. I'm evidence that the organization is good and that it works. And I see a need for it.

The organization was never set up to sustain itself long term. I am honest about the hurdles. It doesn't help that the legacy of MOVE continues to be the fallout from the 1985 bombing more than knowledge about the organization itself. The outrageous example of what happened with the University of Pennsylvania and Princeton University still haunts me.

Penn is in West Philly, maybe two or three miles from Osage Avenue and the site of the bombing. Princeton is a little farther north, in central New Jersey. Both are well-moneyed, well-known, first-rate, prestigious, Ivy League institutions. Unthinkably, two anthropologists associated with the schools kept the remains of one or more MOVE bombing victims for decades. Without family notification or consent, the professors used the victims' bones to teach class. It was fucking vile. And at Penn, the bones were stored at a campus museum and put on a YouTube channel by Penn Museum's anthropology professor Janet Monge. I found out about this when a journalist called to get my comment on the story. I didn't know what she was talking about. News about what Penn and Princeton had done was just breaking.

To this day, it's unclear where some of the remains are and if they've been respectfully laid to rest. It's shocking beyond all reason. Makes it hard to heal. But I've been trying.

In 2023, I bought my great-aunt Louise's house at 6221 Osage Avenue. After the bombing, the city rebuilt homes on the block a few times. They kept hiring shoddy contractors, so the homes kept needing to be reconstructed. I first tried to buy it in 2017. But the city would sell it only to a developer. I asked why I couldn't buy back the property where my family was killed. "It's because your last name is Africa." The city didn't want anybody from MOVE back in that house.

I began protesting. #ReclaimOsage was my hashtag. I wanted to own what had been taken from the people I loved. This got attention in the city. The homeowner on Osage called me up. He said he was getting too many unsolicited visits from people sympathetic to MOVE. He wanted out and offered to let me buy it. It wasn't an easy process, even from that point. But finally, I was able to get it back. In the last conversation I had with Louise, she told me she wanted her house back. I remember asking her why, after all that had happened. Her answer was simple: "Because it's mine." The last time she lived there was 1983. She died in 2019. It's bittersweet that she didn't live long enough to see the house back in our family. She dreamed of living there again.

Mayor Wilson Goode apologized for the bombing the day after it happened, in a televised address. Thirty-five years after the bombing, in 2020, Goode continued to express his deep regrets, by writing an op-ed in *The Guardian*, apologizing again, and calling for city officials to issue a formal apology. The Philadelphia City Council, led by Councilwoman Jamie Gauthier, did just that a few months later. It's a step.

I'll never stop thinking that it's despicable how the legacy of MOVE has reverberated in the city of Philadelphia and for future generations of Africas. But I am clear that the progress we've made over the years has come from dedicated people without whom none of our achievements would have been possible.

My parents are doing great. They lived with me for a year and then got their own place. Newlyweds definitely need their own space. They created a film company called New Hori-Zens. The company's mission is to "shatter stigmas by creating empathy." Their films tell the stories of people who have returned home from prison and made positive contributions to society or those who are simply overcoming traumatic pasts.

Despite my parents' reunion, the story of MOVE hasn't been a happily-ever-after. I wish my grandma LaVerne could have lived to see her children come home from prison. I wish Louise and Frank could have made up before Frank was killed in the bombing. I wish Delbert and Chuck could've enjoyed more of their lives outside of prison, after their release.

In September 2022, when Chuck was dying of cancer, his doctors told him that to relieve his terrible pain, they could sedate him. But the sedation needed to be so strong that once he went under, he would probably not be able to come back from it. Chuck agreed to the sedation, but before he went under, he took a couple of deep breaths, threw his fist to the sky, and said, "Long Live John Africa!"

Living a MOVE life is like a roller coaster. It has its highs and lows. Sometimes it's fast enough to take your breath away. Other times it's so slow you're bracing yourself for the inevitable drop that can send you spiraling down hard and fast.

Only this is not a thrill ride. This is real life. Forty years after the nuns stuffed chocolate in Taylor's mouth, Taylor still can't stand the taste or smell of the stuff. Whenever Allen hears the sounds of helicopters, he keeps a close eye on them in case they're coming to bomb him. Whit became so angered by her entire life experience in MOVE that she disassociated herself from everything MOVE-related, and she hasn't spoken to me or our parents since 2021. It's been a mixed bag of perspectives and reactions.

Just like everyone has theirs, I have mine. For me, I see great value in inspiring people to resist injustice. You don't have to be a MOVE member to do that. But you certainly can be. It's the path I've chosen and will continue to choose. Because I know the only way to get anything done is to get On a Move.

ACKNOWLEDGMENTS

I would like to acknowledge my wife, Robin, without whose presence my life and world would be dark and gray.

To my kids, Alex, Koby, Tommy, and Alia: you make my life worth living.

To my parents: You are the reason I exist. Your example is a testament to true love.

To my extended family, my MOVE brothers and sisters (especially the second generation): I love you all and would not be the man I am today without you.

To my revolutionary brothers and sisters around the world: stay on a move!

To my awesome literary agent Jaidree Braddix, Park & Fine Literary & Media, the incredible team at Mariner Books, and my writer D. Watkins: this book would not be the success it is today without your hard work.

Special, special thanks to my editor Rakia Clark for leading a singular and clear vision for *On a Move* from the very beginning and for bringing her relentless work ethic to meeting the goals we set out to achieve. Rakia's contributions, from top to bottom, were critical. I am grateful.